MARSHAL OF
THE ROYAL AIR FORCE
SIR CHARLES
PORTAL

Disclaimer

The conclusions and opinions expressed in this document are those of the author. They do not reflect the official position of the British Government, the Ministry of Defence, the Royal Air Force, the United States Government, the Department of Defense, the United States Air Force (USAF) or the USAF Air University.

MARSHAL OF THE ROYAL AIR FORCE
SIR CHARLES PORTAL

ONE OF THE GREATEST ALLIED
LEADERS OF WW2

RICHARD MILBURN

AIR WORLD

AIR WORLD

MARSHAL OF THE ROYAL AIR FORCE SIR CHARLES PORTAL
One of the Greatest Allied Leaders of WW2

First published in Great Britain in 2023 by
Air World
An imprint of
Pen & Sword Books Ltd
Yorkshire – Philadelphia

ISBN 978 1 39904 439 4

Typeset by SJmagic DESIGN SERVICES, India.
Printed and bound in the UK by CPI Group (UK) Ltd.

Pen & Sword Books Limited incorporates the imprints of After the Battle, Atlas, Archaeology, Aviation, Discovery, Family History, Fiction, History, Maritime, Military, Military Classics, Politics, Select, Transport, True Crime, Air World, Frontline Publishing, Leo Cooper, Remember When, Seaforth Publishing, The Praetorian Press, Wharncliffe Local History, Wharncliffe Transport, Wharncliffe True Crime and White Owl.

For a complete list of Pen & Sword titles please contact

PEN & SWORD BOOKS LIMITED
George House, Units 12 & 13, Beevor Street, Off Pontefract Road,
Barnsley, South Yorkshire, S71 1HN, England
E-mail: enquiries@pen-and-sword.co.uk
Website: www.pen-and-sword.co.uk

or

PEN AND SWORD BOOKS
1950 Lawrence Rd, Havertown, PA 19083, USA
E-mail: uspen-and-sword@casematepublishers.com
Website: www.penandswordbooks.com

FSC
www.fsc.org

MIX
Paper | Supporting
responsible forestry
FSC® C013604

Contents

Acknowledgements

While this is a relatively short work, I have received enormous assistance in its production. First and foremost, at the School of Advanced Air and Space Studies (SAASS), I wish to thank Dr Tom Hughes and Dr Rich Muller for their thought, care and encouragement in providing the sage advice needed to assist a novice biographer. I will always appreciate their delicate brutality. At the Air War College, Colonel Patrick Budjenska and Dr Corbin Williamson ensured the financial burdens of travel were lessened. I am also grateful to Dr Seb Cox for allowing me access to the Portal Archive at Christ Church, Oxford, and for providing RAF subject matter expertise that corrected some of my more egregious errors.

I must also thank David Freeman, editor of *Finest Hour*, who provided encouragement, as well as an introduction to Portal's niece, Lady Jane Williams. The brief time I spent with Lady Williams and other members of the Portal family was invaluable in humanising him even more. I hope I have done them justice.

As well as my dissertation committee, Mr Gary Mennell, Dr Ann Mezzell, Dr J.T. LaSaine and Group Captain John Shields provided invaluable editorial assistance. Their attention to detail is exceptional, and they resolved numerous grammatical and some factual errors. Dr P.J. Springer's 'Great Captains' elective class provided an analytical framework to assess Portal's performance, and was just great fun! Dr Tammi Davis Biddle also provided encouragement that this was a project worth pursuing during a brief car journey after she lectured at the Air War College (AWC) at Maxwell AFB, Alabama.

I have spent seven very happy years at Maxwell, and both students and faculty at the Air Command and Staff College (ACSC), SAASS and AWC have contributed to my education and enabled this work to have the rigour it does. I am immensely thankful for the experience, which I will always treasure. Deserving of special recognition is Lieutenant Colonel Jamila Fitzpatrick,

ACKNOWLEDGEMENTS

my battle buddy during SAASS, a fierce editor and wonderful writer. I am grateful for all her assistance.

The Special Collections team at Christ Church College, Oxford, helped enormously, before, during and after my visits to the archive in January 2019 and February 2020. I am particularly grateful to the Keeper of the Collections, Dr Christina Neagu, for her friendly encouragement during the weeks there, and for facilitating access to the collection. Elizabeth Piper rendered assistance above and beyond any that could be expected of an archivist, and I am grateful for both her infectious enthusiasm and depth of knowledge of the Portal Papers. Both made writing this study easier. Staff at the Liddell Hart Centre, King's College London; the Royal Air Force Museum; the Churchill Archives in Cambridge; the Imperial War Museum, London; the National Archives at Kew; and the Air Historical Research Agency at Maxwell AFB all provided exemplary assistance.

Throughout this process I have relied upon the unstinting support of my wife, Mandy, and my two boys. They have all sacrificed time and effort, allowing me the freedom to think and write without undue distraction or a guilty conscience. Any and all errors herein contained are my own.

Foreword

Throughout history leaders and commanders have been honoured, lauded and vilified for their leadership, their bravery, their cunning and their example, but, most often, for their successes or losses. However, sometimes, our leaders have gone unacknowledged, either because of the turn of events or because others have grabbed the limelight and the leadership role of an individual has not attracted the critical eye of historians or chroniclers. Charles Portal is just such a man. As Chief of the Air Staff during the Second World War, he was instrumental in the strategic leadership of the still young, talented and resource-strapped Royal Air Force. His leadership and skill were in navigating and negotiating the optimum way through the myriad of operational, logistical and aviation development that was challenging the Royal Air Force and demanding detailed understanding of the factors and the ability to frame effective arguments at the very top of the British Government and with its allies. It is particularly important to recognise the high-level strategic relationships that Portal engendered, and which were so critical to the ultimate Allied victory. The author of this book has captured the essence of that role and highlighted just how important Portal was to the strategic effectiveness and capability of the Royal Air Force in its most challenging period, both in its own right and as a capable ally. I thoroughly recommend those with any interest in the history of the Royal Air Force or of the role of the most senior government advisors to read and digest this insightful and effective analysis of the vital and understated role Portal played in the ultimate success of the Royal Air Force, Great Britain and its allies in 1940–45 as outlined by the author.

Air Chief Marshal Sir Stephen Dalton
His Excellency Lieutenant Governor of Jersey

Introduction

Strategy is a series of relationships
Richard Betts

This is a book about a man most people have never heard of: the Chief of Air Staff of the Royal Air Force during most of the Second World War, Sir Charles Frederick Algernon Portal. Portal is the youngest Chief of Air Staff to have been appointed in the last 100 years, and retired from the military aged fifty-one, younger than the age at which most chiefs are appointed. Portal led the Royal Air Force with distinction for more than five years during the war and, though feted in the hour of victory, has been largely forgotten over time. I want to start by telling the unlikely tale of how I came to be Sir Charles's second biographer, because doing so will help to illuminate why he has slipped from the public's gaze despite having been a member of Churchill's inner circle during the war.

In the summer of 2016, I graduated from the Air Command and Staff College (ACSC) in Montgomery, Alabama, and moved on to the faculty as the Royal Air Force exchange officer. One of my two outstanding office mates was Dr John T. LaSaine, a diplomatic historian who, oddly, happened to be writing a biography of Hugh Dowding, architect of Britain's victory in the Battle of Britain.

In the course of writing his biography of Dowding, Dr LaSaine and I enjoyed many hours reminiscing about the wartime RAF and its leaders. One day he casually remarked that someone ought to write another biography of Charles Portal. I knew Portal was the leader of the RAF during most of the war but could have told you little else. I thought nothing more about this comment until much later, and just continued to enjoy our daily discussions as his work proceeded. Following the end of my assignment to ACSC, I was fortunate enough to be selected to attend the School of Advanced Air and Space Studies (SAASS), also in Montgomery, Alabama, where one of the requirements for graduation is a thesis of at least fifty pages. Initially I thought I would attempt to write a grand theoretical masterpiece bringing the work of Carl von Clausewitz into the twenty-first century. It was not to be, as none of the SAASS faculty were willing to support my outlandish ideas. Percolating in the back of my brain were the words of Dr LaSaine about Portal, so I purchased the sole existing work on him from an online book store.

There is only one biography of Portal, written by the RAF's official historian at the time of Portal's death, Denis Richards. I thoroughly enjoyed the book, and must admit feeling more than a little guilty I had not read more about Portal before. Richards was the pre-eminent RAF historian of the time, and amassed every feasible document relating to Portal, to paint a thorough picture of the man and his contribution. Without Richards' sterling efforts in amassing files and conducting interviews, this project would have been extremely difficult, if not impossible. This is not an attempt to replace Richards' biography, which is both longer and more thorough than my own. But this work represents a more focused approach than the first biography, which quite rightly tells the whole story of Portal's life. This book, by contrast, concentrates on Portal's military service and, in particular, his leadership of the RAF during the Second World War. If there is a single moment when I knew I had to write a book about Portal, it was after reading a single line, contained in a footnote, on page 215 of Richards' book. The footnote described the retirement of Lord Plowden from his post as Chairman of the Atomic Energy Agency in 1959, a post previously held by Portal. Lord Plowden made a farewell call to President Eisenhower, who said to him, 'And don't forget to remember me to Peter Portal. You know, I always think that Peter was the greatest of all the British war leaders – greater even than Churchill.'[1]

I was dumbfounded by this line of text, and re-read it several times. I then wondered how I, a Royal Air Force officer with twenty years of military experience (and, I thought, fairly well educated), could be barely aware of a man who President Eisenhower considered Britain's greatest wartime leader? Why would Portal not be renowned in the history of the RAF? It was hard to dismiss the comment, coming as it did from Eisenhower, a man with

---

1 Richards, Denis, *Portal of Hungerford: The Life of Marshal of the Royal Air Force, Viscount Portal of Hungerford, KG, GCB, OM, DSO, MC*. New York, N.Y.: Holmes & Meier, 1977, 215.

enormous military and political credibility, and delivered in an informal remark not designed for public consumption. I had previously assumed that Portal's anonymity was a reflection of his sub-par performance as Chief of Air Staff. Surely, if it were otherwise, the RAF would remember him much more fondly than they do, which is to say they do not at all. Eisenhower's assertions called into question my own thoughts about Portal, and I had to know more.

SAASS afforded me that opportunity. Part way through the course, I applied for the Air University PhD programme, and was lucky enough to be accepted. This allowed me to continue the work on Portal after completing SAASS. This book is the product of my labours for the programme and the pursuant Air University PhD. The Royal Air Force also has a PhD programme; ironically it is called the Portal Fellowship. The point of this story is that a combination of luck, intellectual curiosity, and a sense of injustice (regarding our 'unknown victor') led to the writing of this book. The work is primarily designed to investigate the veracity of Eisenhower's assertion. That is why the book concentrates on Portal's military service. Many labels could be attributed to Sir Charles Portal. He was a diplomat, a leader, a manager, a logistician and a technologist. However, the description most befitting Portal, that encompasses all these roles, is that of strategist.

In *The Soldier and the State*, Samuel Huntington wrote, 'The modern officer corps is a professional body and the modern military officer a professional man.'[2] He considered the unique professionalism of the officer to be 'the management of violence.'[3] Huntington's use of the term management was deliberate, because he viewed the profession to be much more than merely the tactical battle. It is also interesting, and potentially provocative, that he chose the term management, which, in military circles, is often considered the poor relative of leadership. Yet in Huntington's description of the duties of the military officer, it is management that predominates rather than leadership:

1. The organising, equipping and training of the force;
2. The planning of its activities;
3. The direction of its operation in and out of combat.[4]

---

2 Huntington, S., *The Soldier and the State; the Theory and Politics of Civil-Military Relations*. Cambridge: Belknap Press of Harvard University Press, 1957, 7.
3 Ibid., 11.
4 Ibid.

Only the last of the three tasks pertains to leadership rather than management, suggesting managerial competence is at least as important in becoming an effective military officer as leadership skills. While management may be the appropriate term at the lower levels of the military, in the higher echelons what Huntington was really talking about was strategy.

The distinction between leadership and management is made even more clearly by Morris Janowitz, Huntington's contemporary. Janowitz divides the military establishment into two historic tribes and a third emerging one. 'The history of the modern military establishment can be described as a struggle between heroic leaders, who embody traditionalism and glory, and military "managers", who are concerned with the scientific and rational conduct of war.'[5] The emerging third group are the military technologists, who are increasingly important in an environment where rapid technological advancements must be harnessed for military use. The first two groups occupy different spheres of respect in the eyes of the public, with the third attracting increasing fascination that reflects western society's technological underpinnings. Janowitz similarly ignored the moniker of strategist, though a combination of technologist and manager at the highest levels of the military is a strategist.

Strategy is the most important aspect of military and indeed political life. As some say, 'tactics without strategy is the noise before defeat.' Strategy is the linking of political goals to the available resources, whether military, diplomatic, informational or economic. Perhaps most importantly, strategy is about understanding the limitations of what is achievable with the resources available and setting goals accordingly. Strategy can broadly be divided into military strategy and grand strategy. The latter involves the use of diplomatic, informational, military and economic instruments of power, the former is just the military element of the overall grand strategy. Yet strategy is about more than just formulation. It is also about understanding the changing environment and adapting to emerging conditions.

In a long conflict such as the Second World War, conditions change frequently. Technological advances, for example, can affect battlefield performance from one day to the next. One such instance was the arrival of the P-51 Mustang to assist the US Eighth Air Force bombing effort in early 1944. Missions during autumn 1943 were prohibitively costly in

---

5 Janowitz, M., *The Professional Soldier, a Social and Political Portrait.* Glencoe, Ill.: Free Press, 1960, 21.

loss of airframes and aviators, notably during raids on Schweinfurt and Regensburg. The Mustang changed the offence–defence balance, making high-altitude precision daylight bombing (HAPDB) not only possible, but militarily profitable. Even the best German fighters, such as the BF 109, proved instantly outmatched.[6] The strategist must understand technology and its effect on the offence–defence balance to grasp what is operationally feasible at any given moment.

Both tacticians and strategists are vital for the success of modern militaries, yet there is a constant tension between the two. Battlefield leadership requires quick thinking and decisiveness. Strategy needs patience and emotional intelligence, particularly when operating with alliance partners whose interests may be different, necessitating policy compromises. Persistence and self-confidence apply to both roles, but often manifest themselves in different ways, and are affected by the other qualities. Examples of military officers who were vastly successful at both are rare. General Curtis LeMay was an infinitely more successful wartime leader than he was Chief of Staff of the United States Air Force. Hugh Trenchard, by contrast, was an average operator, but an exceptional administrator of the newly formed Royal Air Force. Leaders who excel in one realm are sometimes ill-suited to the other.

Napoleon Bonaparte exhorted us to read 'the great captains.' In doing so, we ought to learn where they failed as well as where they succeeded. Napoleon recommended studying the great battlefield commanders such as Julius Caesar, Hannibal Barca and Alexander the Great. What is intriguing about all three historical giants is that they all excelled tactically and were legendary battlefield commanders, but each failed in some way at the strategic level. Julius Caesar, Hannibal Barca and Alexander the Great each lacked the ability to compromise. They may have defeated the enemy, but they failed to maintain support from their own side at crucial times.

Hannibal Barca was a Carthaginian general who masterminded decisive victories at the battles of Lake Trasimene and Cannae. Cannae may be the most revered battleplan in history, the immortal double envelopment and subsequent massacre of a huge Roman Army that led to the defection of several city-states, such as Capua, to Carthage. Hannibal is exalted for his genius in battle and was so intimidating, to even the Romans, that Consul

6 Tooze, Adam, *The Wages of Destruction: The Making and Breaking of the Nazi Economy.* Penguin: New York, 2006, 626.

Fabius famously avoided engaging in battle against Hannibal, preferring to frustrate and stymie his forces. However, Hannibal suffered from a lack of support from Carthage, whose political leaders felt threatened by his success. He failed to secure adequate forces to defeat Rome, and this was the ultimate cause of his downfall.

Alexander amassed the greatest geographic empire in world history, but also failed at the political level. Though accounts of Alexander's death are disputed, poison is considered a likely cause. A recent study showed poisoning with veratrum album would produce the symptoms and death described in the historical record.[7] Alexander was probably killed by his countrymen, the Macedonians, because they either feared him so much, or wanted to return home, something Alexander was unwilling to do. Not one for compromise, Alexander paid the ultimate price. The Macedonian Empire splintered in the wake of his death, because he had failed to plan for his succession.[8]

Julius Caesar's story is similar; Caesar effected immense battlefield performance while cutting across great swathes of Europe, quelling all in his way. However, Caesar was undone by his own hubris following his self-appointment as 'consul for life.' The method of his demise is so iconic that Agatha Christie borrowed it for the plot of *Murder on the Orient Express*.

Napoleon also has blemishes on his record despite implementing sweeping military and political changes in Europe. He transformed the scale of war in Europe by nationalising it, arming the entire French people to fight the small private armies of other states. However, Napoleon did not instigate an effective educational programme whereby the next generation of divisional commanders would be ready to replace his aging ones, which caused problems in later campaigns. Most crucially, he failed to see the inevitability of the coalition that rose to defeat him. It was his own grand strategic folly. Such decision-making should perhaps lead to caution, not exaltation, regardless of the victories that preceded such action.

Napoleon was one of the last warrior statesmen, who had total control of both the military and political aspects of war. Napoleon was responsible for a

---

7 Schep, Leo J., Slaughter, Robin J., Vale, J. Allister & Wheatley, Pat (2014), 'Was the death of Alexander the Great due to poisoning? Was it Veratrum album?', *Clinical Toxicology*, 52:1, 72–77, DOI: 10.3109/15563650.2013.870341 accessed on 15 June 2021 at 11.00.

8 Barry S., *Masters of Command: Alexander, Hannibal, Caesar and the Genius of Leadership*. 1st Simon & Schuster hardcover ed. New York: Simon & Schuster, 2012, Introduction. This section, although written from memory, owes a great deal to Barry Strauss's introduction and framing of the failures of history's great captains.

fundamental change in the character of war in Europe. He nationalised the scale of conflict such that all other countries had to follow suit or face ruin. In doing so, Napoleon sowed the seeds of the death of many European monarchies and the birth of liberal democracies. Combine this political change with the industrial revolution that took place during the nineteenth century, and the conditions were created for states to conduct war on an unprecedented scale. Another result of these changes was civilian control of a professionalised military, which evolved over the nineteenth and early twentieth centuries. The roles of military leaders changed in the twentieth century with the advent of total war. A divide was created between those military personnel who were primarily leaders on the battlefield, and those who had to liaise with politicians and sister services, as well as organise logistics to enable this state-funded leviathan. The strategist has become more important over time, especially as the military becomes ever more reliant on the integration of complex technology.[9] Recently, the importance of administrative positions has been entrenched in bureaucracy on both sides of the Atlantic through the Goldwater–Nichols changes and the creation of Joint Forces Command (now Strategic Command) respectively. There is now a doctrinal divide between the war-fighting general and the military politician. These different paths are not, though, equally reflected in the published military historiography.

Most military biographies concentrate on controversial battlefield leaders because they make more dramatic studies. Heroic battlefield leadership and 'military genius' form the basis of interest. If the subject is controversial, all the better. There are endless biographies of colourful battlefield commanders such as Patton and Montgomery, but significantly fewer of people like General Hap Arnold, who oversaw the build-up of American air power during the Second World War. Arnold was inarguably more important to the American war effort than Patton. Biographies of Arnold exist primarily because of his crucial role as the father of the United States Air Force. While there are various such biographies, the one that has been seen in the syllabus of the leadership course at the United States Air Force Air Command and Staff College is *Architects of American Air Supremacy: Gen Hap Arnold and Dr Theodore von Karman*.[10] This book specifically examines Arnold's role as a technologist, rather than his role

---

9 Janowitz, *The Professional Soldier*, 22.
10 Daso, D., *Architects of American Air Supremacy: Gen. Hap Arnold and Dr Theodore von Kármán*. Maxwell AFB, AL.: Air University Press, 1997.

as a strategic leader. While an engaging read, it may not provide the most useful basis for the development of strategic leadership thought.

Across the Atlantic, Bernard Montgomery has attracted much more biographical attention than the Chief of the Imperial General Staff, Sir Alan Brooke. A quick search for Montgomery reveals more than twenty biographical results. By stark contrast, for Brooke there is only one true biography, plus his war diaries. There is also *Masters and Commanders*, in which Brooke is one of four leaders credited with winning the war in the west.[11] Roosevelt and Churchill appear to be the main selling points, with George Marshall and Brooke mere afterthoughts to lend a military flavour to the title.

The RAF in general is extremely poorly served with biographical material. Hugh Dowding, Commander-in-Chief of Fighter Command, has the most biographies of a senior RAF leader by a short head over Arthur 'Bomber' Harris. Neither of these men rose to the top of the service, and Trenchard, who led the RAF through the 1920s, has only three books with his name atop them. Trenchard was essentially a bureaucrat, a man who unquestionably saved the RAF from being reabsorbed into the British Army and Royal Navy during the austere years following the First World War. Yet he is of less biographical interest than those who led Fighter Command and Bomber Command respectively for periods during the Second World War. Harris attracts great controversy because of his refusal to alter course from the city bombing campaign in 1945. He is also often given the credit for devising the 'strategic bombing' campaign that attacked German cities, a blatant historical inaccuracy, as the campaign predates Harris's time at Bomber Command by more than a year.

For the military scholar there is simply a dearth of available material discussing the qualities and histories of successful military strategists. In fact, the most common RAF biographical subject is Douglas Bader, who captivates because of the adversity he overcame to continue to fly. Bader biographies are concerned primarily with neither leadership nor management, but a very personal victory. It is a true British underdog story. Guy Gibson also attracts significant attention, because of his leadership of the storied Dambuster raids by 617 Squadron. The man who led all these wartime airmen (barring Trenchard) through most of the war, Air Chief Marshal Sir Charles 'Peter' Portal, merits nary a mention in most of these books.

---

11 Roberts, Andrew, *Masters and Commanders: How Roosevelt, Churchill, Marshall and Alanbrooke Won the War in the West*, London: Penguin, 2008.

Portal's place in the historiography is paltry; he is often quickly overlooked in a rush to concentrate on the subject of a given thesis. Even fine historians such as Dik Daso make basic errors such as getting Portal's rank wrong. In his brief biography of Jimmy Doolittle, Daso writes, 'The question of whether or not to pursue the objectives of the Combined Bomber Offensive (CBO), as established during the Casablanca Conference in mid-January from both England and Italy was hotly contested by American and British air leaders. Lt. Gen. Ira C. Eaker, Eighth Air Force Commander, along with Air Vice Marshal Sir Peter Portal, and Air Chief Marshal Sir Arthur Harris, feared the build-up of a new strategic air force would cripple the CBO and jeopardize Operation OVERLORD, the invasion of Europe.'[12]

In this brief passage, Daso demotes Portal two ranks to air vice marshal while correctly stating Arthur Harris's rank. Neither Harris nor Eaker were even conference participants, because they were subordinate commanders with no agency in strategic decision-making. They made decisions at the operational level, but Daso awards them fictitious strategic agency, a job that ought to be reserved for Hollywood directors, not historians. Demoting Portal two ranks is a glaring oversight, illustrating the lack of importance even esteemed writers frequently attach to Portal. Similarly, in his biography of Carl Spaatz, David Mets refers to 'the Chief of the Air Staff, Sir Hugh Portal', while correctly identifying the name of Portal's deputy, Sir Wilfrid Freeman.[13]

More insidiously, in *One Christmas in Washington*, David Bercuson and Holger Herwig deliberately misrepresent a meeting between Portal and Hap Arnold, the head of the US Army Air Corps at the time. They state Arnold was 'greatly offended' at Portal's suggestion Britain needed American bombers to help attack Germany, despite this already having been formally agreed. They then describe the meeting as having ended in acrimony, which is suggested neither in Arnold's notes from the meeting, nor in his autobiography, *Global Mission*.[14] They continue to mischaracterise the

---

12 Daso, Dik A., *Doolittle, Aerospace Visionary*, Military Profiles, Washington, D.C.: Brassey's, 2003, 76.

13 Mets, David R., *Master of Airpower: General Carl A. Spaatz*. Novato, CA: Presidio Press, 1988, 130.

14 Bercuson, David Jay, and Herwig, Holger H., *One Christmas in Washington: Churchill and Roosevelt Forge the Grand Alliance*. Toronto: McArthur, 2005, 136–137; Arnold, Henry Harley, *Global Mission*, London: Hutchinson, 1951, 276–278; United States Department of State, *Foreign Relations of the United States: The Conferences at Washington, 1941–1942, and Casablanca, 1943*, Washington, D.C.: US Government Printing Office, 1941–1943, 222–224.

Arnold–Portal relationship throughout the book to artificially create tension where none existed. In fact, Arnold and Portal knew and liked one another prior to the ARCADIA Conference in December 1941–January 1942. All too often, Portal has been sacrificed on the altar of storytelling. Charles Portal has received meagre recognition as one of Britain's greatest wartime leaders. He was also, despite the claims of Bercuson et al, an exceptional diplomat during all Allied conferences.

Portal's anonymity cannot, however, be solely laid at the door of military biographers. He must shoulder some of the blame himself. Portal was a sporadic diarist, which makes it difficult to grasp his impression of events. For a biographer, this makes a study of Portal challenging and open to different interpretations. Most of the diaries that do exist are concerned with Portal's teenage pastime of hawking, rather than his military career. The extremely colourful *War Diaries of Field Marshal Lord Alanbrooke* have, by contrast, left an indelible impression of what Brooke thought about a variety of his colleagues, notably Churchill and de Gaulle. Churchill was so upset when he read the unredacted diaries that he reportedly burst into tears and exclaimed, 'I never realised they hated me so much!'[15] It is unclear if de Gaulle ever read the diaries, but had he done so, he may have been similarly afflicted, as Brooke paints a scathing, yet hilarious, picture of the future French president.

Had Portal written a diary, it seems unlikely he would ever have endorsed its publication. Portal was an intensely private man, who had no interest in stoking controversy. He was even quick to walk back what he considered erroneous conceptions of Alan Brooke when the opportunity arose. Following Brooke's death in 1963, the BBC commissioned a programme to discuss his wartime contribution. When asked about the diaries, Portal remarked firstly that it was astonishing Brooke had the energy to write them, as he must have been exhausted on most nights. He secondly pointed out that the diaries were only ever intended for Brooke's wife to read. Portal also observed that Brooke toned his rhetoric down later, and regretted what he had sometimes written in the heat of the moment when exhausted. Portal went on to describe how the diaries did not accurately reflect the man he had worked alongside for four years, and under the most immense pressure. Portal attested that Brooke was neither petulant, nor self-pitying nor disloyal. He fought hard but

---

15 Interview author and Lady Williams of Elvel, 24 January 2020.

fair and with good humour and cheerfulness.[16] Even eighteen years after his retirement, Portal stoutly defended his wartime colleague, trying to defuse any controversy or faulty interpretations Brooke's diaries might cause. This may have been disappointing to radio listeners expecting Portal to belatedly 'dish the dirt.' It would be easy to assume Portal was boring, yet nothing could be further from the truth. Portal was a complex character, who is the more fascinating for his indifference to his own legacy, and a humility that rarely accompanies someone of such immense talents.

Portal was almost alone among senior figures in not publishing a self-congratulatory autobiography at the end of the war. Churchill took six volumes to do so, and most of the surviving leaders wanted to get their points of view across. Portal was very different. Even during the war, he largely shunned the limelight, remaining behind the scenes and allowing his operational commanders to enjoy the accolades. Portal's war was fought across the conference table with other military leaders and politicians, not on the battlefield. His is not a story of military genius in a moment of adversity but of wrestling with alliances, logistics and big personalities, both military and political.

Despite having been one of Trenchard's boys, and having seen how Trenchard continued to exert influence on the RAF long after his military retirement, Portal did not mimic his mentor following his own retirement. When the war ended, Portal had little direct influence on his successor, Arthur Tedder, other than recommending him as his replacement. But he largely considered his time as being done, and when he did lecture to the military, at Cranwell or staff colleges, he was extremely careful to express wherever his view was his own. But mostly, he towed the party line. Were it possible to interview Portal today, it is extremely unlikely he would ever let the mask drop. He was meticulous in preserving the legacies of others, even to his own detriment. This remains a remarkable feat of humility.

The purpose of this work is to try to reintroduce the little-known Portal as a central military figure in the Second World War. It examines what led Eisenhower to hold Portal in such high esteem. Is this view of a man broadly forgotten in the historiography of the war justifiable? Was Portal an effective leader during the war? More importantly, how significant was

---

16 Brett-James, Anthony, *Portrait of Field Marshal Viscount Alanbrooke*, recorded 22 January 1964, Portal Papers, Christ Church College, Oxford (Hereafter referred to as CC), CC/3/A/A5.

Portal's role in the construction and execution of British and Allied strategy during the war? The work seeks to provide a case study of military strategy to plug what seems to be a significant gap in the available literature on military leaders. This specific focus on strategic leadership during total war is unusual and hopefully enlightening regarding the qualities needed to be a successful military officer once promoted beyond the battlefield.

The study will focus on key relationships Portal developed during the Second World War. This was an archetypal global modern war: a possible, if unfortunate, situation in which nations might find themselves in the future. The war was both a joint campaign and a combined one, involving complex alliances and differing national interests. Chapters 1 and 2 cover Portal's career up to the time when he was appointed Chief of Air Staff (CAS). Thereafter five key relationships are examined, exploring the manner in which Portal was able to influence those around him. These relationships show the gamut of Portal's engagement: up to Churchill, across to sister services with Brooke, Alliance dynamics with Hap Arnold, and two very different subordinate relationships with Tedder and Harris.

The foundational relationship is with Churchill, the subject of Chapter 3. Credibility with political leaders is crucial to modern military leaders, and Portal's method of engagement set him apart from his peers. Churchill could be stubborn and impulsive, acerbic and charming. Portal managed this crucial relationship expertly, becoming one of Churchill's most trusted lieutenants. Staunch Churchill supporters may find the portrayal of Churchill here to be unnecessarily defamatory. Churchill is among England's finest, yet what he unquestionably gave England in heart and fight was not matched by his strategic contribution. Churchill's daily battle rhythm made it extremely difficult for others to keep up. It was crucial, with his enormous responsibilities, that Churchill set the pace. His schedule and method of engagement broke other, lesser, men.

No relationship in this work is exclusive, and several events are revisited from differing perspectives in different chapters. But Portal's relationship with Churchill affects all of the following chapters to a greater or lesser degree. Had Portal been unable to influence Churchill, his significance to the overall war effort would have been severely reduced. Chapter 3 demonstrates how Portal was able to sit at the top table, the breadth of his influence, and how he could be instrumental in British decision-making despite being much younger than both his fellow Chiefs of Staff and the Prime Minister.

This leads naturally into Chapter 4's discussion of Portal's relationship with Alan Brooke, the Chief of the Imperial General Staff from Christmas

1941. Portal and Brooke were vastly different characters. Brooke was very quick to think and speak; Portal was much more considered and patient. Yet together, they formed a partnership that, although littered with disagreements, formed the strategic nexus of British military thought during the war. Churchill biographers have sometimes painted the man himself in this light, but Churchill was the heart and not the brains of the war effort.

On the military side, it is often Brooke who is credited as Britain's premier strategist. This is a natural conclusion, because he was the Chairman of the Joint Chiefs of Staff (COS) Committee, and so their spokesperson whose decisions were recorded in meetings. He was also the primary British military spokesperson during Allied conferences. Nevertheless, strategy came from the joint brains of Brooke and Portal, and their respective staffs. It was frequently hotly contested in the daily British COS meetings. There was a long, drawn-out process during 1942 when the two forged the British approach, and how to sell this, primarily European theatre strategy, to the US Joint Chiefs of Staff (US JCS). The two British naval leaders, Dudley Pound and Andrew Cunningham, who replaced Pound following the former's death in 1943, played a lesser role. Pound was loath to engage in discussion outside the maritime domain,[17] and Andrew Cunningham entered the fray only once the strategic die was cast. The Portal–Brooke relationship involved frequent, heated debate in British COS meetings, but during Allied conferences they spoke with one voice. Brooke's acerbic and confrontational approach was complemented by the more conciliatory tones and compromising approach of Portal. They were, despite their differences, a team.

Having considered how Portal managed a challenging peer in Brooke, Chapter 5 looks at Portal's relationship with Arthur Tedder, Air Officer Commanding in the Middle East theatre, and overall Deputy Commander for OVERLORD. The relationship between the two men was crucial and bled over into the Portal–Brooke relationship. Because Tedder was operating in the primary theatre of war, Portal was desperate to gain an air perspective on what was going on in the Mediterranean and North Africa, especially given some Army commanders' penchant for blaming the RAF for their own operational failures. The fact that there were sections of the British press doing likewise made Portal's job more challenging, and his close relationship with Tedder was crucial in maintaining the RAF's credibility in Whitehall. Tedder's correspondence with Portal allowed

---

17 Richards, *Portal of Hungerford*, 199.

the latter to give an informed perspective on the deficiencies of the land component, which balanced Brooke's land-centric views and gave Portal political ammunition.

In return, Tedder received Portal's unwavering support, which he required since Churchill was initially unconvinced Tedder was the right man for the job following the dismissal of Arthur Longmore as the Air Commander in the Mediterranean in 1941. The Portal–Tedder relationship may be as close to the ideal as possible for a leader–subordinate relationship under such intense pressure. Tedder was a vital cog in providing Portal with situational awareness regarding what was happening in the Mediterranean and North Africa, long the British strategic focus. This theatre was also chosen for the first major Allied operation following the US entry into the war. The correspondence between Tedder and Portal was prodigious, enabling Portal to attend COS meetings better informed than he would otherwise have been.

Portal's relationship with Hap Arnold is examined in Chapter 6. Arnold was head of the US Army Air Forces and responsible for the enormous industrial build-up of American wartime air power. The difficulties Portal and Brooke experienced in determining British strategy were often mirrored in the Portal–Arnold relationship, because they had different priorities and concerns. Portal was exceptionally strategic in his outlook, which enabled him to win almost everybody over in the end. Despite the fact Portal's requirements for the RAF almost always worked against Arnold's desire to create an independent United States Air Force, Portal was able to develop a productive working relationship with him. Arnold's initial Anglophobia was overcome, in no small part due to Portal's efforts, and together the men delivered the Arnold–Portal agreement, which assisted in ensuring Allied logistical superiority. This agreement was absolutely crucial, as the earlier Slessor–Arnold agreement needed fundamental revision after the Japanese attack on Pearl Harbor on 7 December 1941. There were areas of contention that continued through the war, yet the two men mostly worked harmoniously together, though across the Atlantic Ocean from one another. Portal and Arnold led the integration of Allied Air Forces for the Combined Bomber Offensive, in which another Portal subordinate would play a key role.

Arthur Harris, perhaps the most challenging and prickly of Portal's subordinates, is the subject of Chapter 7. Harris and Portal met when they were both squadron commanders at Worthy Down, and Harris succeeded Portal as Deputy Director Plans in the Air Ministry in the 1930s. During the Battles of France and the Battle of Britain, when Portal was the Commander-in-Chief of Bomber Command, Harris was his trusty lieutenant at No. 5 Group. After a brief period in the Air Ministry when Portal became CAS, Harris was sent to the US, where he cultivated highly productive working relationships with senior American airmen. Harris's relationship with such key figures made him a natural leader of Bomber Command, as did his remarkable technical expertise. However, Harris was an immovable object regarding bombing strategy and this caused great tension later in the war. Portal has been criticised for not firing Harris, yet Portal's ability to continue working with a subordinate with whom he fundamentally disagreed should be seen as a positive leadership trait, not a black mark.

Much of this work is concentrated in the first half of the Second World War, during the establishment of these key relationships. Much as the logistical plan for Allied success was in place following the ARCADIA Conference in December 1941–January 1942, so were most of the key relationships. After this point, Allied victory was likely, if not assured. In many regards the CASABLANCA Conference in January 1943 is the last point during which fundamental strategic disagreements needed resolution. After this, the question was where to apply Allied power for the maximum effect and at the lowest cost. This caused great consternation between the British and Americans during 1943. Yet the British were largely of one mind by this time, so the frequency of correspondence between Portal and even Churchill drops precipitously in the second half of 1943 and again in 1944. Having established the foundations for success, other leaders took up the baton.

This study will illuminate Portal's personal qualities. These qualities differ greatly from those required of a battlefield commander. Modern military leaders should pay attention to studies of strategic leaders whose traits reflect the requirements of contemporary warfare. All military leaders must lead up, down and across, just as Portal did. This study does nothing to degrade the heroism or genius of battlefield generals. It is not an attempt to denigrate the contributions of Churchill, Harris, Brooke, Dowding, Tedder, Ismay, Cunningham, Freeman, Douglas or a host of others who all gave a tremendous amount to deliver victory during the most difficult circumstances. In the real world, and in a national (and arguably global) fight for survival, there ought to be plenty of room to acknowledge the contributions of more than a few feted heroes. Portal did not succeed alone, something he was at pains to point out whenever asked. Yet of all members of the RAF, Portal did contribute most to victory during the Second World War. He did not do so through the mystical application of his *coup d'oeil* to, in a moment, see the magical path to victory. He toiled his way through endless papers, countless meetings and spent day upon day, week upon week, and month upon month considering what strategic path Britain must follow.

In the end, this work attempts to better serve the needs of military education. Learning how Portal navigated the Second World War and how he cultivated productive relationships with impetuous prime ministers, Anglophobic Americans, impatient Army officers, and both prickly and humble subordinates, ought to illuminate the important traits of a strategic military leader. It is doubtful whether anything other than inspiration can be drawn from the biographies of the heroic leaders but, even if it can, this is probably of little or no utility at the strategic level. Military genius, as Clausewitz described it, may mostly be a tactical and at best an operational gift. Or perhaps there is no such thing as military genius. Arthur C. Clarke once wrote, 'Any sufficiently advanced technology is indivisible from magic.' Perhaps military genius is the same. It is not genius per se, but the ability to see patterns that others cannot, forged through a challenging and engaging programme of education. I hope this study fulfils part of the needs and priorities of a broader military education, relevant to the future employment of military professionals.

This study is unapologetically brief regarding Portal's post-military career and later life. It is a military biography in the truest sense, concerned with military strategy, diplomacy, logistics, and leadership. There is an entire industry dedicated to business leadership literature, which has little to no value for military officers. Businesses are there to make money; the military deals in the blood of nations where decisions are of infinitely greater consequence. The execution of war in the modern age is also almost exclusively carried out in alliances, not independently as most businesses operate. Portal's greatest gifts were diplomacy and compromise, which are not qualities Steve Jobs, Elon Musk et al are noted for. The subject matter also reflects a specific sphere of interest. In researching and writing about Portal, I have tried to illuminate areas where he may have erred, to paint a fair portrait of a man I greatly admire. I prefer my heroes to be flawed; it makes them more relatable. Portal was not perfect, but that does not mean Eisenhower was wrong.

Chapter 1

The Early Years

But the old man would not so, but slew his son,
And half the seed of Europe, one by one.

Wilfred Owen

Charles Frederick Algernon Portal was born at the family home, Eddington House, Hungerford, on 21 May 1893. His Christian names were homage to his godparents, but he was never known by any of them. When his grandmother laid eyes upon him, she exclaimed, 'Oh! What a shock-headed Peter!' The alliteration stuck and the future Chief of Air Staff became Peter Portal, a name used by both family and friends throughout his life.[1]

The Portal family was of Huguenot origin; Peter's father, Edward, was an Oxford graduate, barrister, squire, Master of the Craven Hunt, and Deputy Lieutenant. Edward was a singular man of typical Portal looks: dark hair and eyebrows with the ample Roman nose that would later distinguish Peter, and still survives in some of the Portal descendants to this day. Edward also knew what he wanted, and abandoned the family business of paper manufacturing to live among the country set and build a family life. The business performed extremely well during the second half of the nineteenth century, fuelled by demands from the Boer War, and Edward had no need to work.[2]

Edward's first marriage to Rosie was short-lived, as she died three months after giving birth to a stillborn third son. Though greatly saddened by the passing of his wife and progeny, Edward knew he needed a mother for his surviving offspring. Fairly soon he began courting the daughter of

---

1 Richards, Denis, *Portal of Hungerford: The Life of Marshal of the Royal Air Force, Viscount Portal of Hungerford, KG, GCB, OM, DSO, MC*. New York, N.Y.: Holmes & Meier, 1977, 11.

2 Portal, Sir Francis, *Portals*, Oxford, Oxford University Press, 1962, in Portal Papers, Christ Church College Oxford (Hereafter referred to as CC), CC/3/I/A.

Captain Charles West Hill, Ellinor Kate, affectionately known as Lil, with whom he would have five further sons, of whom Peter was the eldest.

Lil was the glue the Portal family needed, and the perfect parental foil to Edward. The Portal clan grew rapidly: Reginald in 1894, Hubert the following year and the twins Mervyn and Nigel in 1902.[3] These four joined Peter and his two half-brothers John-Leslie and Gervas at the vibrant Eddington House. Lil treated none of the boys any differently, taking on Rosie's two as if they were her own, and managing a challenging and boisterous brood of seven boys after just a few short years. Her adopted son John said she could not have been any kinder or taken any more interest in him had she been his biological mother.[4] Edward was an extremely strict, though kind, parent, and occasionally a little vociferous. Lil filled the house with love and affection during the blissful but dying embers of peaceful upper-middle class British life that would be so rudely arrested by the First World War.

Eddington House afforded the Portals a degree of luxury, and Peter a varied and privileged upbringing. The country pile had about 400 acres and was staffed by six or seven servants inside the house and a similar number for the grounds.[5] Freed from career distractions, Edward was focused entirely on raising the boys, and he set about introducing his children to a raft of activities. The entire family was involved in hunting, cycling, swimming, golf, shooting and fishing, which stoked the competitive fires in Peter from a young age. He did not care for equestrianism, one of his father's favourite pastimes, preferring to ride a machine rather than an animal with its own notions. Edward was Master of the Hunt, but never pressed his children to partake in an activity they did not wish to, so Peter was allowed to abstain. Reginald remarked it was the only thing he was aware of at which Peter was not good, so although the rest of the family took part in riding parties, Peter gradually dropped out of them.[6] Even at a young age, Peter Portal knew his own mind.

Peter did participate in other family pursuits: shooting, ferreting and any ball games, yet his real love was hawking.[7] His interest came from a chance meeting with Gilbert Blane, the chairman of the Hawking Club Headquarters at Salisbury Plain, when his father was camping with the

---

3 Mervyn died aged six.

4 Interview between John Portal and Denis Richards, 13 Aug 73, CC/3/VIII/A, 3.

5 Interview: Vice Admiral Sir Reginald Portal and Denis Richards, 15 October 1973, CC/3/I/B, 2.

6 Ibid, 4.

7 Richards, *Portal of Hungerford*, 16.

Berkshire Yeomanry.[8] Though all the family enjoyed hawking, Peter took his interest to the next level. Hawking appealed to his patient and meticulous nature and he set his mind to mastery. Ironically, though Portal never kept a wartime diary while head of the Royal Air Force, he did keep a detailed hawking diary during his teenage years, and was a published author on the subject by the age of sixteen. He was obviously not seeking public recognition, as he used the pseudonym 'Tinnuculus' to conceal his real identity.[9] Such modesty truly made him an atypical teenager.

In his love of ball sports, he was perhaps more typical. Of the range of activities promoted by Edward Portal, it was cricket that united everyone at Eddington. There was an occasional cricket pitch at Eddington that was sometimes rolled to allow play, and Edward would assemble a team of both the Portals and the servants. Opposition came from Hungerford and other neighbouring towns to play, and Peter became the most adept of the Portals at cricket as well as other sports to which he set his mind. The inclusion of the servants reflected Edward's staunch belief in showing respect to his staff. The children would be severely chastised should they waste the servants' time, which on one or two occasions they did.

Freedom to roam the house and grounds at Eddington sometimes led to boyish mischief. Edward was peculiarly lenient in allowing the boys to gallivant all over the grounds, including the roof. The boys were always warned to be careful, but never forbidden from exploring.[10] In the course of such endeavour the boys one day discovered all the wiring for the bells on the roof, the means by which the servants could be called from around the house. On the roof, through which the wires ran, the boys could jerk a whole series of wires at once, sending servants scurrying in all directions, and the boys into peals of laughter that did not necessarily reflect their father's perspective.

Nevertheless, Edward's overall philosophy was to let 'boys be boys' and to allow them to enjoy both the many activities on offer, and to bask in the comfort of kith and kin. In this environment of friendly sibling competition, catalysed by the sometime strict overtures of his father and cosseted by the unfettered love of his mother, Peter developed his personal creed. Honourable conduct, physical toughness, and a keen sense of competition

---

8 Interview between Vice Admiral Sir Reginald Portal and Denis Richards, 15 October 1973, CC/3/VIII/A, 5.

9 Portal, Charles, 'Falconry', *The Field*, No. 3095, 20 April 1912, in CC/3/1/C.

10 Interview: Vice Admiral Sir Reginald Portal and Denis Richards, 15 October 1973, CC/3/VIII/A, 7.

were married to a lack of ostentation and a calmness that must have been inherited from Lil rather than Edward.

Peter's idyllic rural homelife was interrupted somewhat by the requirements of a formal education. At twelve, he sat the entrance exam for Winchester, scoring high for his age. Winchester provided a larger group against whom he could test his mettle, and a focus for his burgeoning intellect. Yet hawking remained his first love. Peter and his friend John Selby-Bigge had a secret mews in the loft of a disused mill adjoining the grounds of Winchester School.[11] Hawking provided an outlet for Peter and also a subject for academic work. *The Wykehamist* (the Winchester School journal) records several papers Peter wrote on the subjects of the peregrine falcon, eagles and smaller hawks from 1909 to 1912. The journal remarked upon the instructiveness of the first paper, based on sound personal observation; upon Peter's vivid descriptions of his observation of two eagles in the second, and his quoting of personal experience to add interest to his 'delightful' third paper.[12] This commentary reflected Peter's overall standing in the class, as he came top of his form in his first year and later finished as second commoner prefect in his house. Though time-consuming, hawking was by no means the sole focus of Peter's time at Winchester. He followed a frenetic sporting calendar.

Peter's love of sports was clear for all to see, as was his boundless determination. Nowhere was this demonstrated more clearly than in his becoming the school fives champion. Having reached the final in 1912, Peter had to face A. Hayhurst-France, comfortably the school's best player for the trophy. He lost the first game easily, but gradually clawed his way back into the tie through sheer guts and determination. *The Wykehamist* reported that France seemed certain to win in two, but Portal brought the match to thirteen all through excellent play and then just won the tie break despite being four to one down. In the deciding set, France tired, and Portal won out comfortably, becoming the recipient of the Watney Cup.[13] He also represented the school at fencing, part of a talented threesome, including the later infamous Oswald Mosley. The team crushed Eton fifteen hits to love and went on to win the Public Schools' Championship with both foil and sabre. Mosley recalled Peter as having a quiet dignity of demeanour and

---

11 Letter: Sir John Selby-Bigge to Denis Richards, 5 August 1972, in CC/3/I/D.
12 *The Wykehamist*, No. 471, 21 December 1909, 189; No. 482, 25 November 1910, 309, No. 503, 26 June 1912, 22.
13 Ibid, No. 500, April 1912, 496.

being likeable in every way.[14] Peter also represented the school at cricket, mostly for the second XI until his final year. He was a miserly left-arm spin bowler, but his success in his final year was cut short by a bout of mumps that sidelined him for the final month of the season.[15]

His sporting successes had been significant, but it was Peter's academic endeavour that enabled him to follow in his father's footsteps and earn a place at Christ Church College, Oxford, in 1912. Following a healthy sporting holiday with the family in Skye, Peter arrived at Christ Church. He embarked upon reading law amid the dreaming spires and splendour of the Great Quadrangle, overlooked by Christopher Wren's iconic tower where life was marked by the regular pealing tongue of Great Tom. There Peter met the Steward of the College, Captain Slessor, father of another future Chief of Air Staff, and prepared himself for the 'shadow of work' that would soon fall upon him. He studied law, classics, physics, mathematics, and divinity, yet remained more engaged with his sporting interests of hawking, beagling and, latterly, motor cycling. His friend from Winchester, John Selby-Bigge, accompanied him to Christ Church, and they repeated their old trick of finding mews for the hawks, this time in some faculty stables.[16] There was little, if any, indication of a successful military career to come.

Thrust into unfamiliar surroundings, Peter remained self-assured. One acquaintance recollected him being silent and slightly severe in aspect, but one who knew his raison d'être.[17] Another, who shared a weekly seminar with the College Law Don, could not recall Portal ever addressing a remark to him. 'I don't think he meant to be unfriendly, but he struck me as being too self-sufficient, and with everything under control, that I did not risk any advance.'[18] Though reserved, Peter did make friends at Oxford.

He was one of a group of seven intimate friends who breakfasted together at Christ Church. In March 1913, Christ Church meadow froze, and they played ice hockey while winter endured. When the weather eased, Peter spent an increasing amount of time with Jim Brocklebank, working on his small Mathis car and later their two motorcycles.[19] Peter bought his first motorcycle, a BAT Jap, encouraged by Jim, sometime in 1913 and

14 Letter: Sir Oswald Mosley to Denis Richards, 31 May 1973, in CC/3/I/C.
15 *The Wykehamist*, No. 504, 26 July 1912, in CC/3/I/C.
16 Letter: Sir John Selby-Bigge to Denis Richards, 5 August 1972, in CC/3/I/D.
17 Letter: Reverend R.A. Rawstone to Denis Richards, 30 July 1972, in CC/3/I/D.
18 Letter: G.K. Thompson to Denis Richards, 31 July 1972, in CC/3/I/D.
19 Letter: Sir Fergus Graham to Denis Richards, 2 August 1972, in CC/3/I/D.

joined the Oxford University Motor Cycling Club. In November, Peter took part in the club's speed trials, which determined participation in the varsity match against Cambridge.[20] He achieved a respectable 64.5mph, but this was eclipsed by the Zenith of fellow Christ Church student L.P. Openshaw, who flew down at a remarkable 82.2mph. Nevertheless, amid atrocious road conditions on 27 May 1914, Peter won the inter-varsity hill climb at Kop Hill. While the win may have been more due to Peter's fearless riding than the machine itself, the feat inadvertently brought him to the attention of the authorities.

Peter was the only one of the six surviving Portal boys who did not immediately choose a life of service, yet before long fate interjected. On Bank Holiday Monday, 3 August 1914, the War Office telephoned Oxford to request the names of those who could ride motorcycles. This message was received by the Vice Chancellor, who instructed a locksmith to break open the Proctor's chest wherein lay the list with Portal's name on it. A mere three days later Peter enlisted, embarking upon the humble beginnings of what was to be a glittering military career.[21] As he provided his own motorcycle, and having trained in the Officer Training Corps (OTC), Peter was promoted immediately to corporal and joined the British Expeditionary Force (BEF) in France as a despatch rider on 14 August 1914. Before long, young Portal came to the attention of his superiors, though not initially in the way he would have wished.

The working hours of the BEF despatch rider were long and arduous. One former despatch rider described it as, 'Hell, no sleep, no food and mud for breakfast, dinner and tea.'[22] Seriously undermanned, the riders provided the primary means of communication between headquarters and the field, and were pushed to the brink of exhaustion. On one occasion, having been riding for almost three days without rest, Peter was ordered to shadow Sir Douglas Haig's staff car in case his services were required. When the staff car pulled up at HQ, there was a loud crunch as his motorcycle careened into the back of the general's car; Portal had fallen asleep while riding.[23] Sir Douglas was fortunately understanding of the

20 Richards, *Portal of Hungerford*, 33.
21 Recollections of Sir John Masterman, told at a luncheon at the Savoy Hotel, London, 25 July 1972, given by Mr Harald Peake, CC/3/X.
22 Letter: Dr John Doyle to Sir Charles Portal, 15 August 1945, in CC/3/II/A.
23 Air Commodore Harald Peake, 'Marshal of the Royal Air Force Lord Portal of Hungerford,' *The Royal Air Forces Quarterly, Vol. 11, No. 3 Autumn 1971*, CC/3/X.

incident and it may even have spurred him to request augmented numbers of riders on 28 September 1914.

Such weariness was not localised to the riders, as French and British forces alike were pushed back further and further in the face of the German Schlieffen Plan onslaught. Sir Archibald Murray, Chief of Staff to Sir John French, on one occasion sat for thirty minutes incapable of thought or action, with perspiration streaming down his face.[24] This was a combined result of not having slept for seventy hours and receiving two letters from the respective commanders of the British First and Second Armies, stating that neither could be extricated.

Despite the combination of fatigue and the morale impact of the retreat, Portal flourished. He rose through the ranks rapidly due to his resourcefulness and quick thinking. On one occasion, Portal and a fellow despatch rider were trapped behind German lines. The pair held up a German lorry and disposed of its driver, before stowing the bikes in the back and driving back to GHQ. It may have been this action that brought Portal to the attention of Haig; in early October Portal was promoted to lieutenant.[25] Shortly thereafter he was also mentioned in despatches as one of many whose service was considered particularly meritorious by General French, the Commander of the BEF.

The early days of the war were particularly hazardous and, in addition to the narrow escape above, Portal was also fortunate to survive the German shelling of a town in which he was billeted. In a candid letter home, Portal wrote:

> We have been having exciting times lately. We are in a town and, as usual, within range of the German heavy artillery. I was coming out of the signal office, talking in the doorway, when a huge 'Black Maria' shell fell in the street just outside. We were all blown through the door. I was not touched. Two men on my right were killed, two on my left were frightfully wounded, and three more were killed in the street outside. It was the most awful ten minutes I have ever had trying to help the poor men who had been hit … We got stretchers and a doctor, and moved the wounded to the hospital. One despatch rider was killed, and one slightly wounded.[26]

---

24 Extract from diary of Colonel T.W. Sheppard, 1st King's (Liverpool) Regiment, in CC/3/II/A.
25 Richards, *Portal of Hungerford*, 36.
26 *Newby News*, 5 November 1914, in CC/3/II/A.

Portal's ability to operate under these conditions reflected his attitude of feeling fortunate to have survived, rather than fearing what may come. It also echoed his fearlessness when riding a bicycle as a child and his motorcycle at Oxford. Fortunately, after this close brush with death, the front began to stabilise and the missions of the despatch riders became more mundane. Despite being given the additional responsibility of Motorcycle Officer, in charge of all the riders in his company, Portal yearned for more.

Staff work, at least at this stage of his life, did not suit young Portal, so he requested a secondment to the Royal Flying Corps. Absent any flying experience, Portal was initially assigned as an observer to No. 3 Squadron in July 1915, based in Auchel and working with the 1st Corps. The early days of military aviation saw rapid advances, as the combatants came to realise the value of control of the air. However, the No. 3 Squadron Morane Parasols were yet to be fitted with the Lewis gun, so the observers were armed with stripped rifles and 100 rounds of .303 ammunition to fight off attacks.[27] Hazards to life were exacerbated by the tricky aircraft itself, in which 'the chances of death by misadventure on the aerodrome were infinitely greater than by enemy action.'[28] New to the RFC, Portal endured a steep learning curve that involved assimilating the Artillery Code, airborne navigation, and the operation of the Lewis gun (despite its absence from the cockpit). With a dearth of flying personnel available, Portal's duties centred almost exclusively on the flying task, and particularly artillery observation. The level of training available reflected the embryonic nature of both the service and the task as, following a half hour's talk from the departing artillery pilot and two 'demonstration shoots' with 6 and 9.2in Howitzers, Portal was deemed a specialist in artillery observation.

The Royal Flying Corps was desperately short of manpower and plagued by inexperience. Portal's pilot was Captain Hubbard, who had never flown over the lines either, and had only once before flown the Morane, which he had wrecked.[29] Fortunately, Hubbard proved to be a competent pilot and despite the engine missing frequently and the constant interruptions from anti-aircraft fire, the pair arrived safely back at base following their first mission over enemy lines.

---

27 Portal, Charles, *War Experiences 1915–1918*, essay produced at RAF Staff College, Andover in 1922, in The National Archives, Kew (hereafter referred to as TNA), TNA/AIR/1/2386/228/11/1, 1.

28 Portal, *War Experiences*, 2.

29 Ibid.

This incident was symptomatic of the general struggles of the military coming to grips with emerging technology. The arrangement of pilot and observer was awkward, with the observer in front and the pilot behind. Artillery support, which became Portal's primary task, was done by signalling with a lamp, a task thoroughly inhibited by the wash from the propeller being directly in his face. The job of the aircrew was threefold: to choose targets from the air, report results of fire, and detail new enemy dispositions to friendly brigade commanders.[30] The pilot flew back and forth between the batteries and the targets to conduct battle damage assessment and then permit the observer to signal, with his rather cumbersome lamp, the success or otherwise of the firing.[31] So began Portal's remarkable career as an aviator, and his first steps in understanding the value of air and land working in tandem.

The rate of technological change during Portal's year with No. 3 Squadron was prodigious. It was not possible to war fit the Moranes prior to arrival at the squadron, so significant alterations were made in situ. Gun mountings, bomb racks both for the undercarriage and on the wings, bomb sights as well as instrument boards were all retro fitted by squadron engineers.[32] Photo reconnaissance began to play a part in squadron activity and the development of wireless improved communications between ground and air.

Following the first leave he had taken in almost a year, Portal returned to France and a changing air battle. The effectiveness of single-seat fighters during the early part of the First World War was hampered by the inability of pilots to shoot effectively through the propellers. Once Roland Garros fitted steel plates to the inside of his two-bladed propellers, the fight for air superiority began in earnest. Garros's enhancement was improved by a German-employed Dutch inventor, Anthony Fokker, who devised the interrupter gear to stop the gun firing when the propeller was in the way. Thus began the fabled 'Fokker Scourge.' Portal had several encounters with German Fokkers, and these became more common as 1915 waned. The additional danger had convinced Portal that his automatic Winchester

30 Jones, H., & Raleigh, Walter Alexander, Sir, *The War in the Air: Being the story of the part played in the Great War by the Royal Air Force: Appendices* (History of the Great War). Oxford: Clarendon Press, 1937, 124.

31 Douglas, Sholto, *Years of Combat; the First Volume of the Autobiography of Sholto Douglas.* London: Collins, 1963, 74.

32 *No. 3 Squadron Diary 1914–18*, TNA AIR 1/687/21/20/3, 8.

rifle would not suffice and he persuaded his pilot to let him carry a Lewis machine gun. This proved to be a fortuitous decision as, on 19 December 1915, a No. 3 Squadron formation was set upon by no less than Max Immelmann, the German fighter ace. Immelmann attacked two of the three Moranes, one of whom fired half a drum of Lewis at the Fokker from a range of 300 yards. It may well have been the superior firepower of the Lewis, trained on Immelmann, that deterred him from a closer approach to the Morane, and he retreated to a distance of 500 yards.[33] Immelmann shadowed the Moranes until he became short on fuel, awaiting any engine problems upon which he could capitalise. Thereafter he dived away, which was fortunate for Portal and Captain Harvey-Kelly, the pilot, as the Lewis gun in their Morane was inoperable.[34] As the German push for air superiority intensified, Portal decided he wanted a more direct role in the fighting and applied to train as a pilot.

If expertise was lacking at the front, it was equally scarce in the flying school at Castle Bromwich. Portal reported upon the prevailing ignorance of 60 per cent of the instructors, whose meagre performance in the aircraft was often quickly outstripped by their students.[35] Though there was a surprising absence of serious accidents, morale among the students was nevertheless very low. On 27 April 1916, Portal graduated from the Central Flying School as a flying officer, RFC with a total of twenty-nine hours as a pilot. His final assignment as a trainee was to fly a Martinsyde Scout to Gosport, where he would join No. 60 Squadron and proceed to France. Portal's experience as a trainee pilot was not one that sat well. Morale on No. 60 Squadron was noticeably better though, and the standard of instruction from Captain R.R. Smith-Barry a great improvement.[36] Portal conducted twenty-six further training flights at Gosport before the squadron departed for France, observed by a young Cecil Lewis, who noted:

> We stood on the tarmac watching them go. And still, after twenty years, my heart swells at the memory of the sight. I can hear the strong engines and smell the tang of the burnt oil. I can see them as they came hurtling up, their goggled pilots

---

33 McCudden, Major James T.B., *Flying Fury: Five Years in the Royal Flying Corps*, New York, Doubleday & Co, 1968, 84–85.

34 Richards, *Portal of Hungerford*, 45–46.

35 Portal, *War Experiences*, 5.

36 Ibid., 6.

and observers leaning down to wave a last farewell before they passed in a deafening flash of speed and smoke fifty feet overhead. One by one, they came up as if saluting us – drum, roll crescendo, cymbal crash, rapid diminuendo. One by one, they disappeared behind the sheds.[37]

For some, it would mark the last time they saw England's green and pleasant land.

Portal arrived back in France for the disastrous beginning of the Battle of the Somme. Though the strategic aim of the battle, to relieve pressure on the French at Verdun, was achieved, the human cost was exorbitant. The RFC was used more heavily than ever before and Portal, reunited with old friends at No. 3 Squadron in July, was in the thick of it. Portal was appointed temporary captain and flight commander, a mark of the regard in which his commanding officer and former pilot, Major Harvey-Kelly, held him. Portal claimed thorough ignorance of administrative matters but set to work on both keeping the flight going and mastering his operational craft.[38]

During the next eleven months, Portal flew no fewer than 326 times as a pilot with the squadron. He was soon recognised as an 'artillery spotting' expert.[39] The excellence of his counter-battery work made him the subject of everyday comment within the corps.[40] Before long, his work was formally recognised. On 10 January 1917 *The London Gazette* announced the award of the Military Cross to:

> Temp. Lieut. (temp. Capt.) C.F.A. Portal, RE Special Reserve and RFC. For conspicuous gallantry in action. He has done excellent artillery work in the air, often in bad weather and at low altitudes; he has always set his flight the best of examples. On one occasion he shot down a hostile machine.[41]

This latter point was significant as the Army co-operation aircraft of No. 3 Squadron were not equipped to engage in air-to-air combat but to spot

---

37 Lewis, Cecil, *Sagittarius Rising*, Great Novels and Memoirs of World War I, Harrisburg, P.A.: Stackpole Books, 1967, 28 and republished Barnsley: Pen & Sword, 2009.

38 Portal, *War Experiences*, 7.

39 Richards, *Portal of Hungerford*, 55.

40 *Recommendations for Honours and Awards*, TNA/AIR 163/15/142/7.

41 *Supplement to the Edinburgh Gazette*, 12 January 1917, 126.

and to bomb enemy batteries. Even in this latter regard, Portal remained incredibly humble. In a war filled with pilots overclaiming kills, Portal did the exact opposite. In a combat report from 10 November 1916, he reported engaging a large biplane, diving on its tail as it prepared to attack a No. 3 Squadron Morane. Portal closed to 150 yards and fired a drum from his Lewis gun. Though others saw the machine out of control, Portal stated that he did not see this, and only watched for five seconds before turning away having heard firing behind him.[42] Despite such humility, a few short months later, Portal was once again recognised, this time with the more auspicious Distinguished Service Order:

> For many months he has done magnificent work in co-operation with the artillery. During an attack he succeeded in silencing nine active hostile batteries, ranging our artillery. His splendid example has been of the greatest value.[43]

Still in his early twenties, Portal enjoyed a burgeoning reputation in the RFC, and it was time to take the next natural step.

The award of the DSO came shortly following Portal's appointment as the squadron commander for No. 16 Squadron and promotion to rank of major. Portal had risen, in three short years, from being a corporal despatch rider to being a decorated front-line squadron commander at the heart of the fight in France. Even at this stage, Portal was becoming renowned and his subordinates greatly respected both his coolness and leadership.[44] In no way did Portal rest upon his laurels. He saw it as his duty to provide the best example he could for his men, and set about doing so. In the following few months, working in support of a Canadian artillery brigade, Portal distinguished himself once more. The General Officer Commanding the Royal Artillery of the Canadian Corps wrote of the 'very gallant and useful work' performed by Portal, asserting that, 'whenever extremely difficult or dangerous work had to be carried out this officer has done it himself.'[45] Coincidentally, working with the Canadians at this time was a young Army officer, Alan Brooke, with whom Portal would later derive and drive Britain's military strategy in the next world war. Portal did not recall the

---

42 *Combats in the Air*, TNA/AIR 2248/209/43/15.
43 *Edinburgh Gazette*, 17 July 1917, 1385.
44 Reed Douglas, *Insanity Fair*, Cape: London, 1939, 37.
45 Peake, *Marshal of the Royal Air Force*, CC/3/X, 5.

two having met at that time, but Brooke must have been aware of the RAF's sterling support and Portal's remarkable leadership of No. 16 Squadron.[46]

The role of the squadron commander was an extremely challenging one. Portal had to run the squadron on the ground, attending to all the matters of administrivia, as well as understanding the changing battle in the air, all while maintaining touch with the corps staff, heavy artillery and some of the batteries.[47] Unable to do all these things, Portal wisely delegated some of the paperwork and concentrated on the operational activities of the squadron. The variety of missions was significant, and Portal took full part in artillery observation, special reconnaissance duties, engine tests, weather tests, test flights, artillery registration, fighting duties, and bombing raids.[48] He truly led from the front and by example, so it was little surprise when he was mentioned in despatches once again in December 1917.[49]

It was perhaps 16 February 1918 that saw Portal's finest hour during the First World War. Flying with Captain C.T. Cleaver MC, Portal escorted his squadron formation over enemy lines to target a German long-range gun. Around twenty German machines attacked the formation and Portal engaged no fewer than five single-handedly. He lured the Germans away from the bombing aircraft and enabled a successful attack on the German artillery. During a frantic ten minutes, he drove down three enemy aircraft, earning the rare accolade of a bar to his Distinguished Service Order.[50] The full award citation from July 1918 illustrates Portal's massive contribution during his final months with No. 16 Squadron:

> For conspicuous gallantry and devotion to duty. During a period of four months, chiefly under adverse weather conditions, he repeatedly carried out successful raids by day and night, his ingenuity and daring enabling him to drop many tons of bombs on important enemy posts. One night he crossed the lines five times, only landing between each flight to replenish with bombs. Another day he took on single-handed five enemy machines, and drove down

---

46 Interview: M.C. Long with Sir Charles Portal, 1952, in Alanbrooke Papers, King's College London (hereafter referred to as KCL/AB), KCL/AB/11/7/1.

47 Portal, Charles, *War Experiences*, 9.

48 *No. 16 Squadron R.F.C. Record Book Oct-Dec 1917*, TNA/AIR/1/1346/204/19/36.

49 *Supplement to the London Gazette*, 11 December 1917, 12924.

50 *Supplement to the London Gazette*, 23 July 1918, 8739.

three of them – a most gallant and splendid feat. On another day, despite thick mist, he registered one of our batteries on an enemy battery, causing the destruction of one pit and obtaining one fire and two explosions; and another day, flying for 5¼ hours, he carried out two very successful counter-battery shoots, observing 350 rounds. He has always set the most magnificent example to the squadron under his command.[51]

Portal's bravery and competence were clear for all to see, yet as squadron commander his duties were much broader and often more difficult.

If Portal was somewhat fortunate to have made it this far through the war, some of his men were not. On 22 October 1917, Portal lost one of his pilots. Francis Marchant was also a family friend. The squadron commander wrote immediately to Francis's father and then three days later to Francis's mother. In this letter Portal wrote:

Since I wrote to Mr Marchant about the death of your son, I have found out a great deal which I should like to tell you … It may be some comfort to you to know that his body is not in the very slightest degree disfigured. I wish you could have seen his face. Never in the six months I have known him have I seen him look more happy and peaceful. I have never had a friend I loved more dearly than Francis and I know that this convincing proof that his death was painless and happy means as much to you as it does to me.

It is terribly hard for me to know your wishes but I hope I did right in saying he should be buried just as he died in his flying clothes and uniform. I took the great risk also of cutting a lock of hair from his dear head, and I enclose in this letter. If I hurt you by sending it please forgive me. I had no-one to consult and merely did what my own people wished to be done …

Sharing in your great sorrow I know well that this letter will be hard for you to read as it is for me to write but I cannot finish it without telling you that of all the friends I have ever

---

51 Ibid.

made there was never one I loved as dearly as Francis. He was the straightest, cleanest, kindest, and best, and I shall never know another like him.

In his work, which he adored, he was perfectly splendid, and all our lives were brightened and made better by knowing him. I never knew him unhappy and now that I know he died in peace I can only think it was not he who suffered but we who are for the time being separated from him.

I can only pray God to comfort us all.[52]

Though some considered Portal standoffish and aloof, the care and compassion Portal demonstrated in his letter writing convey his deep sense of humanity. Rather than being arrogant, as some perceived, Portal was simply introverted and found the written word more easily than the spoken. Professor R.V. Jones, one of the chief British scientists during the war, considered that 'speaking did not come very easily to him, especially when he had to say something particularly complimentary, but when the words came, they were good.'[53]

As the German Spring Offensive of 1918 petered out, and the Allies prepared for a decisive counter-attack, Portal's war drew to a close. On 17 June 1918 he was promoted and posted to No. 24 Wing near Grantham, passing command of No. 16 Squadron to Major A.C.K.W. Parr. Portal's fighting during the First World War was complete, and he was well on the path to success. Having distinguished himself through his bravery, leadership and pursuit of excellence, Portal was now marked for advancement by none other than Trenchard, who would lead the RAF through the next decade.

---

52 Richards, *Portal of Hungerford*, 57.
53 Recollections of Professor R.V. Jones, Savoy Hotel, London, 25 July 1972, luncheon given by Mr Harald Peake, CC/3/X/2.

Chapter 2

The Interwar Years

He who would trade liberty,
For some temporary security,
Deserves neither liberty nor security.

Benjamin Franklin

Amidst the swingeing post-war defence cuts, a high-level sponsor was essential if a permanent commission was to be obtained. Portal could have returned to his legal studies in Oxford, but he was forever changed by his experiences in France. He was awarded a permanent commission (one of around only 1,000) on 1 August 1919, a week after his wedding to Joan Welby, daughter of Sir Charles Welby.[1] Following a honeymoon in Scotland, the Portals set up house in Rauceby, an idyllic village a couple of miles from RAF Cranwell, where Peter was posted. Portal was to be the chief flying instructor at the flying training wing, led by Wing Commander L.B.W. Rees VC. Both Portal and Rees kept hawks on tethers outside their offices. Peter was remembered by members of the school as both enigmatic and hawkish, much like the birds he so adored. Portal was not in the habit of explaining things that were apparent to him, but expected his wishes, unspoken or not, to be obeyed.

One evening, Portal gave his clerk a secret document to return to Rees's office with the added instruction to obtain a signed receipt for it. The clerk, W.H. Warman, found the office empty so secured the document in a locked drawer and left for home. The next day Portal enquired if Warman had obtained a receipt for the document and the clerk reasonably explained that Rees had already left for the day. 'You must always get a signature,' Portal insisted.

---

1 Richards, Denis, *Portal of Hungerford: The Life of Marshal of the Royal Air Force, Viscount Portal of Hungerford, KG, GCB, OM, DSO, MC. New York, N.Y.:* Holmes & Meier, 1977, 73.

'Please Sir you do have my word for it, that it was safely delivered and secured.'

'Warman, I trust you most implicitly but there is just one thing.'

'What's that Sir?' he quickly retorted most hopefully.

'You could drop dead and then we would have no proof.'

This exchange puzzled Warman for years, and it was not until he was in his sixties that the answer occurred to him. Had he placed the receipt book with the secret document in the locked drawer, a signature would have been ready for him in the morning.[2] Portal clearly knew the solution to the conundrum but did not feel it necessary to explain this to the clerk at the time, or at any future point! Such quirks were endearing to some, but vastly frustrating to others, who viewed them as evidence of Portal's intellectual arrogance.[3] More likely is that Portal enjoyed these logical puzzles and used them as both tests of his staff and amusing asides. According to Sir John Cordingley, even at this early stage, Trenchard had Portal in mind as a potential future Chief of Air Staff. Cranwell was Trenchard's creation and he attached great importance to the men sent there.[4]

Following a successful tour, Portal was selected to be a student at the brand-new RAF Staff College. The first intake at the Staff College was an exalted group, destined to scale the heights of the new service. Future Chief of Fighter and Coastal Command, Sholto Douglas, Future Chief of Bomber Command, Richard Peirse and, most famous of all, Air Officer Commanding 11 Group during the Battle of Britain, Keith Park, were among Portal's classmates. Their spartan surroundings did not befit the future fame of the group. Parliament allotted a paltry £18.4 million to both the RAF and civil aviation in 1921–22 and reduced this to an eye-watering £11 million the following year. The first Air Staff College operated from brick buildings at Andover Airfield with minimal heating, where the cold often bit in the heart of winter. One of the students, John Baldwin, reported that, 'Many ... found it advisable to consume copious draughts of hot rum and milk during the morning break to avoid complete "icing-up" during the second lecture spell. The routine was a wild rush to the anteroom, and while the required stimulant was being ordered and consumed, a round of whisky-poker was played. The

---

2 Letter: W.H. Warman to Denis Richards, 15 October 1972, in Portal Papers, Christ Church College Oxford (Hereafter referred to as CC), CC/3/III/B.

3 Anthony Furse, *Wilfrid Freeman*, Spellmount, 2000, 160.

4 Interview: Denis Richards and Sir John Cordingley, 14 November 1972, CC/3/III.

first player to lose three lives was host to the rest.'[5] Despite the austerity, the group engaged in the college's aim to provide its students a general education, and to teach them how to think, in preference to what to think. The student body responded well, engaging fully while enduring the minimalistic living arrangements at Andover, whose conditions were, nevertheless, infinitely preferable to those its students had encountered a few short years earlier in France. Following successful completion of the course, Portal moved to the Air Ministry, where the significant figure of Trenchard loomed large.

Portal's new role fell in the Directorate of Operations and Intelligence, where he was responsible for domestic flying operations. A few weeks later Joan gave birth to their second child, Rosemary Ann, who thankfully was born healthy. Their first baby, Richard, had died shortly following birth in autumn 1921. A posting to the Air Ministry was an essential rung on the ladder for a future leader and Portal quickly got to grips with the machinations of Whitehall and the machinery of government. Because there were only seven squadrons in Britain at that time, Portal became a self-styled operational requirements branch. His detailed technical knowledge enabled him to draw up requirements for new aircraft that would then be built by industry in very small numbers. Portal would frequently observe the testing of these prototypes with Trenchard. If the test pilots were complimentary of the new aircraft, Trenchard would consider a larger order, but such orders were extremely limited given the political conditions.[6]

Amid a governmental policy of 'no war for ten years,' and a bitter inter-service fight, the RAF was battling for its survival and Trenchard was its knight in shining armour. In such economic circumstances, Trenchard's pursuit of economy demonstrated extreme political savoir faire. He laid the foundations for the future service, understanding well that the finances for a large organisation simply did not exist at the time. For example, of the 4,000 commissions he created after the First World War, only about 1,000 were permanent. This allowed the RAF to reduce costs but keep the personnel. Moreover, Trenchard expertly manipulated the British Army's failure to economically suppress a revolt in Iraq in 1921 (it cost around £40,000,000) and convinced Churchill to hand over control to the RAF, both expanding its role and ensuring its independence.[7] Though Portal, as a co-operative

---

5 Richards, *Portal of Hungerford*, 79.

6 Richards, *Portal of Hungerford*, 83.

7 Corum, James S. and Johnson, Wray R., *Airpower in Small Wars: Fighting Insurgents and Terrorists*. Modern War Studies. Lawrence, Kan.: University Press of Kansas, 2003, 55.

joint officer, may not have entirely approved of this adversarial approach, he could not fail to learn some salient lessons from it. Trenchard had patiently waited for his opportunity and then ruthlessly exploited it for the benefit of the junior service. While Portal would always remain a co-operator at heart, he saw at first-hand the cut-throat nature of inter-service politics. As one historian noted, 'The only place the navy was prepared to bury the hatchet was in Trenchard's back.'[8]

Further education for Portal came through attendance at a series of conferences held in Trenchard's office in July 1923. Even here as a relatively lowly squadron leader, Portal showed his grit by disagreeing with Trenchard regarding the appropriate balance between fighter and bomber squadrons. Trenchard insisted there was no such thing as a correct ratio and, being offensively minded, wanted as many bomber squadrons as possible. Trenchard viewed France as Britain's likely next opponent and thought that in a bombing war the French would 'squeal before we did.'[9] While Trenchard favoured a mere thirteen fighter squadrons, out of a total allocation of fifty-two, Portal's branch recommended twenty. Portal was mindful of ensuring the protection of the British people from enemy bombers, a factor Trenchard vastly underrated. The fact that Trenchard settled on a figure of sixteen fighter squadrons says much for both men.[10]

Portal spent three years with the Air Ministry, including a stint at the senior officers' war course at the Royal Naval College. This early exposure to the Air Ministry was a vital grounding in Portal's professional development. He had seen Trenchard walk a fine line to ensure the survival of the RAF, amid the stinging attacks of the other services. This experience would stand Portal in good stead when he had to continue the battle in the early 1930s as Deputy Director Plans. However, in the interim, he was assigned as commander of No. 7 Squadron at Worthy Down, where he would first encounter a key ally in the future fight against Germany.

Having supported night bombing in Trenchard's discussion group, it was fitting that Portal was assigned to the home of night flying – Worthy Down. The primary exponent of this activity was Arthur Harris, the commander of No. 58 Squadron. Both squadrons flew Vickers Virginias, which were slow and lightly armoured. They had little to no survivability flying

8 Smith, Malcolm, quoted in Miller, Russell, *Boom: The Life of Viscount Trenchard: Father of the Royal Air Force,* London: Weidenfeld & Nicolson, 2016, 279.
9 Russell, *Boom,* 279.
10 Richards, *Portal of Hungerford,* 90.

in the daytime, so Harris concentrated on night flying training, and No. 58 Squadron was considered the best.[11] Portal's competitive edge quickly came to the fore as he challenged his boys to outstrip Harris's at their own game. Portal's spirit and determination infected the squadron and a rapid improvement in morale and effectiveness ensued.

The acid test of this improvement came when competing for the annual Laurence Minot Memorial Trophy, awarded for the most accurate bombing squadron of the year. The trophy was named after a bomber pilot killed in 1917 and a donation made in memoriam funded the Air Ministry prize. Harris's squadron was the reigning champion, but Portal fired up his troops for their yearly visit to the North Coates Fitties bombing and firing ranges, where they would be assessed. The competition to represent No. 7 Squadron for the trophy was fierce, but Portal was 'without any shadow of doubt the Squadron's best bomb aimer.'[12] Portal's attention to detail played into this, as he was observed at night, polishing his practise bombs, presumably to ensure a more aerodynamic and predictable drop pattern.[13] No. 7 Squadron won the trophy in consecutive years with Portal as the bomb aimer, establishing a tradition of excellence that the squadron carried through the 1930s, during which time they won on several more occasions. Portal's leadership of the squadron greatly enhanced his growing reputation, and he was fondly remembered by all. Sir John Whitley stated, 'I can honestly say that in all my service life I have never served on a station where the morale was so high – we worked hard and we played hard.'[14] Many echoed these sentiments and there was a sense of sadness across the station when the Portals left Worthy Down, initially for the Imperial Defence College, and then back to London.

Portal's second posting with the Air Staff was as the Deputy Director Plans (in the Directorate of Operations and Planning once again). His remit included both single service and joint projects. In the latter vein, Portal was a member of the Joint Planning Sub-Committee that sat underneath the Committee of Imperial Defence. The acrimonious character of inter-service relations had not dissipated in Portal's absence and is succinctly described by Portal's number two at Plans, Squadron Leader (later Air Chief Marshal Sir) Ralph Cochrane:

---

11 Richards, *Portal of Hungerford*, 94.
12 Ibid., 95.
13 Letter: L.T. Carruthers to Denis Richards, 7 October 1972, CC/3/III/F.
14 Richards, *Portal of Hungerford*, 95.

At that time, one was writing papers and trying hard to propagate new ideas which were totally opposed by the accepted ideas of the other two services. There were no points of agreement that I can really think of between the other two services and the Air Force. Everything was in dispute. Even the very existence of the Air Force was in dispute, with both the other two services ganging up to try to divide it between them. Anyone who was head of Plans at the time was in the forefront of that battle – they couldn't help but be –and it was entirely due to the skill and intelligence of Portal and Harris that the Royal Air Force survived.[15]

Harris followed Portal into the Plans job. The combined work of the two men, coupled with the fact that the Navy and Army were often pulling in different directions, saved the RAF and possibly the country. Portal recalled discussions that took place regarding the defence of Singapore. The Royal Navy had been approved to build a large base there in 1921 to combat future Japanese aggression, but there was little agreement between the services regarding the defensive measures needed. The Army argued for six large 15in guns pointing seaward, while Trenchard desired a more flexible response using torpedo-bombers, fighters, and reconnaissance planes that could be reinforced from Iraq and India in the event of a crisis. Unfortunately, there was no air route from Calcutta at the time and the squadrons did not exist so, as an interim measure, three of the six guns were installed in 1926. These guns were followed by a flying boat squadron in 1929 and a torpedo bomber squadron in 1931. This was the state of play when Portal entered the fray and sensibly argued that 'any base on the east coast of Malaya would be liable to capture and use by the enemy unless adequately defended or capable of destruction at short notice.'[16] Portal's argument permeated the dense foliage of Army and Navy minds over time, and shortly after his departure from Plans, a lay down of five and a half squadrons in peacetime and nine and a half in war was established. In the event, this proved horribly inadequate when the Japanese invaded in December 1941.

---

15 Saward, Dudley, *Bomber Harris: The Story of Marshal of the Royal Air Force, Sir Arthur Harris*, 1st ed. in the USA ed. Garden City, N.Y.: Doubleday, 1985, 79.

16 Richards, *Portal of Hungerford*, 101.

Despite the seriousness of the work at the Air Ministry, Portal's dry wit sometimes burst forth. Squadron Leader (later Air Marshal Sir) Gerald Gibbs was a close observer of Portal's humour during this period at the Air Ministry. 'He sometimes enjoyed transposing the clichés of officialise in drafts of letters – for example in place of the frequent stereotyped opening phrase "You will remember that" – he suggested "You have forgotten, if indeed you ever knew".'[17] Gibbs also recollected asking Portal why he insisted on returning from leave (Portal was in the habit of taking his entire sixty-one-day allocation in a single block) on a Thursday. Portal replied, 'so that the weekend arrives before I am struck with the full horror of being back.'[18] These asides helped to humanise Portal to his colleagues as he was exceptionally dedicated to work and somewhat introverted.

Portal's reputation was further enhanced during his time in Plans. He had a tireless work ethic, and was an outstanding staff officer who wrote in simple, easily comprehensible language. His habit was to write in the mornings before sending a proofed copy to CAS in the early afternoon. The output coming from a single source strengthened the message and the RAF was able to survive broadsides from both the Navy and Army. Portal was regarded as sometimes hard, but never seen as unfair. His diligence was rewarded with promotion to group captain in 1931 and further reward was to come in the form of command. This was no less than Portal deserved following a remarkable staff tour, summed up by Sir Ralph Cochrane. 'Portal's contribution to the Air Force during this period was immense.'[19]

Portal's upcoming command in Aden was reported in the *Daily Telegraph* as, 'the most important command a Group Captain can obtain.'[20] That an airman was now in charge of Aden, and had been since 1927, was a resounding endorsement of Trenchard's policy of Air Control. He had successfully wrestled more responsibility from the hands of the British Army and arguably made the RAF more indispensable in the Empire than it was at home. Naturally, the RAF was not alone in Aden; there was both a residual Army presence and local levies, for whom Portal was also responsible. He did not form a favourable opinion of Aden at first, which was likely due to the short-term absence of his family. Nevertheless, he quickly got to grips with the business of joint command.

---

17 CC/3/VIII/A, Richards, *Portal of Hungerford,* 105.
18 CC/3/VIII/A.
19 Richards, *Portal of Hungerford,* 104.
20 *Daily Telegraph,* 29 September 1933, CC/3/III/H.

Before long, Portal had to execute the doctrine of Air Control. Some members of the Quteibi tribe had attacked a Yemeni caravan, which required the protectorate to act. The crime was the more serious because the tribesmen had actually been paid to protect the caravan during an earlier part of the route. Operations against the tribe lasted two months from 22 March to 21 May 1934, and Portal later lectured on Air Control at the Royal United Services Institute.[21] Portal acknowledged the requirements for Army units to take the lead in urban areas where the guilty and innocent lived side by side. However, in the large hinterlands of the British Empire, aircraft came to the fore. Portal was also at pains to illustrate the difference between Air Control and punishment bombing, a distinction lost on many. Portal asserted that Air Control involved significant dialogue between the tribe and an RAF liaison officer, and bombing only occurred when villagers refused to acquiesce to British demands. There would then be a warning to clear the village, followed by a bombing strike to teach the tribesmen a lesson. What ensued was a form of psychological warfare, to outlast the tribesmen.

Most important in the theory of Air Control was to establish the guilt of the tribe in question, as they may merely have had the finger pointed at them by another group. Once attribution was proven, a meeting was set up with the Quteibi Sheikh, who was offered a reasonable alternative to the bombing. In this case, the Quteibi Sheikh was ordered to surrender those responsible, pay a fine, and was given ten days to do so. Having failed to comply, the tribe was then ordered to take its people and animals and leave the village until the government told them they could return. The bombing then began, but not as wholesale destruction, just enough to keep the villagers from their fields and homes. Thus began the psychological element. The tribe went through various stages of defiance, boasting, anger and finally acceptance before returning to the bargaining table. The government then explained they only wished the Quteibi to become, once again, lawful members of the larger community. The action was a complete success and cost the lives of only three Quteibi tribesmen who attempted to take a delayed action bomb apart.[22]

Portal's time in Aden was busy, challenging, and personally rewarding. In his spare time, he took up sailing, at which he naturally excelled.[23]

---

21 Portal, C.F.A., 'Air Force Co-operation in Policing the Empire,' lecture at RUSI, 17 February 1937, *Royal United Services Institution Journal*, Vol. 82, Issue 526.

22 Portal, C.F.A., 'Air Force Co-operation,' 354.

23 Notes on Portal: Air Vice Marshal W.M. Yool, 6 October 1972, CC/3/III/F.

He ordered a 4-ton sailing boat from England, which arrived only ten days before the first race of the 1934 season. Nevertheless, he was able to report to his mother that he won the first race. The ease with which Portal appeared to master this tricky sport astonished his friends in Aden.[24] The secret of his success lay in characteristically meticulous research. This careful preparation should come as no surprise from a man who polished his bombs prior to the Laurence Minot Trophy run to ensure a more uniform distribution. Where sailing was concerned, Portal studied the local winds and learned the race regulations to discern any possible advantages that could be gleaned. He became so adept that he was able to carry off the Aden 'aggregate cup' in 1935. Life was idyllic as Joan and the girls joined in the gamut of sporting activities in which Portal engaged: sailing, fishing, swimming, and surfing. The family safaried in British Somaliland, attended the local church, and entertained visiting dignitaries. In early 1935, Portal was promoted to air commodore, becoming the youngest in the service. Life was good; however, this blissful existence was soon interrupted. The rise of dictators caused a growing unease in Europe, and before long its spectre approached Aden, as Mussolini planned his assault on Abyssinia.

The Abyssinia Crisis was precipitated by the ambition of Mussolini, the naivety of the British and the French, and the indifference of the Americans. Mussolini wanted to expand the Italian Empire in Africa, and set his sights on Abyssinia, modern-day Ethiopia, and Eritrea. A disputed border area led to several skirmishes, to which the League of Nations largely turned a blind eye. Mussolini continued to build up his forces, mobilising two divisions in February 1935 amidst growing Ethiopian nervousness. While Mussolini agreed to a League of Nations arbitration of the dispute, he had no plans to call off the invasion and talks fell apart in mid-July. The League of Nations took insipid action even after Ethiopia declared war on Italy. It was only on 7 October 1935, following Italy's invasion, that the League finally declared Italy as the aggressor but none of the great powers took any serious action to deter or roll back the Italian action. Worried about its credibility, and fearing Italy's withdrawal, the League applied economic sanctions, but crucially excluded sanctions on oil and coal for Italy, which may have resolved the crisis.[25] Uncertain how far Mussolini would go, and

---

24 Richards, *Portal of Hungerford*, 113.

25 Strang, G. Bruce, "'The Worst of All Worlds:" Oil Sanctions and Italy's Invasion of Abyssinia, 1935–1936.' *Diplomacy and statecraft* 19, No. 2 (2008): 210–211.

conscious of the Italians' dependence on Aden for water supply, Portal's fears of an assault on Aden grew.

By late October, Portal had received reinforcements from all three services, including a squadron each of fighters, bombers, and flying boats. The immediate danger had passed, but Portal had worked tirelessly to integrate these new forces into the limited space at Aden. Most significant was the arrival of the warships on 11–13 September, after which Aden was defensible. For once, and in great contrast to his experiences in the Air Ministry, Portal was pleased to see the Royal Navy. His calm deportment was remarkable during a period in which he was under extreme pressure.[26] Characteristically, once the crisis had passed, Portal began to feel bored; he was ready for the next challenge.

Portal's successor in Aden arrived in December 1935 and the Portals returned to England and the Imperial Defence College once more. The college consisted of three directing staff, one from each service, working under the commandant, Air Marshal Sir Arthur Longmore. The student body consisted of thirty-two handpicked senior officers including Keith Park. The course was based on a series of syndicated joint exercises, running various war scenarios. The faculty had to be broad-minded, strategic, and balanced; Portal was exceptional in all three regards. Though there was still inter-service rivalry, Portal displayed a measured approach to war and limited his output to discussion of the air weapon. Service parochiality would have been understandable because the Army and the Navy representatives were preaching their respective gospels about the superiority of the 'British Tommy' and the battleship.[27] Portal demonstrated his more holistic strategic view in an exchange with a civil servant, Charles Evans. Evans sent Portal a paper on the controversial topic of air versus battleship. Rather than decrying the battleship in his response, Portal pointed out the requirement for powerful ships to take on the German Navy in the Atlantic, but questioned their utility in the Pacific theatre, where a battle fleet would be less useful against Japan.[28] He also astutely realised that it was only Germany and not Japan that represented an existential threat to the UK. Promoted once more in July 1937, Portal was next off to be Director of Organisation and a third stint at the Air Ministry.

---

26 Clarke, Dudley, *A Quarter of My Century*, Unpublished Biography, held at Imperial War Museum, London, 524.

27 Notes on Portal: Air Marshal Sir Ralph Sorley, CC/3/III/G.

28 Letter: Portal to Charles Evans, 17 August 1936, CC/3/III/G.

Portal's return to the Air Ministry was at a key time in Britain's preparations for war. Following the secret rearmament of Germany, Hitler had annexed the Rhineland in 1936, whereupon Britain belatedly began to grasp the nature of the growing threat. Portal's earlier emphasis on fighter aircraft had proven prescient, in particular his support in 1932–33 of the eight-gun fighter, long before Dowding realised its importance.[29] He was now to be a key player in the mobilisation of some 1 million additional people in a period of just two years.

Several matters led to what was, thus far, the most challenging period of Portal's career. The RAF expansion had been planned, but not necessarily funded, since 1934. A series of sequential schemes represented by letters described the ever-evolving requirements for the future air force. By the time Portal arrived, Scheme F was in operation, with H additions. Partially a result of the Abyssinia Crisis, this scheme allowed for 124 squadrons and 1,750 front-line aircraft.[30] By the time Hitler took the Sudetenland in 1938, Scheme M was approved, with a front-line force of 2,550 aircraft; the requirement to plan and then plan again was extremely taxing for Portal's relatively small team. The good news in Scheme M was the more generous apportionment of resources to fighter aircraft: 25 per cent more than scheme L.[31] In addition to this central work, Portal also found more innovative ways to fuel expansion.

Chief of these was the Empire Air Training Scheme whereby Canada, Australia, New Zealand, and the like were used to train pilots to fight for the British. Portal's description of the birth of this scheme was typically understated. 'Two or three of us, we got round the table, and it started just like that.'[32] A mission was established under Lord Riverdale, and the scheme was born in Canada, New Zealand, Australia, South Africa, and Rhodesia, all of which contributed pilots to the war.[33] Portal was also involved in the more efficient organisation of RAF auxiliary squadrons and the development of the RAF Volunteer Reserves, which was only founded in 1936. He visualised the widespread use of women in various

---

29 Interview: Denis Richards with Air Marshal Sir R. Cochrane, 22 August 1973, CC/3/VIII/A.
30 Found at www.heritage.norfolk.gov.uk/Data/Sites/2/media/scottow/historicalappraisal pt2rafexpansion.pdf accessed on 24 February 2021 at 13.00 Central Time.
31 Richards, *Portal of Hungerford*, 123.
32 Interview: Denis Richards and Sir John Cordingley, CC/3/VIII/A.
33 Cordingley Interview, CC/3/VIII/A.

RAF trades but lacked the accommodation at that time to implement appropriate changes. Infrastructure was perhaps the knottiest problem of all, as the dramatic expansion of the RAF necessitated many new main and satellite airfields. The work that went into this was complicated by the fact that most of the allocation could not be met by taking over civil airfields; land had to be requisitioned from the estates of extremely reluctant and resourceful landowners.[34] One particularly determined landowner in Norfolk lobbied Cabinet ministers, wrote to other MPs and peers and raised questions in the House of Commons. Eventually, the exasperated wife arrived at the office of Lord Balfour of Inchrye, Undersecretary of State, to plead her case tearfully. Portal, ignoring his previously informal relationship with Balfour stated firmly, 'Under-Secretary of State. If you do not now authorise this requisition you will be failing in your duty to your country.'[35] Balfour signed.

Portal's appointment as Air Member for Personnel (AMP) demonstrated the trajectory of his rise through the Service. He was now at the top table for RAF leadership: the Air Council. In this role Portal continued the work he had begun as Director of Organisation, now bearing overall responsibility for both personnel and training, including the Empire Air Training Scheme. His remit also included postings, appointments, promotions, discipline honours and awards.[36] However, he escaped the need to recommend any new appointees at command level. Amid growing fears of an impending war, both Bowhill and Dowding were extended in post, as AOC Coastal and Fighter Commands respectively.[37] Portal was AMP for only fifteen short months and, though Britain was by no means on a seamless war footing by the time hostilities began, he did make some significant improvements.

Shortages in key trades led Portal to recommend the formation of the Women's Auxiliary Air Force (WAAF). A disruptive thinker, Portal subsequently convinced the Air Council to break the new organisation away from War Office control and had a female director, Miss J. Trefusis Forbes, appointed. Recruitment was steady thereafter, and both in terms of numbers and breadth of expertise, the role of the embryonic service grew exponentially (from five trades in 1939 to over eighty in 1943).[38] The

---

34 Richards, *Portal of Hungerford*, 127.
35 Balfour Harold, *Wings over Westminster*, Hutchinson: London, 1973, 108.
36 CC/3/III/K.
37 Richards, *Portal of Hungerford*, 131.
38 Ibid., 132.

WAAF provided crucial expansion potential for British forces just when it was needed.

Portal also recognised another problem in RAF organisation. It was policy in the interwar period for pilots to have a second speciality and to alternate between flying appointments and technical matters if serving on a full commission. Trenchard had instigated this approach because a small service could not support a raft of specialisations. Portal grasped that the approach was no longer apposite with the rapidly expanding RAF. Moreover, during an existential war every pilot would be needed in the cockpit. He, therefore, recommended new and permanent branches of commissioned service within the RAF: initially engineering, signals and armament officers.[39] This reflected not only the need for specialist pilots but also the increasingly complex nature of the modern technology being integrated into the RAF, such as radar and other electronic warfare systems. This resulted in economies in training and utilisation, but also opened up the possibility of a full career in the RAF to personnel unsuitable for flying duties. Additional space for pilot training was supplied through Portal's Empire Air Training Scheme, but this had stalled at inception in 1937.

The outbreak of war in September 1939 gave the Empire Air Training Scheme the shot in the arm it needed. A lack of a sense of urgency in the Commonwealth led to severe procrastination, with virtually the sole agreement being Canada's commitment to train fifty pilots per year. This was nowhere near enough and, by war's outbreak, the RAF had many more aircraft than it could use, being short of pilots, observers, and air gunners. Portal was utterly dissatisfied with this paltry return, and resolved to exponentially increase the output of the scheme. Working based on an aircraft output of 2,550 per month, Portal calculated that 20,000 pilots per year were needed. There was no way this could all be accomplished in the UK. Around fifty flying schools were needed in the dominions of Canada, Australia, and New Zealand, with the side benefit that excess capacity could be used to train pilots from those countries.[40] The dominions agreed to the scheme on 17 December 1939 and, by 1942, it was producing 11,000 pilots and 17,000 other aircrew each year. This number was bolstered once Southern Rhodesia and South Africa joined. Though success in the war was

---

39 Ibid., 133.
40 Ibid., 134.

not ensured through the scheme, one of the RAF's glaring problems had, belatedly, been resolved. This was another period of resounding success for Portal, in what Trenchard considered the RAF's most difficult job.[41] Portal's record of unfettered success resulted in the plum job of Air Officer Commander-in-Chief of Bomber Command, the RAF's second most prestigious role.

The bomber force, which Portal commanded from April 1940, was not fit for its stated purpose: attack on the German mainland. Historian Tami Davis-Biddle noted this period as one of crisis for the RAF during which, 'the gap between rhetoric and reality proved to be nothing less than an abyss.'[42] While successful execution of Air Control in the Empire had proven both militarily and economically effective, the realities of war with an industrialised western nation were vastly different. The British bomber force had problems with navigation, survivability, range, bombing accuracy, and night flying tactics, to name but a few.[43] Portal's predecessor, Air Chief Marshal Sir Edgar Ludlow-Hewett, understood these problems, and evinced them to higher levels. For his honesty, and his exposure of the 'sins of omission of … politicians,' Ludlow-Hewitt was removed from command to become the RAF's Inspector General, where he again rendered invaluable service.[44] Replacing the man did nothing to solve Bomber Command's problems, which hove into Portal's view as he came to grips with his new responsibilities.

Portal had barely been at Bomber Command a week when the illusion of the 'Phoney War' was shattered by the devastating Blitzkrieg attack on Denmark and Norway. Denmark capitulated with barely a whimper, leaving no time for allies to mount a defence. Resistance in Norway was piecemeal, and British support was not planned as an integrated, joint campaign. Allied ground troops were left to face an unopposed Luftwaffe, with Junkers dive-bombers and Heinkel He 111s wreaking

---

41 CC/3/XIV/B.

42 Biddle, Tami Davis, *Rhetoric and Reality in Air Warfare: The Evolution of British and American Ideas about Strategic Bombing, 1914–1945.* 1st. pbk. ed. Princeton Studies in International History and Politics. Princeton, N.J.; Woodstock: Princeton University Press, 2004, 183.

43 Biddle, *Rhetoric and Reality,* 88–91.

44 Harris Arthur, *Bomber Offensive,* Barnsley: Pen & Sword, 2005, 36; Connelly, Mark. *Reaching for the Stars: A New History of Bomber Command in World War II.* London; New York: I.B. Tauris. Distributed by St Martin's Press, 2001, 25.

havoc in the British ranks.[45] It was a stunning illustration of how tactical bombing could be a force multiplier for a well-executed joint campaign. In slightly less than two months it was all over. Even had the will existed for Bomber Command to support British ground troops in similar manner, the capability was absent at that time. As Ludlow-Hewitt had warned, Bomber Command was far from ready for strategic bombardment, and fit only for an escorted interdiction role.[46] Far from Britain, RAF bombers shorn of fighter support would have been ripped to pieces by a rampant Luftwaffe. Bomber Command had to cut its cloth in line with what was considered achievable. Even with more limited aims, the results were depressing.

The period of Portal's tenure was a voyage of discovery for Bomber Command. The so-called heavy bombers of 1940, Wellingtons, Whitleys and Hampdens, would be superseded by the infinitely superior Lancaster, Halifax, and Stirling later. Ranges and payloads in 1940 were thoroughly inadequate for the dreams of bomber advocates, and the German monoplane fighters reduced bomber survivability immeasurably. In the words of Arthur Harris, 'Even a bad fighter is bound to catch the average bomber.'[47] Unfortunately for the RAF, the Luftwaffe's fighter aircraft were state of the art.

Bomber attrition was high, yet missions remained politically expedient if militarily unwise. A counter-attack was essential for British public morale, and Bomber Command provided the sole available means. Despite all the deficiencies in capability, the British press aided and abetted papering over the cracks to paint a rosier picture. The *Daily Express* declared, 'That is the way the public wants to see Britain fight the war. For every crack they give us we pay it back double.'[48] This was a gross exaggeration of British efforts at the time and Portal was unconvinced it represented productive output for his crews.

Survivability was one of Portal's primary concerns; another was the inability to actually carry out effective bombing. Two problems were apparent: operations in bad weather and bombing accuracy, or the lack thereof. The first phase of the Battle of Norway illustrated the problems perfectly. Acting on Coastal Command intelligence on 9 April 1940, twelve

---

45 Terraine, John, *A Time for Courage: The Royal Air Force in the European War, 1939–1945*. New York, N.Y.: Macmillan, 1985, 115–116.
46 Verrier, Anthony, *The Bomber Offensive*. London: Batsford, 1968, 59.
47 Harris, Bomber Offensive, 42.
48 Connelly, *Reaching for the Stars*, 26.

Wellingtons were sent to sink two cruisers at Bergen. Despite best efforts, no ships were sunk and only a few German sailors injured.[49] Perhaps the ultimate indignity for Bomber Command was that, following the escape of the *Köln*, her damaged sister ship, the *Königsberg*, was sunk the following morning by Coastal Command. Most of the remaining German fleet, ordered back to home bases having dropped off the invasion forces, made it home safely. Adverse weather precluded any successful attack on the *Gneisenau* and *Scharnhorst* on 12 April 1940, despite Portal sending out ninety-two bombers to locate and engage them. Twelve Hampdens continued to Kristiansand to attack another warship but were met by German fighter resistance. Only five of the Hampdens landed back at Waddington, and all had taken fire. Another crash-landed at Acklington, but the crew were unhurt. It was a gloomy portent for Portal of what was to come, as well as a sobering reminder of the dangers of daytime bombing. Portal ought to have known better, as Bomber Command had suffered severe losses the previous year during daytime raids over Wilhelmshaven.[50]

More successful was a plan to conduct aerial mine laying of German sea lanes, which took place under the code name GARDENING. From mid-April 1940, Bomber Command laid magnetic mines in the Great and Little Belts, the Sound, the Kiel Canal, the Elbe Estuary, and other areas beyond the reach of the Royal Navy.[51] Over the following six weeks around 300 mines were laid at the cost of eleven aircraft. The results of these operations (twelve German vessels were sunk) were not fully known to Portal or Harris (whose No. 5 Group had conducted the operations) at that time. However, both men argued strongly in support of the effectiveness of these operations throughout the war.

Despite capability deficiencies, there was great pressure on Bomber Command to perform, exacerbated in May 1940 when Chamberlain was replaced as Prime Minister by the irrepressible Winston Churchill. Churchill thought the Allies were, 'Better equipped for war than was Germany, with more trained men, more guns, more and better tanks, more bombers and fighters.'[52] What Churchill did not fathom were the details that rendered this

49 Richards, Denis and Saunders, George, *Royal Air Force 1939–1945 Vol. I: The Fight at Odds*, London: York House, 1953, 84.

50 Terraine, *A Time for Courage*, 117.

51 Richards, *The Fight at Odds*, 89.

52 May, Ernest R., *Strange Victory: Hitler's Conquest of France*. 1st ed. New York: Hill and Wang, 2000, 7–8.

numerical superiority irrelevant. The Allies planned in isolation; the French and British were forbidden from entering Belgium until it was invaded. The French had little ability to conduct air–land co-operation; interwar service resentment had burned until the French Air Force gained independence in 1933. Until then, the air forces had been reluctantly subjugated to a tactical role. By 1936, they preferred a doctrine of strategic bombing at odds with both their tactical responsibilities to support the French Army and France's strategic defensive posture at the Maginot Line.[53]

More seriously, the divisions the French left to defend their centre, to the west of the Ardennes Forest, were bereft of anti-tank and anti-aircraft weapons, because it was assumed the terrain was impassable for tanks. The British, in turn, were only partially committed to the defence of France because, following defeat in Norway, they fully expected Britain, and not the Low Countries, to be subjected to the next Nazi assault.[54] The combination of these strategic blunders led to a rapid series of setbacks. Nevertheless, Churchill demanded to be on the attack immediately, with Bomber Command his primary instrument. Portal was given ample opportunity to squander his force in the defence of France. Though separated by layers of bureaucracy from one another, the following five months would be a window into Portal's future.

Initially, bombers enjoyed some success, and in a single day 204 German transport aircraft, 130 bomber and reconnaissance machines and 13 fighters were destroyed by combined action, much of it from French and British bombers. This lone high point did little to mask the grave difficulties for exposed bombers operating where the enemy had an increasingly ironclad grasp on air superiority.

Once the reality of the German thrust through the centre became apparent, the French begged for maximum effort against the bridgeheads.[55] On 14 May 1940, seventy-two bombers were put to the task; forty-three were lost. Later in the day twenty-eight Blenheims attacked and only seven returned. Equally concerning was the bombers' inability to impact the pontoons, which remained largely intact. An Air Ministry note to Portal on 4 June pointedly described the problem. 'The strenuous and gallant efforts of your squadrons

---

53 Young R.J., 'The Strategic Dream: French Air Doctrine in the Inter-War Period, 1919–39.' *Journal of Contemporary History.* 1974; 9(4): 57–76.

54 Orange, Vincent, *Churchill and His Airmen*, London: Grub Street, 2013, 119.

55 Read, Simon, *The Killing Skies: RAF Bomber Command at War.* Stroud (England): Spellmount, 2006, 30.

against objectives in collaboration with the land battle since 10 May have not always had results commensurate with the effort exerted.'[56] In simple terms, Portal's force was ill-suited to the task, and Portal and the Air Ministry knew it. Portal's vision was for a strategic air force, not a tactical bombing force. Though this might have appeared a mistake watching the Blitzkrieg rampage across France, Germany's inability to knock Britain out of the war in the ensuing Battle of Britain lent more credibility to Portal's own strategic views.

Portal was unconvinced that his lightly armed Blenheims could arrest a German advance, and gamely fought political pressure to sacrifice them needlessly. Churchill pleaded on 17 May, 'Is there no possibility of finding out where a column of enemy armoured vehicles haunts during the dark hours, and then bombing. We are being ripped to pieces behind the front by these wandering columns.'[57] Portal had already expressed grave doubts about such action to Chief of Air Staff Sir Cyril Newall, stating, 'I feel justified in expressing serious doubts whether the attack of 50 Blenheims based on information necessarily some hours out of date are likely to make as much difference to the ultimate course of the war as to justify the losses that I expect ...'[58]

Even as the final British formations were evacuating Dunkirk on 2 June 1940, Churchill was planning the next attack should Italy enter the war. 'We should be able to strike back with our heavy bombers at Italy the moment she enters the war ... These Squadrons should be flown to their aerodromes in Southern France at the earliest moment when French permission can be obtained.'[59] Churchill was living in an alternate reality. Portal was grounded in strategic reality, and agreed with Dowding (among others) about the futility of the further defence of France. During the evacuation, Portal infuriated Dowding. He insisted daylight bombing missions would only be authorised if there was a fighter escort. Dowding wanted his fighter squadrons to remain in Britain, where they held the advantage over the Luftwaffe. Portal was conscious his bombers were sitting ducks without an escort. The Air Ministry sided with Portal and ordered Dowding to comply, preserving the bomber force for the rigours of the later war, while assisting the hard-pressed British Expeditionary Force (BEF). The tension between Dowding and Portal

---

56 Orange, *Churchill and his Airmen*, 127.
57 Churchill to Chief of Air Staff, 17 May 1940, Chartwell Papers, Churchill College, Cambridge (hereafter referred to as CHAR), CHAR/20/13/2.
58 Richards, *Portal of Hungerford*, 147.
59 Churchill to S of S for Air, 2 June 1940, CHAR/20/13/3.

belied their broadly similar strategic views, albeit from differing vantage points. They both needed to preserve and build their respective forces for the campaigns to come: in Portal's case the strategic bombing of Germany, and for Dowding the more imminent defence of the homeland.

Following the ignominy of defeat in the Battle of France came Britain's 'Finest Hour': the Battle of Britain. This was, of course, Dowding and Park's victory, but Bomber Command played a vital, if somewhat unheralded, role. Though Bomber Command conceived of its role as an offensive one, the Battle of Britain would afford it the chance to demonstrate the defensive merits of bombing. This was apposite as Portal was well aware that Bomber Command was ill-suited to its intended role in the summer of 1940.[60] As the threat of invasion grew, any objections Portal had to a defensive emphasis melted away. In fact, the change of role was rather fortuitous for Bomber Command. Portal directed his bombers against the Luftwaffe and its lines of communication; against ports and shipping; and at the growing concentration of barges in the Channel that foreshadowed the German invasion: Operation SEALION. The Wehrmacht generously presented a large target area, right on the coast, which was well lit, something within Bomber Command's limited wheelhouse even then. With 36 per cent of Bomber Command's sorties flown against the gathering invasion force between July and October, the bombers were able to destroy some 12 per cent of the invasion fleet.[61] This effort, compounded by that of Coastal Command, helped convince Hitler only a decisive victory against Fighter Command would enable the invasion. Without defeating Fighter Command, the invasion barges would be ripped to pieces by the twin-engine 'heavy bombers' of the RAF.

Bomber Command also changed the course of the Battle of Britain. The attack on Berlin led to Hitler's unwise strategic decision to switch the point of attack from RAF airfields to London. AOC 11 Group, Air Vice Marshal Keith Park observed the results of the Luftwaffe raid on London on the night of 7 September. The following day he wrote, 'It was burning all down the river. It was a horrid sight. But I looked down and said: "Thank God for that."'[62] Germany's change of emphasis eased the pressure on Fighter Command airfields, hastening the German defeat, and ensured the

---

60 Bungay, Stephen, *The Most Dangerous Enemy: A History of the Battle of Britain,* London: Aurum Press, 2001, 90.
61 Bungay, *Most Dangerous Enemy,* 91.
62 Hastings, M., *Winston's War: Churchill, 1940–1945* (1st Vintage Books ed.). New York: Vintage Books, 2011, 89.

cancellation of SEALION. It was Britain's first victory, and it belonged, in part, to Bomber Command and Portal.

Portal had proven his worth as an operational commander in the difficult circumstances of the two battles. With sub-standard equipment, and a prime minister always demanding more, Portal's quiet resolve shone through. It was a challenging time for the Command, which lost 103 aircraft in April and May over enemy lines.[63] Harris wrote, 'At Bomber Command his calm confidence during the Battle of France, when the bomber force was enduring heavy casualties and it was clear that its efforts could do no good, was exactly what was needed to sustain the courage of those under him.'[64] During the Battle of Britain, and the early strategic assault on Germany, Portal gently brought Churchill onside regarding the limitations of his Command. By mid-July, Churchill acknowledged, 'The long-range bombing of Germany should be conducted with a desire to save the machines and personnel as much as possible while keeping up a steady attack. It is very important to build up the numbers of the bomber force, which is very low at the present time.'[65] This represented a small victory for Portal: Churchill was gradually coming to grips with the scale of the task that lay ahead, rather than seeking the next 'finest hour', as was sometimes his wont.

As the battle waned in October, Portal left Bomber Command for Whitehall to replace Newall as Chief of Air Staff. Nothing could halt Portal's inexorable rise; he was 'the accepted star of the Royal Air Force.'[66] Portal, writing some years later, commented, 'I can only say that I was completely surprised and my first thoughts were serious doubts as to whether I could tackle the job as I knew it meant dealing with some rather formidable people at the political level, of which I had no experience.'[67] Foremost among these formidable politicians was, naturally, Churchill. The continuing relationship between these men would prove crucial to Britain's eventual wartime success.

---

63 Hastings, Max, *Bomber Command,* New York: Dial Press/J. Wade, 1979, 353.
64 Harris, *Bomber Offensive, 57.*
65 Churchill to S of S for Air, 11 July 40, CHAR/20/13/4.
66 Churchill Winston S., *The Second World War, Vol. II, Their Finest Hour,* The Educational Book Company Ltd: London, 1951, 17.
67 Peake, *Marshal of the Royal Air Force,* CC/3/X, 10.

Chapter 3

Portal and Churchill

*Although he had brilliant ideas, he was hardly susceptible
to reason and could not follow a consecutive argument when
presented to him by others.*
Anthony Storr about W.S.C.

It must have been with a sense of trepidation that Portal approached his initial duties as Chief of Air Staff (CAS). Having become somewhat acquainted with Churchill's ways during his time at Bomber Command, Portal knew how different the two men were. Impatient, impetuous, and idealistic, Churchill's decision-making process stood in stark contrast to Portal's calm, logical approach. Would Portal hold sway with the Prime Minister and be able to direct the RAF as he wished? Compounding Portal's difficulties was that his fellow Chiefs of Staff, John Dill, and Dudley Pound, were both more than a decade older than him. Churchill already knew Pound very well from his time at the Admiralty, so Portal was the outsider, stepping into the lion's den. However, Portal was at least from the same social class as Churchill. His abundant self-assurance, that came in part from upbringing and in part from his nature, would be essential to deal effectively with the upcoming challenges. With the Royal Air Force in a parlous state, notwithstanding Fighter Command's recent victory, Portal had a tough time ahead. And Churchill was not a man who gave anyone an easy ride.

Winston Spencer Churchill was born at Blenheim Palace on 30 November 1874 into a life of exceptional social privilege but relative economic poverty. The son of Lord Randolph Churchill, future Chancellor of the Exchequer and third son of the seventh Duke of Marlborough, Churchill's financial woes were born of the British aristocratic tradition to bequeath everything to the eldest son, leaving any remaining progeny to fend for themselves. His father's astonishing political rise to Chancellor and Leader of the House of Commons at the age of just thirty-seven was perfectly mirrored by its cataclysmic demise less than five months later when he resigned over an economic disagreement with the Prime Minister, Lord Salisbury. Lord Randolph proposed military budgetary cuts to finance improvements at home. He mistook his public popularity for political security and was sidelined by Salisbury permanently. He had spent a total of eleven months in office and 'was without rival in attracting so much attention and achieving so little.'[1] Young Winston, watching with a close eye, would go on to match his father in boldness, and greatly outstrip him in political survivability.

Winston was educated at Harrow, where he underperformed consistently, resulting in his father putting him in the Army class there. He subsequently failed to win a commission in the infantry. Only after Lord Randolph had him tutored did Winston finally achieve a cavalry cadetship in 1893, and entry to the Royal Military Academy at Sandhurst.[2] Lord Randolph's death two years later spurred Winston to greater effort, and he graduated a respectable twentieth of 130 cadets in his Sandhurst class. Moreover, Winston realised his desire to follow his father and grandfather to higher office. He, therefore set out to make a name for himself in the British Army, and began a rigorous regime of self-education.

Churchill travelled to India in 1896, which was unhelpfully peaceable at that time. Only through war could he earn the reputation he craved. Churchill immediately sought a posting to a frontier to further the chances of adventure, and quickly saw action in the Makaland region, where he showed courage under fire. This also led to a first published book that began to put his name in the public sphere. He followed this up with a sojourn to Sudan as part of Kitchener's Anglo-Egyptian forces and was involved in a cavalry charge against the local dervishes during which more than 20 per cent of his regiment was lost. Having survived the campaign, and gained enough material for a second book, *The River War*, Churchill returned to London, resigned his commission, and decided to run for Parliament.[3]

An unsuccessful, if not historically anomalous, campaign led to Churchill sailing for South Africa. He was employed as the *Morning Post*'s war correspondent during the Boer War. Churchill was officially a non-combatant, yet failed to act the part. In November 1899, the Boers ambushed an armoured train carrying Churchill. He proved pivotal in the

1 Jenkins, Roy, *The Chancellors*. London: Macmillan, 2015, 36.
2 Schoenfeld, Maxwell Philip, *Sir Winston Churchill: His Life and times*. 2nd ed. Malabar, Fla.: R.E. Krieger Pub., 1986, 5.
3 Schonfeld, *Sir Winston Churchill*, 8–9.

liberation of the engine despite his own capture. Churchill's bravery was reported by British escapees, and his fame was bolstered when he promptly broke from prison in Pretoria and made his way back to British forces with considerable panache. His war reports were read widely, and his renown sufficient to secure a successful second parliamentary campaign, enabled by a magnanimous gesture from the Liberals, who split their ticket in a two-member constituency as a mark of respect for Churchill's heroism.[4] Churchill entered Parliament having been part of two wars, and having published four books and numerous articles, all at the remarkably tender age of twenty-five.

The new Conservative Member of Parliament for Oldham wasted no time in trying to make his mark. He made his first speech in response to another future Prime Minister, David Lloyd George, who criticised the government's policy on South Africa. A political rival later claimed that Churchill had 'spent the best days of his life preparing impromptu speeches.'[5] Churchill worked hard at public speaking, a task made more difficult by his slight speech impediment.

Other problems also arose; his ideological beliefs, as a Conservative Progressive, put him at odds with the party leadership. By 1903, his liberal bias and disillusionment were apparent when he wrote in a letter, 'I hate the Tory Party, their men, their words and their methods.'[6] Shortly thereafter, Churchill crossed the Houses of Parliament to sit with the Liberals, an act of political treachery that infuriated and outraged both the Conservative Party leadership and his constituents. Shortly afterwards he wrote, 'Great men, at the height of their power, often to their cost refuse to recognise the ability of newcomers.'[7] Churchill had seen the winds of political change, and supported the plight of the common man, if only to forestall the rise of the Labour Party. He galvanised Liberal support in the Manchester constituencies, winning all seven seats from the Conservatives in the process.[8] The Liberals swept the 1906 General Election; Churchill was both re-elected and given his first significant post, in the Colonial Office.

---

4 Ibid., 11.

5 Ibid., 13.

6 Charmley, John, *Churchill: The End of Glory: A Political Biography*. London: Hodder & Stoughton, 1993, 31.

7 Churchill, Winston, *Lord Randolph Churchill*. New. ed. London: Odhams Press, 1952, 222.

8 Stewart, Herbert Leslie, *Winged Words: Sir Winston Churchill as Writer and Speaker*. New York: Bouregy & Curl, 1954, 9.

Churchill was well-suited both to his new appointment and to his new party. His experiences in the Boer War also gave him insight into the region's problems. The changing relationship, to one of dominion rather than colony, was acceptable to Churchill's grand view of Britain, and his energy earned him promotion to President of the Board of Trade after Asquith succeeded Campbell-Bannerman as prime minister. This took Churchill out of his comfort zone, in foreign affairs, and into less-trodden ground of social reform, but he took to it well. Churchill worked tirelessly for old age pensions, for unemployment insurance, for reducing the powers of the unelected House of Lords, and for taxing the 'unearned increment of land.'[9]

Churchill was promoted to Home Secretary in 1910, during which he cemented a reputation for somewhat erratic and emotional behaviour. There were numerous strikes during the period, and Churchill sometimes overreacted, as when he sent in troops to quash a miners' strike in Tonypandy in 1910. Though no lives were lost, the gesture was unwise in the extreme, and demonised him to the political left. He attended a police shootout with two anarchists in 1911, unnecessarily dramatising the event. His penchant for conflict led Asquith to wisely move him to the Admiralty, yet the heart still sometimes ruled the head. In 1914, as head of the Admiralty, Churchill sent warships to Irish ports to resolve the impasse between Ulster Unionists and Irish secessionists, attempting to bring the Unionists in line with governmental policy for Irish Home Rule. It took Prime Minister Asquith to recall the ships.

The First World War did not go well for Churchill as Lord of the Admiralty. He failed to effectively instigate long overdue naval modernisation, and the strategic failure in the Dardanelles defined his war. As early dreams of a quick war faded into distant memory, each side sought to devise a grand strategic move to break the deadlock. Churchill believed that Turkey was the answer, as an attack could drive it from the war, bring Italy into line with the Allies, and re-establish communications with Russia. As later, Churchill ignored salient strategic realities in preference for romantic notions of decisive victory. A calamitous naval incursion, in which one third of the ships entering the strait were sunk, preceded a stagnant land invasion that led to the death of 44,000 Allied troops. Churchill bore the blame, resigned from office, and left for the trenches. Extraordinarily, he returned to government in early 1917 following a stirring speech that encouraged

---

9 Stewart, *Winged Words*, 11.

new Prime Minister Lloyd George to bring him back into the fold. Lloyd George did so, despite the stringent objections of over 100 Tory MPs.

Following victory in the field and at the ballot box in late 1918, Churchill became Secretary of State for War and Air. In this post-war role, two things greatly concerned him: demobilisation and Russia. The former would occupy much of his energy, and his effective performance went some way to rebuilding his parliamentary credibility. Unfortunately, in a war-weary Britain, his casting of Russia as the next great threat antagonised both the Labour Party and the Prime Minister. Churchill was violently anti-Bolshevik. His claims that Russia, 'with victory in her grasp fell upon the earth, devoured alive, like Herod of old, by worms,' did nothing to alleviate his reputation as untrustworthy, unbalanced, and extreme in many eyes.[10] Churchill's ability to see things in black and white was both his greatest strength and his greatest weakness. In domestic politics, it made him unpalatable to great swathes of his parliamentary colleagues yet, in foreign policy, it sometimes enabled him to see more clearly than most.

Following the 1922 General Election, Churchill was out of Parliament, but he reunited with the Conservative Party to return as Chancellor of the Exchequer in 1924. He was ill-suited for the task. He accused the Trade Union Congress of challenging the constitution during the General Strike of 1926, losing further face with the Left. He had food convoys escorted by armed troops with bayonets fixed and rifles loaded, entirely inappropriate for the situation. As Chancellor, he was also intimately involved in the 'no war for ten years' policy that contributed to Britain's strategic atrophy in the 1920s and early 1930s. Churchill once said that he would rather be right than consistent. While he had been in favour of generous post-war terms with Germany initially, by 1929 he had already perceived 'the drum-beats of the new antagonisms.'[11]

From the back benches in the 1930s, Churchill crowed time and again about the growing Nazi threat. He was dismayed at the poor state of the Royal Air Force, a distant sixth in global size by the 1930s. Some thought him 'wild' or 'preposterous,' yet a growing number gradually recognised the wisdom of his world view. Hitler's reoccupation of the Rhineland, Mussolini's excursion into Ethiopia, and the Spanish Civil War in 1936 all indicated Churchill's pessimism was well-placed. His influence grew, and the failure of Chamberlain's appeasement policy, roundly criticised by Churchill, was

---

10 Schoenfeld, *Sir Winston Churchill*, 42.
11 Ibid., 52.

conversely a political victory for Churchill. He called Munich a 'total and unmitigated defeat' and 'a disaster of the first magnitude.'[12] This Churchillian rhetoric, thought anachronistic by many, befit times of existential crisis. Two days after Germany invaded Poland on 1 September 1939, Churchill was back in the Cabinet, as head of the Admiralty once more. The Royal Navy signalled all the ships at sea the following: 'Winston is back.'[13]

Britain's political humiliation was complete when Hitler invaded France on 10 May 1940, and Chamberlain's political career was over. The only remaining question was who would be the next prime minister? The choices were either Churchill or Lord Halifax, a proponent of appeasement along with Chamberlain. Thankfully, Britain chose the clenched fist over the bended knee. Churchill roused the nation, and made the lion roar once more. Britain needed a catalyst, and Churchill provided it. The rhetorical excesses that hampered him domestically with the Labour Party were exactly what Britain needed to begin to meet the German military behemoth. His indomitable spirit infused the nation.

Britain now had thrust, but Churchill was a man of erratic strategic vector. He was a man given to excesses of opinion, of wild and inaccurate strategic assessments, of great impatience and occasional fits of pique. He incorrectly predicted the obsolescence of the tank, the defensibility of single vessels against aircraft, and the likely static nature of land warfare in the future.[14] As Roosevelt once observed, 'Winston has fifty ideas a day, and three or four are good.'[15] Churchill needed a stabilising voice, to curb his excesses, a man of true strategic vision to direct Churchill's legendary energy and magnetic personality. Peter Portal was Churchill's perfect foil.

Portal's major role, as head of the RAF, was to represent the service on the Joint Chiefs of Staff (COS) Committee, where General Sir John Dill and Admiral Sir Dudley Pound were the Army and Navy representatives. The infusion of new blood on to the committee was no accident as, following one late meeting involving the chiefs, Churchill remarked, 'I have to wage modern war with ancient weapons.'[16] Those who heard this could not have

---

12 Ibid., 67.

13 Ibid., 68.

14 Ibid., 62.

15 Rubin, Gretchen Craft, *Forty Ways to Look at Winston Churchill: A Brief Account of a Long Life.* 1st ed., New York: Ballantine Books, 2003, 29.

16 Kennedy, John, *The Business of War: The War Narrative of Major-General Sir John Kennedy*, (London: Hutchinson, 1957), 60.

failed to spot the irony of the remark, as Churchill was senior in years to all three chiefs. Portal represented the first element of change, but others would follow. Both Sir John Dill and Sir Dudley Pound were subsequently replaced; in Pound's case, this followed his untimely death in 1943. Younger men were needed, because having Churchill as a taskmaster was extremely taxing, both physically and mentally.

Churchill's modus operandi allowed him to operate throughout the war and survive intact where many younger men fell by the wayside. He read in his bed during the morning, took a nap in the afternoon and worked late into the night. His COS meetings typically started at 21.30 hours and finished in the early hours of the morning.[17] These hours would already have been challenging, but were more difficult for the military chiefs who did not take afternoon naps. It would not have been an appropriate way to lead the armed forces, and the service leaders had to deal with their subordinates during working hours. Nevertheless, they had to dance to Churchill's tune.

If Churchill's battle rhythm was a challenge, this was certainly exacerbated by his manner. Churchill relentlessly questioned the chiefs about all areas of the war: strategy, tactics, technology, and logistics. Churchill did not wish to divine every fine detail of the activities of each service, but he did want to ensure that his chiefs were on top of things. The avalanche of minutes emanating from the Prime Minister's office led to outpourings of frustration by some of the chiefs. Alan Brooke, Dill's replacement on Christmas Day 1941, was the most acerbic in his commentary. Brooke kept diaries throughout the war, initially intended only for his wife to read; his irritation at the inscrutable Prime Minister came across in waves. In September 1944 he wrote, '[Churchill] has got only half the picture in his mind, talks absurdities and makes my blood boil to listen to his nonsense ... Never have I admired and despised a man simultaneously to the same extent.'[18] Brooke found Churchill equally exasperating and inspiring, his passion for operational details only matched by his ignorance of them. Yet, in person, Foreign Secretary Anthony Eden records that Alan Brooke was, except on rare occasions, 'patient, even tempered and untiring.'[19] Where patience may have come at some personal cost to Alan Brooke, to Portal it was natural.

---

17 Ibid., 61.
18 Cohen, Eliot A., *Supreme Command: Soldiers, Statesmen, and Leadership in Wartime*, New York: Anchor Books, 2003, 98.
19 Fraser, David, *Alanbrooke*. 1st ed. New York: Atheneum, 1982, 504.

Churchill, never satisfied with a first answer from a Chief of Staff, often asked the same question repeatedly. One favourite hobby horse early in Portal's tenure was the ratio of aircraft to personnel. In Portal's very first month as CAS, Churchill directed a query to him regarding the 'very large excess of crews' in the Army Co-operation Squadrons; they had 177 crews and 147 aircraft. Churchill suggested in his minute that the excess might be used to offset the marked shortage of pilots in Bomber Command at that time.[20] Portal's response was, perhaps, surprising. Instead of jumping at the opportunity to reinforce the RAF's premier offensive output, the command of which Portal had just relinquished, he defended the manning levels of Army Co-operation Command with logical aplomb:

> It is true that there are more pilots than aircraft in Army Co-operation squadrons, but there are sound reasons for this. In the first place, there are no O.T.U.s for these squadrons other than No. 112 Canadian squadron, which is used as a training squadron to No. 110 Canadian squadron. In all the other squadrons, it is necessary to train pilots in the squadrons themselves to hold a reserve against possible casualties. The main task of these squadrons at present is training in co-operation with Army Commands, but they have many additional duties laid upon them. They are called on to provide rescue services for fighter pilots shot down over the sea, to provide pilots to fly communication aircraft for the Army Command, and to train future glider pilots in Moth aircraft.
>
> In spite of this, we have recently reduced our commitment to Home Forces by 30% in order to free pilots for operational commands, and we have economised in pilots by not filling up Army Co-operation training courses for some time past, the pilots thus made available being released for Fighter Command.
>
> The present provision of pilots is therefore not excessive for the existing commitments, and I feel certain that the War Office would be most reluctant to accept any further decrease in the scale of air co-operation provided for the Army.

---

20 Churchill to Portal, 24 October 1940, Sir Charles Portal Archive, Christ Church College, Oxford, hereafter referred to as CC, Archive 1 of 3, Box 1 of 13, Entry 4, CC/1/1/4.

> On the day you mention it is true only 147 aircraft were shown as available for immediate operations, but the squadrons were in fact very nearly up to establishment. As in all squadrons, a number of aircraft were undergoing routine overhauls and minor repairs.[21]

There are several salient elements to Portal's communiqué that précis how he would think during his time as CAS. In the first place, and entirely coherent with his formative experiences, Portal was, first and foremost, a joint officer. He refused to score cheap points over one of the other services if it would detract from the overall fight. Secondly, Portal had an excellent grasp of the nuanced differences between his organisations, and how their requirements differed. Because Army Co-operation Command had no Operational Training Units (OTUs), they needed a greater number of front-line pilots. Portal understood some of these pilots would be in training in the squadrons; in the absence of OTUs, that was where the training was taking place. As such, there were also instructors within the squadrons to provide the training, so they would need more pilots per aircraft than other organisations within the RAF. Moreover, Portal pointed out that an adjustment had already been made in the allocation of pilots and Portal did not believe the War Office would support another change. This situation keenly demonstrated Portal's inclination to precisely analyse each individual situation and prescribe appropriately. Churchill abandoned this battle but chose another avenue of attack: the Mediterranean.

On 17 November 1940, Churchill wrote to Portal regarding the 'astounding disparity between operational fighting strength and the total ration strength personnel' in North Africa.[22] Churchill's main contention was that Arthur Longmore, the Air Officer Commanding in the Mediterranean, had just reported having 200 operationally fit aircraft and 17,000 personnel, or about seventy-seven airmen per serviceable machine:

> The pilot question is even more pointed. Here we have just under 1,000 pilots for only 220 serviceable Operational machines, or between 4 and 5 pilots for every machine. It is surely not necessary, and when we see how very short we are

---

21 Portal to Churchill, 31 October 1940, CC/1/1/4b.
22 Churchill to Portal, 17 November 1940, CC/1/1/14e.

of pilots at home, it would seem a duty to transfer some of these great numbers of pilots for whom there are no machines fit to fly, or any use for fighting, to home establishments.[23]

Churchill was typically pushy about this matter; Portal's reply was characteristically detailed and logical:

> The disparity between the number of men and the number of aircraft on charge is always striking but it is not really so great as you suggest. In addition to the 220 operationally fit aircraft of modern types, which you mention, there are 530 serviceable aircraft of older types, some of them obsolescent. A proportion of these are still engaged on active operations and the rest in training co-operation with the Army, communication and other similar duties; all have to be maintained in a serviceable condition. There are, therefore, 750 aircraft to compare with the 17,000 personnel. The latter of course include all the officers and airmen employed on· staffs, on transport, on defence of aerodromes and on administrative and other duties.[24]

Portal was equally versed in the unique conditions of the Mediterranean Air Command, as he had been Army Co-operation Command. In this case, there were two main factors affecting the aircraft to pilot ratio: that the number of aircraft in theatre was much greater than reported to Churchill, and that, being overseas, there was a vast staff and defence network that inflated the numbers compared to domestically based commands. Portal continued:

> The actual number of heads per serviceable aircraft, therefore, works out at something under twenty-three. This is about 60% of the number found necessary for the Air Force working with the British Army in France and is actually less than the number per machine on the battle front in the last war, when aircraft and engines were far more easily repaired and maintained than they are today. The fact that the figure is smaller than in the last war shows the improvement in organisation that one would

---

23 Ibid.
24 Portal to Churchill, 1 December 1940, CC/1/1/14g.

expect, but, at the same time, it must not be forgotten that the men themselves have to be more skilful. With rapid expansion, dilution is always necessary, and this is bound to increase the number of men per aircraft, at least for a time; further, as more of the larger and more complicated aircraft come into service in the Middle East, this tendency is, naturally, accentuated.[25]

Portal was quick to point out the unique features of the theatre and mitigating factors that altered any calculus. Given the long lines of communication in the enormous theatre, and thus the time required for sending reinforcements, Portal explained, the changing flux of war necessitated a generous allocation of personnel.[26] This missive showed one of the hallmarks of Portal's leadership. He was consistently unwilling to make rash adjustments anywhere, ever conscious of the elements of friction inherent in any move of personnel between command or theatre. Churchill was, however, correct to keep raising these objections, to ensure Portal was the master of his brief.

On 28 February 1941, Churchill returned to the fray, this time with an assault on Coastal Command. His basic complaint was similar. Churchill was concerned about the disparity between available crews and aircraft, noting an apparent surplus of 221 crews.[27] Portal again moved to reassure Churchill regarding the prevailing ratios, but explained them in a different way. On this occasion, Portal described how aircrew in contrast to aircraft, do not, routinely, fly every day. Portal estimated that an average crew would fly three times per week. He also pointed out the average figure for number of aircraft available (345), compared to the 202 Churchill had used as an extreme example in his figures. This instance reflects the habits of both men during their long correspondence. Churchill would use a single statistic that highlighted a problem he perceived, whereas Portal would look at the overall picture, take an average figure, and make his calculations from there. Using the average figure, and the calculation of how often aircrew fly compared to their aircraft, Portal showed that there were only 181 crews available each day and an average of 345 aircraft, meaning that crews not aircraft were the limiting factor on operations. Portal knew this well from his time as AMP. Churchill was not done yet.

---

25 Ibid.
26 Ibid.
27 Churchill to Portal, 28 February 1941, CC/1/2/33A.

On 1 May 1941, Churchill queried why Fighter Command had 442 more crews than aircraft, with a gap of 126 when only 'fully operational' crews were considered. Portal responded, 'I am sorry that I have not already made clear the reason for this gap. It is that, owing to the fact that at any one time, a number of pilots in each squadron are resting or on leave or sick, it is necessary to have a larger number of pilots on establishment than aircraft.'[28] He went on to explain how the greater number of pilots allowed Fighter Command to deal with casualties during heavy periods of fighting. The message was clear; crews not aircraft were the limiting factor in operations. Nevertheless, Churchill responded later in the month citing 1,504 fighter crews and only 1,371 aircraft, and how this disparity distressed him, when both Bomber Command and Coastal Command were more balanced.[29] Portal responded that, in fact, Bomber Command and Coastal Command were under-strength in operational crews, reiterating for the umpteenth time that crews not aircraft limited output.[30]

Churchill's method of engagement with Portal, indeed with all the Chiefs of Staff, was one of persistent questioning. Churchill did what many military leaders do at lower levels of command. Technical and subject matter expertise lies with subordinates, so effective leaders use detailed questions, about tactics, technologies, logistics etc., to probe subordinates for signs of ignorance. Alan Brooke became more frustrated (privately) by this process than Portal, who revelled in the intimate details, which often allowed him to confirm in writing what he had mused over during solo lunches at the Travellers' Club. In fact, Churchill's niggling persistence ensured Portal would reconsider any assumptions he had made, allowing Churchill to check the strategic logic of his CAS. While this strategy frayed the nerves of the brilliant but brittle Sir John Dill, Portal, Brooke and, later, Andrew Cunningham saw the battle through to the end of the war.

Early in his tenure, Portal displayed his grit, dealing with prime ministerial badgering with eloquent detail, patience, and occasional humour. Resilience was certainly necessary to remain in Churchill's inner circle, but it was Portal's strategic awareness that really caught the Prime Minister's eye.

Portal was regarded by some as 'the real brains' of the COS Committee.[31] He had received the most thorough military education of all the chiefs, spending

---

28 Portal to Churchill, 4 May 1941, CC/1/2/22a.
29 Churchill to Portal, 20 May 1941, CC/1/2/54.
30 Portal to Churchill, 24 May 1941, CC/1/2/54a.
31 Tedder, Arthur William, *With Prejudice: The War Memoirs of Marshal of the Royal Air Force, Lord Tedder.* London: Cassell, 1966, 532–3.

several years in the professional military education establishment, an experience that served him well. Sir Noel Hall, who served in the Ministry of Economic Warfare in 1938–43 observed, 'If some disaster, physical or political, overtook Churchill, an effective successor to his overall military responsibilities would be at hand in Portal.'[32] Portal certainly had influence with Churchill, and his involvement in discussions stretched to the whole of the military, enabled by his joint experience during the First World War, as well as time well spent in military education. Prior to the arrival of Alan Brooke on the COS Committee, Portal was the only chief who influenced Churchill's broader strategic thought. This was vital, as Churchill was a man of vacillating strategic preferences.

Portal's influence, and measured approach, manifested themselves on many occasions during his tenure. Perhaps most notably, Portal had to defend the agreed policy of strategic bombing in autumn 1941 following the Butt Report's stinging critique of Bomber Command's shortfalls in hitting targets. The report stated starkly that only two fifths of aircraft claiming to have attacked their allocated target during a full moon got within 5 miles of it. On a moonless night this proportion fell to one fifteenth.[33] In September 1941, Churchill complained:

> It is very disputable whether bombing by itself will be a decisive factor in the present war. On the contrary, all that we have learnt since the war began shows that its effects, both physical and moral, are greatly exaggerated. There is no doubt the British people have been stimulated and strengthened by the attack made upon them so far. Secondly, it seems very likely that the ground defences and night fighters will overtake the Air attack. Thirdly, in calculating the number of bombers necessary to achieve hypothetical and indefinite tasks, it should be noted that only a quarter of our bombs hit the target. Consequently, an increase in the accuracy of bombing to 100% would in fact raise our bombing force to four times its strength. The most we can say is that it will be a heavy and I trust a seriously increasing annoyance.[34]

32 Interview, Denis Richards with Sir Noel Hall, 4 December 1974, CC/3/XV/5.
33 Webster, Charles Kingsley and Frankland, Noble, *The Strategic Air Offensive against Germany, 1939–1945. History of the Second World War*, United Kingdom Military Series. London: H.M. Stationery Office, 1961, Vol 1, 78.
34 Churchill to Portal, 27 September 1941, CC/1/2/2d.

Churchill raised some legitimate concerns, including the fundamental question of whether heavy bombing was the correct strategic approach. The needling missive typified Churchill's pattern of repeatedly circling around to confirm the direction of the war. This could easily have frustrated Portal, as Churchill's endless questioning caused a great deal of work for an already beleaguered Air Staff. Instead, Portal composed his response in a logical and constructive manner. He began by reminding Churchill that:

> Since the fall of France, it has been a fundamental principle of our strategy that victory over Germany could not be hoped for until German morale and German material strength had been subjected to a bombing offensive of the greatest intensity. This principle has been re-affirmed by you on several occasions.[35]

Portal also referred to the declared British grand strategy affirmed by the COS:

> It is in bombing, on a scale undreamed of in the last war, that we find the new weapon on which we must principally depend for the destruction of economic life and morale ... After meeting the needs of our own security, therefore, we give to the heavy bomber first priority in production. Only the heavy bomber can produce the conditions under which other offensive forces can be deployed.[36]

Having reaffirmed the stated strategy of both Churchill and the COS, Portal astutely perceived the reasoning behind Churchill's earlier minute and addressed the issue:

> I think it is as easy to underestimate the consequences to Germany of a bombing offensive on the scale envisaged by the Air Staff as it is to over-estimate it. Interception techniques will certainly improve; but so too will the technique of locating targets at night. Bomber defence will also improve. There are no certainties in war, but taking the various factors together,

---

35 Portal to Churchill, 2 October 1941, CC/1/2/2e.
36 Ibid.

> I see no reason to regard the bomber as a weapon of declining importance.[37]

This was not a blind defence of the role of the bomber. Rather, it acknowledged that changes would come, but that there was no present reason to alter the strategic vision. Portal presented a balanced view of the possible technical developments for both defence and attack, an essential element of strategic assessment. Portal continued:

> It is not the purpose of this minute to justify the contention that the bomber offensive will prove the decisive weapon. My object is to suggest the necessity for a clear picture of our aim. As I have said, existing directives afford such a picture and give a clear-cut definition of the kind of Air Force we must create if victory is to be won. But these directives rest on the assumption that – given the necessary production – the Royal Air Force is capable by itself of carrying the disruption of Germany to a very advanced stage. If this assumption is no longer tenable, we must produce a new plan.[38]

Portal coolly conveyed the strategic realities to Churchill, while granting that there could be other ways to pursue victory. Portal was not a blind advocate for strategic bombing, even at this early stage of the war. Nor was he wedded to the strategy for organisational reasons. He readily acknowledged other possibilities but was again aware of the losses inherent in switching approaches. Such strategies would, for example, require a very differently composed Royal Air Force than that being procured. Portal never told Churchill what course to follow but delivered his honest assessment that there was no reason to alter the strategic course at that time. In autumn 1941, Portal was aware of the cold, hard reality: Britain had no other options.

Portal's minute, which rebutted Churchill's critique of bomber strategy while calling for a greater share of resources, served multiple purposes. Portal's argument was firm yet deferential, supportive but not blindly parochial. He extolled the virtues of one of the principles of war: selection

---

37 Ibid.
38 Ibid.

and maintenance of the aim. The calls on bomber aircraft and pilots were many, with the Royal Navy demanding ever greater support for the Battle of the Atlantic. By alluding to the path to victory, for which strategic bombing was a key enabler, Portal put forth his case for a greater allocation of resources to Bomber Command. Portal's chosen approach may have been an attempt to play to Churchill's pathology, who preferred a dashing victory to obdurate defence. The bomber offensive was not quite the former, requiring a massive build-up of materiel, but it did at least afford Britain a point of attack against Nazi Germany. Moreover, Portal considered the war holistically, a consistent theme in his approach. He was even willing to sacrifice the immediate needs of the RAF if it served broader strategic goals. Most notably, Portal was exceptionally, and unusually, broad-minded and diplomatic in considering the role and perspective of the United States and its leaders both before and following their entry into the war.

The United States Congress passed a series of Neutrality Acts from 1921 to 1939 but, from 1937, Roosevelt sought to loosen its suffocating grip on his ability to influence foreign policy. The 1937 Act introduced the provision of 'Cash and Carry' whereby nations at war could purchase provisions from the US, except arms, so long as they paid immediately and transported them away on non-American ships.[39] Superficially neutral, this provision in fact favoured only Britain and France, since Axis powers lacked the requisite control of the sea to instigate the 'Carry' element of the provision.[40] In 1939, Roosevelt's attempt to renew the statute was stymied by Congress, a bitter blow to a beleaguered Britain. However, once fears of an Axis attack materialised, congressional attitudes changed; Cash and Carry was reinstituted, and extended to the provision of arms. The US remained outwardly neutral, but the realities of sea power and geography exposed the lie.

Cash and Carry sufficed for Churchill during the 'Phoney War', but its limitations were laid bare once war was unleashed in all its elemental fury during the Battle of France and the subsequent Battle of Britain. Having virtually exhausted its gold reserves, Britain could no longer afford to pay for its materiel requirements, and desperately needed more help from America. Churchill wrote to Roosevelt on 8 December 1940 and explained Britain's

---

39 https://history.state.gov/milestones/1921–1936/neutrality-acts#:~:text=After%20 a%20fierce%20debate%20in,transporting%20goods%20to%20belligerent%20ports. Accessed on 5 October 2020 at 07.45 Central Time.

40 Churchill Winston S., *The Second World War, Vol. II, Their Finest Hour*, The Educational Book Company Ltd: London, 1951, 424.

parlous financial state. 'As you know, the orders already placed or under negotiation … many times exceed the total exchange resources remaining at the disposal of Great Britain.'[41] Roosevelt spent the remainder of the month pondering his strategic response, formally announcing it during a 'Fireside Chat' on 29 December 1940 broadcast over radio to the American public. He warned, 'A nation can have peace with the Nazis only at the price of total surrender.'[42] Denying that he was putting America to war, he nevertheless said, 'We (America) must be the great arsenal of democracy.'[43] What this meant in practice was a change of policy from 'Cash and Carry' to 'Lend-Lease.'

Lend-Lease represented both a political and military shift, fundamentally changing the terms of assistance to Great Britain. Lend-Lease formally acknowledged the alliance with Great Britain and, although it did not ensure America would enter the war, made this eventuality a probability rather than a possibility.[44] Britain no longer had to pay for the use of American materiel, but could lease it and return it. Roosevelt explained Lend-Lease as follows:

> Suppose my neighbour's house catches fire, and I have a length of garden hose four or five hundred feet away. If he can take my garden hose and connect it up with his hydrant, I may help him to put out his fire. Now what do I do? I don't say to him, 'Neighbour, my garden hose cost me fifteen dollars; you have to pay me fifteen dollars for it.' No! I don't want fifteen dollars. I want my garden hose back after the fire is over.[45]

This more direct assistance proved popular with the American public, but there were mutterings in some circles. In the days following Roosevelt's address, letters and telegrams were a hundred to one in favour of the additional support to Britain.[46] The Act gave Roosevelt carte blanche to

---

41 Churchill, *Finest Hour*, 432.
42 Kimball, Warren F., *The Most Unsordid Act*. Baltimore: The Johns Hopkins Press 2019, 128.
43 Reynolds, David, Kimball, Warren F., Chubar'ian, Aleksandr Oganovich, *Allies at War: The Soviet, American, and British Experience, 1939–1945*. The Franklin and Eleanor Roosevelt Institute Series on Diplomatic and Economic History; 7. New York: St Martin's Press, 1994, 59; Kimball, *Unsordid Act*, 128.
44 Pogue, Forrest C., *George C. Marshall: Ordeal and Hope 1939–1942,* New York: Viking Press, 1963, 71.
45 Smith, Jean Edward, *FDR*. 1st ed. New York: Random House, 2007, 485.
46 Kimball, *Most Unsordid Act*, 129.

assist Britain as much as he wished, with no financial penalty imposed on the UK. Churchill, for his part, described Lend-Lease as, 'the most unsordid act in the history of any nation.'[47]

In the aftermath of the attack on Pearl Harbor, and the resulting American entry into the war, changes in the British allocation of aircraft were inevitable. A visit was, therefore, organised for Portal to meet once more with his American counterpart, General Hap Arnold, who determined the allocation of Lend-Lease materiel for the air domain. Portal knew that some reduction was inevitable, but hoped to maintain a flow of aircraft to the RAF, and Bomber Command in particular. However, to maximise his share, Portal needed the PM to be on his best behaviour with Arnold. Understanding that Churchill was probably furious about the potential reduction in allocation, Portal wrote to Churchill to pre-empt any histrionics during the upcoming meetings. Though Lend-Lease was important to the RAF, maintaining productive Alliance relationships was more significant to Portal. Portal began his missive by empathising with Churchill's point of view, one that it would have been easy for him (as RAF service chief) to share. Portal wrote that:

> There is of course much to be said in reply to his [Arnold's] arguments as we, for our part, feel that any sudden curtailment of deliveries upon which we had counted would involve grave loss to the common effort.[48]

However, Portal then recommended a more constructive course of action:

> You may decide that your reply should not dwell on this aspect of the matter but instead should concentrate on the practical results we hope to achieve from the forthcoming discussions. In that event, I suggest the following would be the principal points to be brought out:
>
> (i) that we recognise and applaud the anxiety of the U.S. Air Forces to throw their full weight into the fight as early as possible;

---

47 Kimball, *Most Unsordid Act*, *236*; Smith, *FDR*, 485, Churchill, *Finest Hour*, 434.
48 Portal to Churchill, 16 May 1942, CC/1/3/35.

(ii) that a common expansion plan is necessary if maximum effort is to be obtained with the forces available;

(iii) that in constructing such a plan the aim should be to secure the maximum impact of air power against the enemy that production and shipping permit – irrespective of whether British or U.S. pilots man the aircraft;

(iv) that the visit of Arnold and Towers is an essential stage in the preparation of such a plan and is heartily welcomed on that account;

(v) that we agree the final stages of the discussion will probably have to be concluded in Washington and that for this purpose I should return to the U.S. with Arnold and Towers.[49]

This magnanimous and selfless approach, ignoring organisational preferences, highlights Portal's broader awareness and ability to disregard tactical and operational concerns in pursuit of grand strategy objectives. In his own account of the negotiations, Arnold describes Churchill and Portal as having been extremely willing to see things from his perspective.[50] Arnold was both surprised and pleased the British chose to take this approach, which further cemented the US–UK alliance and the close working relationship between the RAF and United States Army Air Forces (USAAF) that would become even more crucial during the Combined Bomber Offensive. From Portal's perspective, the reduction was inevitable. It was unimportant who was conducting the bombing over Germany, so long as it was being done. He was, as ever, prepared to play the long game.

Portal was held in extremely high esteem by his American colleagues. His ability to see the bigger picture shone through, and set him apart from other British military leaders. Eisenhower wrote about Portal that, 'His distinguishing characteristic was balance, with perfect control of his temper; even in the most intense argument I never saw him show anger or unusual excitement.'[51] Another who observed Portal keenly, and had an intricate web of influential American connections, was Churchill's then daughter-in-law, Pamela. She wrote:

---

49 Portal to Churchill, 16 May 1942, CC/1/3/35.
50 Yenne, Bill, *Hap Arnold: The General Who Invented the U.S Air Force*. Washington, D.C.: Regnery History, 2013, 100.
51 Eisenhower, Dwight D., *Crusade in Europe*, (Garden City, N.Y.: Doubleday), 1948, 266.

Harry Hopkins and all the Americans thought very highly of him, and he got on well with all the top brass – General Marshall thought very well of him, and they felt he wasn't playing games, he didn't have an axe to grind. Sholto Douglas and Montgomery both had a personal thing, but Peter never wanted anything for himself ... The Americans fought hard with Montgomery, but I don't know any of them who knew Peter who didn't adore him.[52]

Portal's diplomatic approach to Alliance matters continued as the American bomber effort in Europe got off to a very slow start. Portal was ever cognisant of Churchill's acerbic proclivities and did what he could to prevent any outburst that could sour relations. On several occasions, Portal took the time to minute Churchill regarding the improvements in American bombing performance, a matter of great import to the war effort and a sensitive subject for all. On 6 April 1943, Portal wrote to Churchill describing the 'outstanding success' of an American raid against submarine building yards at Vegesack. On 12 July, Portal sent photographs of a successful US attack on the Renault Works in France asserting, 'they seem to have made a very good job of it'. On 12 October 1943, he again applauded 'the best high altitude bombing we have seen in this war' and enclosed reconnaissance photographs to Churchill to meet a query regarding US ability to be accurate enough to hit a target within St James's Park. Portal was ever conscious of the importance of the Alliance and served the greater needs of the war by choosing to highlight American success when he could have emphasised their failures instead and elevated Bomber Command in the eyes of the Prime Minister. Parochialism would have been an understandable course of action as Bomber Command was also under pressure from Churchill; however, Portal understood that grand strategy demanded magnanimity and diplomacy. While this broad vision won him great favour with the Americans, it sometimes resulted in conflict within the COS.

The Battle of the Atlantic was crucial to Britain's survival, yet the Royal Navy made significant missteps in its preparations. The British Armed Services were all unprepared for the Second World War. Having suffered 'unrestricted submarine warfare' during the First World War, the Navy placed a huge amount of stall in the invention of Asdic (sonar) for the detection

---

52 Interview: Mrs A. Harriman–D. Richards, 18 July 1973, CC/3/XV.

of German U-boats. Such confidence was unshaken by poor performance during the Spanish Civil War and at the start of the Second World War.[53] Because modern U-boats operated near the surface, sonar detection was more difficult than surmised. The Royal Navy's operational deficiencies ran much deeper though. Anti-submarine weapons were deficient, and the Royal Navy had no high-speed escort carriers, nor sufficient destroyers to act as convoy escort.

Despite the lack of anti-submarine detection systems or suitable aircraft and weapons in 1939, over time limited-range Coastal Command aircraft proved effective in the deterrence and destruction of both airborne and sub-surface attacks in the Western approaches.[54] German possession of Atlantic ports, following the rapid capitulation of France in 1940, extended the reach of the U-boats. When coupled with Coastal Command's successes in coastal waters, U-boats ventured further west, moving the Battle of the Atlantic beyond the range of land-based aircraft and creating a new menace. In the absence of sufficient escort carriers and destroyers, the Royal Navy blamed the Royal Air Force for the mid-Atlantic gap that emerged.

The Royal Air Force's Bomber Command was given a task of supreme importance by Churchill in October 1940. He designated the German battleships *Bismarck* and *Tirpitz* as the highest-priority targets.[55] This reflected the idea that Bomber Command was more effective at locating and attacking surface rather than sub-surface vessels. In combination with the Royal Navy, action against German battleships proved extremely effective in 1941. The *Scharnhorst* was put out of action for four months during an air raid in July comprising fifteen Halifax bombers attacking the ship at her moorings.[56] The bombers scored no fewer than five direct hits. This followed a successful earlier attack on Brest that damaged the *Prinz Eugen* so badly it could not set sail again until 1942.[57] Bomber Command followed these raids by continuing to apply the pressure and

53 Hughes, Terry, and Costello, John *The Battle of the Atlantic,* New York: Dial Press/J. Wade, 1977, 31.

54 Haslop, Dennis, *Britain, Germany and the Battle of the Atlantic: A Comparative Study,* London: Bloomsbury Academic, 2013, 76.

55 Redford, Duncan, 'Inter- and Intra-Service Rivalries in the Battle of the Atlantic.' *Journal of Strategic Studies* 32, No. 6 2009, 913.

56 Ward, Christopher, *4 Group Bomber Command: An Operational Record,* Barnsley: Pen & Sword, 2012: London, 548.

57 Schmalenbach, Paul, 'KM Prinz Eugen'. *Warship Profile 6.* Windsor: Profile Publications, 1971, 141.

dropped a further 1,200 tons of bombs on Brest before the end of the year.[58] Portal doubled down on involvement in the Battle of the Atlantic through attacks on German naval bases and shipping yards at Hamburg, Kiel, Bremen, Emden, Wilhelmshaven, and Rostock, among others. Over 6,700 tons of high explosive bombs were dropped on these targets in 1941 to degrade German naval output.[59] Portal was husbanding his resources expertly and attacking the most important and achievable targets, ever mindful of the political optics. He advertised the RAF's successes and kept the Prime Minister on side regarding the build-up of Bomber Command.

The Royal Navy was aware of their problems and acknowledged them internally. The Commander-in-Chief of the Western Approaches, Admiral Dunbar-Nasmith VC, wrote to the First Sea Lord, Admiral Dudley Pound, in December 1940 about the issues. The convoy system that had proven so effective during the First World War was failing due to a shortage of escorts, a lack of effective training, poor attack strategy and an inability to locate U-boats either on the surface or under it.[60] Dunbar-Naismith opened training schools, but it all took time. Meanwhile, Portal convinced Churchill in July 1941 to leave the first long-range Liberator bombers with Coastal Command, and not to transfer them to Bomber Command.[61] Regardless, Portal and the RAF suffered scourging criticism for the perceived failure to apportion very long-range (VLR) aircraft to Coastal Command (these did not exist in large numbers at that time), and the failure to attack the U-boat pens in France while under construction. The latter error, by Portal and the Air Ministry, contributed to greater destruction of Allied shipping in 1942.

Although more ships were sunk in 1942 than in the two previous years combined, Britain was never in danger of being knocked out of the war.[62]

---

58 Busch, Fritz-Otto, *Prinz Eugen*. London: First Futura Publications, 1975, 117.

59 Redford, 'Service Rivalries,' 903.

60 Brodhurst, Robin, *Churchill's Anchor: The Biography of Admiral of the Fleet Sir Dudley Pound*, Pen & Sword Maritime: Barnsley, 2015, 176.

61 Bell, Christopher M., 'Air Power and the Battle of the Atlantic: Very Long-Range Aircraft and the Delay in Closing the Atlantic "Air Gap,"' *Journal of Military History*, 79, No. 3, July 2015, 701.

62 O'Connell, John F., 'Closing the North Atlantic Air Gap: Where did all the BRITISH Liberators Go?', *Air Power History*, Vol. 59, No. 2 (Summer 2012), 34; Duncan Redford, 'The March 1943 Crisis in the Battle of the Atlantic: Myth and Reality,' *History*, Vol. 92, No. 1 (305), (January 2007), 67.

The critical factor tipping the balance in the Allies' favour was the entry of the United States into the war on 7 December 1941. After this point, and despite the sinking of more than 1,000 ships in 1942, Britain and America built ships faster than the Germans could destroy them.[63] Admiral Pound's fatalistic pronouncement in December 1941, 'If we lose the war at sea, we lose the war,' was accurate, though not a reflection of Britain's emerging strategic reality.[64] This did not stop him from demanding a four-fold increase in Coastal Command aircraft, to over 1,900, in March 1942.

Pound, who rarely strayed beyond the bounds of naval discussions, had a narrower strategic aperture than Portal, who was dealing with the apportionment of air power to all theatres, and prioritising as best he could. Pound's demands got short shrift from Portal, as did General Alan Brooke's similar request for squadrons to support Army Co-operation training. Portal had a deficit, not a surfeit, of assets, and precise allocation was an exacting process. Building up the pressure on German industry through strategic bombing and ensuring success in North Africa were Portal's priorities. Rampaging Japanese forces complicated these priorities in 1942, when stopping losses in the Far East was added to Portal's list. Portal's approach to the Battle of the Atlantic was to apportion sufficient aircraft so supplies could continue to arrive in the UK but, in a fight where resources were limited everywhere, there could be no surplus anywhere. It was the correct strategic approach, and fully backed by Churchill despite Portal's relatively new acquaintanceship and Pound's long association with Churchill. Portal's strategic outlook won Churchill to his side.

Nevertheless, 1942 was a torrid year. On the western side of the Atlantic, the German U-boats enjoyed their second 'happy time' attacking unescorted American convoys. The United States learned the hard way instead of from Britain's experiences. Moreover, there were now more U-boats than ever in the Atlantic, with 45 operational at the beginning of 1942, rising to 100 by the end of the year.[65] Admiral Karl Doenitz, the Kriegsmarine chief, instigated *Wolf Pack* tactics, attacking in groups and at night, rendering the task of sinking the German U-boats more difficult. The provision of Liberators, newly arrived from the US, might have helped close the mid-Atlantic gap but for two issues.

---

63 Redford, 'Myth and Reality,' 67.
64 Brodhurst, *Churchill's Anchor*, 263.
65 White, David Fairbank, *Bitter Ocean: The Battle of the Atlantic, 1939–1945* New York: Simon & Schuster, 2006, 298.

The first was the significant modifications needed for the standard production model, the Mark II and later Mark IIIA, to become VLR. The Mark II and IIIA models had an operational range of roughly 1,700 miles vice 2,400 for the Mark I.[66] Rather than take the time to modify the Liberators to VLR, the Admiralty, who exercised operational control over Coastal Command assets, chose to operate the Liberators over the Bay of Biscay, attempting to intercept the U-boats en route to their operating areas.[67] This effort was totally unsuccessful in 1942, with not a single U-boat sunk in the Bay of Biscay in the first six months despite 265 transits. The following 6 months were scarcely better with only 7 U-boats sunk for the loss of 100 aircraft.[68] It was, therefore, hardly surprising that Portal stonewalled Pound's pleas for further assistance. It was a waste of valuable RAF assets.

The second problem, as Portal advised Churchill, was American expectations that B-17s (Flying Fortresses) should be used for high-level bombing. Politically sensitive as ever, Portal worried the United States might recall aircraft that were not used as agreed.[69] Meanwhile, Liberators provided sterling service for the RAF in the North Africa campaign, supporting operations in the Mediterranean, where they were the only aircraft with the requisite range to bomb Tripoli.[70] Despite these competing priorities, Portal sent thirty-two Liberator Mark IIIs to Coastal Command between July and September 1942. Unfortunately, the Germans moved the U-boat war further and further west, beyond the range of the Mark IIIAs.

Despite the worsening situation in the mid-Atlantic, which came to be known as the Black Pit, Coastal Command did not prioritise its VLR aircraft for operations in that region. As late as February 1943, Coastal Command allocated only twelve of its thirty-six VLR Liberators to the mid-Atlantic gap, with the others operating in the English Channel and over the Bay of Biscay.[71] Belated analysis from Coastal Command's operational research section showed unequivocally that U-boats were much more likely to be sunk in the vicinity of convoys than in the Bay of Biscay.[72] Portal

66 Goette, Richard, 'Britain and the Delay in Closing the Mid-Atlantic 'Air Gap' During the Battle of the Atlantic,' *The Northern Mariner*, XV No. 4, (October 2005), 29.
67 Goette, 'Air Gap,' 29.
68 Brodhurst, *Churchill's Anchor*, 272.
69 Redford, 'Service Rivalries,' 911.
70 Terraine, *A Time for Courage*, 419.
71 O'Connell, 'Atlantic Air Gap,' 39.
72 Goette, 'Air Gap,' 38.

consequentially took decisive action, determining to convert all ninety newly acquired Liberators to VLR duties, before convincing the Combined Chiefs of Staff (CCS) on 29 March 1943 that 'the greatest practicable number of existing VLR ASV equipped aircraft ... now assigned to other duties, be diverted to anti-submarine operations in the Atlantic.'[73] This action prompted Churchill to appeal directly to Roosevelt, and a strong presidential push finally got the United States to allocate some VLR aircraft to the Western Atlantic.[74] Until that point, precisely zero had been used for this purpose.

Admiral King, the Chief of Naval Operations, defiantly maintained his VLR fleet operating in the Pacific, which he alone of the Combined Chiefs considered the decisive theatre of war. Belated improvements in American VLR allocation between the Pacific and Atlantic, as well as the eventual introduction of carrier escorts, resulted in significant U-boat attrition in mid-1943. With forty-three U-boats sunk in May 1943, Doenitz temporarily removed U-boats from operations. The battle was effectively won, though better prioritisation by the Admiralty could have ameliorated losses sooner. Portal, by contrast, had gauged his strategic priorities expertly, ensuring the RAF contributed to success in North Africa and the Battle of the Atlantic while maintaining direct pressure on German industry through heavy bombing. He correctly refused to overcommit air assets to a failing enterprise in the Bay of Biscay, yet authoritatively supported the Battle of the Atlantic when he saw how the tide could be turned. Portal had been resolute yet shown a keen eye for the intricacies of naval warfare when the opportune moment arose.

While the Battle of the Atlantic, and the allocation of air power assets in general, caused disagreements among the COS, the chiefs often banded together to prevent implementation of some of the Prime Minister's wilder strategic schemes. Churchill never overruled a united COS Committee, though he was more than prepared to wear them down to the point of submission. Only under threat of a public clash could he ignore their advice, though theoretically the chiefs could be overruled on political grounds.[75] Yet the gap between military and political spheres blurred during

---

73 Ibid., 39.

74 Hughes and Costello, *Battle of the Atlantic*, 261.

75 Bryant, Arthur and Alanbrooke, Viscount Alan Francis Brooke, *Triumph in the West: A History of the War Years Based on the Diaries of Field-Marshal Lord Alanbrooke, Chief of the Imperial General Staff.* 1st ed. Garden City, N.Y.: Doubleday, 1959, 22.

the Second World War, so the military advisors were consulted broadly, and their influence was much wider than the public understood. Once Brooke replaced Dill as Chief of Imperial General Staff (CIGS), there was a military bulwark to curtail Churchillian scheming.

The COS and Churchill developed very different ideas about British Pacific strategy in 1943. Churchill's notion was to recapture British Imperial territory lost in 1942 and restore national prestige. Pragmatically, the chiefs considered assisting the United States in the military defeat of Japan to be the priority.[76] Neither side would budge, but heated discussions ran from mid-1943 until mid-1944. The pattern of behaviour Churchill displayed toward the chiefs as a joint body was similar to that experienced by each chief individually. Churchill was extraordinarily persistent, difficult to persuade, and capable of fits of pique when he did not instantly get his way. Brooke records 8 August 1943 as the first time Churchill mentioned the tip of Sumatra as his proposed point of attack, but it was an ongoing battle during which Churchill expected the chiefs to resolutely resist his wishes as he attempted to coax, harass, and browbeat them into assent.[77] On this matter, and despite a concerted campaign, Churchill could not move his COS.

This heated debate led to the most acrimonious time between the COS and Churchill. Brooke described Churchill as behaving 'like a spoilt child that wants a toy' on 19 August 1943.[78] The problem for the COS Committee was that, on this occasion, the Americans wanted Britain to concentrate on Burma and support to China; President Roosevelt had proposed this approach at the TRIDENT Conference in May 1943.[79] What Brooke, Portal, et al knew was that the logistic requirements of such an operation were impossible before the war with Germany ended.[80] Thus the debate raged. The following February when the chiefs insisted on a general approach, Churchill described a comprehensive strategy as 'long term projects that cripple initiative.'[81]

---

76 Alanbrooke, *War Diaries*, 526.

77 Bryant, *Triumph*, 25.

78 Alanbrooke, *War Diaries*, 444.

79 Butler, James Ramsay Montagu, Gwyer, J.M.A., Ehrman, John and Howard, Michael. *Grand Strategy: History of the Second World War Vol. IV*, United Kingdom Military Series. London: H.M. Stationery Office, 1956, 443.

80 Eden, Anthony, The Reckoning; the Memoirs of Anthony Eden, Earl of Avon. Boston: Houghton Mifflin Co., 1965, 536.

81 Alanbrooke, *War Diaries*, 526.

By March there was talk of mass resignations, and Lieutenant General Hastings Ismay, Churchill's chief military assistant, warned him of the possibility.[82] This was unthinkable with OVERLORD only a few months away. In the end, the Joint Planning Staff proposed a compromise that came to be known as the 'Middle Strategy'.[83] The strategy involved an axis starting at Timor, running through Burma and ending in Saigon.[84] The planning work was instigated by direction of the COS on 1 April 1944; it had all the hallmarks of Charles Portal.[85] Though strategically the plan was imperfect, it brought the chiefs closer to Churchill at a vital time in the war – a few short months before the planned liberation of France. The Pacific plan was never implemented, as Japan capitulated before Britain could transfer its martial assets to the theatre. In a sense this was less important than the amelioration of difficulties between Churchill and the chiefs, and Brooke in particular. The plan was built on compromise and diplomacy, which were Portal's greatest gifts. Brooke's key strength was his willingness to argue logically with Churchill. Both approaches functioned, sometimes in tandem, to keep the PM in line. Nevertheless, with vastly different personalities, Portal and Brooke were bound to clash in the cauldron of the COS Committee.

---

82 Ismay, Hastings Lionel Ismay, *Memoirs,* New York: Viking Press, 1960, 400.
83 Fraser, *Alanbrooke*, 389.
84 The National Archives, Kew, (hereafter referred to as TNA), TNA CAB/79/73/10/135.
85 TNA CAB 79/72/17/289.

Chapter 4

Portal and Brooke

I cannot say that we never differed among ourselves even at home, but a kind of understanding grew up between me and the British Chiefs of Staff that we should convince and persuade rather than try to overrule each other.[1]

Winston Spencer Churchill

Portal first worked with Alan Brooke when the latter was on the staff of the Canadian Corps in 1917. Portal commanded the Army Co-operation Squadron attached to them. The two men met occasionally during the interwar period, but were not well acquainted when Brooke took over as CIGS in late 1941. Portal's initial impressions were mixed. Brooke seemed the polar opposite of his predecessor, the charming, tactful, and diplomatic Dill. Life on the COS Committee was going to change with Brooke present.[2] Moreover, Brooke could be abrupt and confrontational. Portal and Brooke were very different characters, so there was a significant possibility of acrimony among the COS, especially regarding the importance and employment of the RAF. Brooke was, unsurprisingly, not a believer in strategic bombing. Challenges lay ahead in this relationship yet, in their differing approaches and modes of thinking, the new composition of the COS Committee offered opportunity as well as risk.

Alan Brooke was born in the French Pyrenees in 1883, the seventh son of an Irish nobleman whose family was known as 'The Fighting Brookes.' The family had produced military men for centuries, with no fewer than twenty-six serving during the First World War and even more twenty

---

1 Churchill, Winston S., *The Second World War, Vol. II, Their Finest Hour*, The Educational Book Company Ltd: London, 1951, 18.
2 Portal interview for Broadcast on BBC 17 September 1963, Portal Papers, Christ Church College, Oxford (Hereafter referred to as CC), CC/3/A/A5.

years later.[3] Further back in time, Sir Arthur Brooke had been a regimental colonel during the razing of the Capitol of Washington D.C. in 1814.[4] It is unclear whether this fact contributed to the United States Chiefs of Staff's (US JCS) initial antipathy toward his direct descendant. Brooke's father died when the boy was only eight years old, leaving him in the care of a doting mother. Initially a delicate child, he gradually grew more robust, becoming an accomplished jockey with the local hunt. He eschewed team sports, being rather shy and preferring solitude.[5]

By the age of sixteen, and unsurprising given family proclivities, Brooke decided to join the Army. He scraped into Royal Military Academy (RMA) Woolwich, placing sixty-fifth of seventy-two during his entrance exam. Nonetheless, he was accepted.[6] The RMA trained cadets for two of the British Army's corps: the Royal Engineers (RE) and the Royal Artillery (RA). Top-performing cadets were sent to the RE and the remainder to the RA. Despite continuously improving his class standing during his two years there, Alan narrowly missed out on entry to the RE, finishing a respectable seventeenth in his class. Alas, only fifteen commissions were awarded in the RE; Brooke was relegated to the Artillery.

Brooke spent his first eleven years in the Army in Ireland and India, where he primarily engaged in sporting pursuits. His equestrian skills were put to the test with steeplechasing and point-to-point races; he also went hunting and fishing frequently.[7] Brooke would later share a love of the last of these pastimes with the heads of his sister services. Fishing dispelled any lingering rancour from meetings and helped forge the COS into a united team.

The British Army believed sport honed the minds and bodies of young officers, and these pastimes were relatively inexpensive for a poorly paid officer as the Army provided both horses and guns. Brooke applied himself thoroughly to sport, as he did to his professional duties, becoming an objective observer of artillery skill and a keen student of military history.[8]

---

3 Roberts, Andrew, *Masters and Commanders: How Roosevelt, Churchill, Marshall and Alanbrooke Won the War in the West*, London: Penguin, 2008, 13.

4 Fraser, David. *Alanbrooke*. 1st ed. New York: Atheneum, 1982, 10.

5 Ibid., 16.

6 Ibid., 17.

7 Ibid., 22–23.

8 Ibid., 20.

Brooke successfully applied for transfer to the Royal Horse Artillery (RHA) in 1909 and joined the Eagle Troop of the RHA at Ambala, where he spent some of the happiest years of his life. During elongated periods of leave back in Ireland, Brooke also became acquainted with, and was subsequently betrothed to, an attractive Irish girl, Jane Richardson.[9] They were engaged for six long years because subalterns such as Brooke had to seek permission to marry from their commanding officers. They finally married in late July 1914. Their honeymoon was six days old when rudely interrupted by the guns of August.

The sudden outbreak of war left Brooke a little disoriented. A curtailed honeymoon was one thing, but all his equipment, his uniform, and even his unit were back in India, to where he was initially recalled. In the event Brooke stopped in Cairo to await the arrival of the RHA, and by mid-September he re-joined Eagle Troop. Fortunately, a thoughtful colleague brought all Brooke's gear with him, which alleviated one concern. His other worry was dispelled when he discovered the unit was bound for Marseilles. Brooke would not miss the war.

More than anything, the First World War educated Brooke in his role as an artillery commander. He was an apt pupil. Brooke arrived in France too late for the Battle of the Marne, and only caught the dying thrusts of the First Battle of Ypres in which the British Army suffered horrendously. Following the cold winter of 1914, Brooke's war began in earnest with the March 1915 attack on Neuve Chapelle. He commanded fifty-four guns, largely because (as described in Brooke's typically sanguine prose), 'My colonel played patience most of the time and he did not take much of the load off me.'[10] Brooke became an artillery expert, noting the overriding problem at the front as the shortage of ammunition. This early exposure to logistics problems provided a salient lesson for high command later, where global supply and lines of communication shaped the construction of British military strategy.

During the Battle of the Somme, in July 1916, Brooke was the Brigade Major Royal Artillery to the 18th Division at Picardy, with direct access to the commander and a vital role in the preparation and conduct of battle.[11] He instigated the first British 'creeping barrage' during the battle, ensuring success in his division's sector. Brooke applied his scientific mind to the

---

9 Ibid., 24.
10 Ibid., 35.
11 Ibid., 41.

task, converting the plan into exact timings and producing precise maps to facilitate easy understanding for all concerned.[12] For Brooke's part in the battle, he was awarded the Distinguished Service Order. His practice would, in time, be adopted across all divisions, but the 18th Division's success was not matched across the front, where British losses were appalling.

In early 1917, Brooke joined the Canadian Corps, to which Peter Portal's Army Co-operation Squadron was attached. Brooke was intimately involved in planning the Canadian attack on Vimy Ridge, including the allocation of positions, communications, and the plan for artillery employment.[13] The daring attack was a roaring success, and Brooke took his fair share of the acclaim. He also fought at Passchendaele in autumn 1917, his last great battle of the First World War, and left the conflict an acknowledged artillery expert, but lacking the rounded joint perspective of Portal. Nevertheless, with reputation firmly established, Brooke was selected for Staff College at Camberley in 1919, where he distinguished himself with his clarity of thought and expression. He was subsequently posted back to Camberley in 1923 as an instructor, following a similar educational path to both Portal and Tedder. He spent four years at Camberley, before becoming one of the first batch of students at the Imperial Defence College in 1927, to where he also returned in 1932 as an instructor. In the meantime, the British Army promoted Brooke from substantive major to brigadier in 1929, above ninety other RA officers, and to the post of Commandant of the School of Artillery at Larkhill.[14] Unintimidated, Brooke set about instigating a thorough reform of training at Larkhill, as well as a comprehensive review and overhaul of the estate.

Brooke rounded out his military education in more practical posts, fulfilling the designation of 'general' officer thoroughly. First, he was appointed brigade commander for the 8th Infantry Brigade, highly unusual for an artillery officer. He then became Director of Military Training, followed by a stint as commander of the British Army's first mobile division. Brooke was experienced in commanding artillery, infantry, and mechanised forces: a true all-rounder.

He further broadened in 1938 in command of the new Anti-Aircraft Corps, where he worked for Air Chief Marshal Hugh 'Stuffy' Dowding, Air Officer Commander-in-Chief Fighter Command. Brooke found Dowding

---

12 Ibid., 45.
13 Ibid., 42.
14 Ibid., 66–67.

not in the least stuffy and spoke warmly about the collaboration. By the time war broke out Brooke had moved on again to command Southern Command. When the 'Phoney War' ended, Brooke was in command of II Corps during the Battle of France, and played a key role in ensuring many of his men escaped Dunkirk. Having returned to London, Brooke spoke to the new CIGS, Sir John Dill, to ascertain his next assignment. Brooke was unamused when told it was to form a new expeditionary force in France.[15]

Brooke returned dutifully to the front, despite knowing the situation was hopeless. Having observed at first hand the total disarray of the French armed forces, he had no doubt the action was futile. The French may have been largely numerically intact, but they were strategically and psychologically paralysed. Brooke learned this personally from General Weygand, the new supreme French commander, and resolved to extricate as many of his forces back to England as possible. When he reported this to Dill, Churchill (who was waiting on the line) told Brooke he had been sent to France to make the French feel supported. Brooke replied acerbically, 'It is impossible to make a corpse feel,' adding that the French Army was basically dead.[16] Churchill, as was typical, argued the issue with Brooke for another thirty minutes, after which Brooke snapped, 'You've already lost one Scottish Division. Do you want to lose another?'[17] Brooke won the point and returned to the UK, division intact.

The following month, Brooke took control of Home Forces and preparations for an anticipated German invasion. In this guise he met with Portal on several occasions to discuss the link between Home Forces and the RAF, which Brooke described as an 'unsatisfactory situation' without elaborating further.[18] In February 1941, Brooke committed a faux pas, summoning Portal, a superior officer, to discuss the matter further. Portal nevertheless appeared at Brooke's office as requested, a display of startling magnanimity.[19] By the end of 1941, Portal's and Brooke's wars coincided, when Brooke was chosen to replace Dill as CIGS. The congenial Dill, who lacked the necessary fortitude to endure the Churchillian firehose,

---

15 Ibid., 135–136.

16 Ibid., 140.

17 Ibid.

18 Alanbrooke, Alan Brooke, Todman, Daniel and Danchev, Alex, *War Diaries, 1939–1945: Field Marshal Lord Alanbrooke*. Berkeley: University of California Press, 2001, 144.

19 Interview: Portal and M.C. Long, 1952, in Alanbrooke Papers, King's College London (hereafter referred to as KCL/AB), KCL/AB/11/7.

was despatched to Washington D.C. There he headed the British Military Mission, rendering such exceptional service that he was accorded the singular honour of being interred in Arlington Cemetery following his death.[20] With Brooke's ascension on 25 December 1941, and Japan's perfidy at Pearl Harbor just six days later, the stage was set. Portal and Brooke would now drive both British and Alliance strategy onward to victory.

Brooke and Portal needed one another for Britain to succeed. While both were strategically minded, neither alone could overcome the resistance of Churchill or the Americans. That Portal could not do it alone was probably best illustrated by the debacle in Greece in early 1941. Britain needed to prioritise activity in North Africa and the Mediterranean, and both Sir John Dill (Brooke's predecessor as CIGS) and Portal believed securing North Africa should precede any incursion into the Balkans and Greece.[21] A united COS Committee would have prevented the action, because Churchill would not unilaterally overrule the advice of his military chiefs.[22] Unfortunately, Sir Dudley Pound, the Chairman of the COS Committee, rarely strayed from naval discussions to discuss broader strategy, which left the matter to Dill and Portal. Where Portal was quietly resolute, Dill was not.

Though he would not outright overrule his military advisors, Churchill actively sought to cajole and convince them to his side. On this occasion he did it with the knowing assistance of his Foreign Secretary, Anthony Eden. Churchill sent Dill and Eden on a fact-finding mission to the Middle East and the Balkans, arming Eden with express powers to send, 'speedy succour to Greece ... He will initiate any action he may think necessary with the Commander-in-Chief of the Middle East, with the Egyptian Government, and with the governments of Greece, Yugoslavia, and Turkey.'[23] Eden worked on Dill during the trip, and effected a change by 19 February 1941 such that Dill then expressed overt support for sending troops to Greece.[24]

---

20 Danchev, Alex, *Very Special Relationship: Field-Marshal Sir John Dill and the Anglo-American Alliance, 1941–44*, 1st ed. London; Washington: Brassey's Defence Publishers, 1986, 1.

21 Ben-Moshe, Tuvia, *Churchill, Strategy and History*. Boulder, Co.: Lynne Rienner Publishers, 1992, 138, 144.

22 Butler, James Ramsay Montagu, Gwyer, J.M.A., Ehrman, John and Howard, Michael, *Grand Strategy: History of the Second World War, Vol. VI*, United Kingdom Military Series. London: H.M. Stationery Office, 1956, 337.

23 Churchill Winston S., *The Second World War, Vol. III, The Grand Alliance*, The Educational Book Company Ltd: London, 1951, 53.

24 Ben-Moshe, *Churchill*, 148.

Dill had not the stomach to oppose Eden and Churchill's combined will. A report from Portal and Pound explaining that 'the risks of failure are serious,' proved too equivocal to dissuade Churchill from his preferred course of action.[25] Brooke considered the campaign that ensued, culminating in a decisive Axis victory, to have been a 'definite strategic blunder.'[26] It comprised action he would never have supported, and it arguably prolonged the North Africa campaign unnecessarily. Dill was not the firewall Brooke would prove to be in the COS Committee. While Dill was charming and polite, Portal needed the more obdurate and stubborn Brooke to help quell Churchill's more eccentric and misguided strategic ideas.

The Portal-Brooke nexus devised and drove British wartime strategy. The authors of *Grand Strategy: The History of the Second World War*, depict Churchill as the arch-strategist: 'For his massive and uneven genius dominated the later, as earlier, stages of the war … These volumes have shown his intimate participation, and commanding role, in strategic discussions throughout the period.'[27] While Churchill was certainly domineering, he did not determine British military strategy during the war. The PM was both overly emotional and too inconsistent to be an effective strategist. Winston may well have proposed or considered every successful Allied stratagem of the war. Unfortunately, he also championed a plethora of strategies that were absolute non-starters.

In particular, Churchill's lack of concern for logistics led to serious British problems. The operation to assist the Greeks in 1941 was doomed from the start, as it took place beyond the range of Mediterranean-based British air support. The Luftwaffe quickly overwhelmed the few squadrons based in Greece.[28] This operation also ripped essential forces from North Africa, contributing to Rommel's successful debut in the theatre. Churchill overextended British forces again in 1943. He devised a plan to take the Dodecanese on the romantic notion that this would draw Turkey into the war.[29] Finally, he became obsessed with Sumatra as the point of attack in the Pacific, despite insufficient maritime transportation to enable the operation, given the demands of the European

25 Ibid., 149.
26 Broad, Charlie Lewis, *Winston Churchill: A Biography*. New York: Hawthorn Books, 1958, 113.
27 Butler, James Ramsay Montagu, Gwyer, J.M.A., Ehrman, John and Howard, Michael. *Grand Strategy: History of the Second World War Vol. IV,* United Kingdom Military Series. London: H.M. Stationery Office, 1956, 334.
28 Ben-Moshe, *Churchill*, 153.
29 Porch, Douglas, *The Path to Victory*, New York: Farrar, Strauss and Giroux, 2004, 471.

war. In a meeting about the proposed plan, Churchill muttered that there were resources available, but presented no evidence to support this view and then accused those present of trying to corner him.[30]

Portal and Brooke had to sift through the mind of the great creator and determine, through rigorous analysis, how to use available resources to meet political goals at a given moment. Churchill was fortunate to find these two men who guided Britain from the beginning of 1942 to a successful end to the war in 1945. It was the COS's role to recommend military strategy to the political leadership, as described by Churchill:

> I do not conduct this war from day to day myself. It is conducted from day to day, and in its future outlook, by the Chiefs of Staff Committee … These officers sit together every day and often twice a day. They give executive directions and orders to the Commanders-in-Chief in the various theatres. They advise me, they advise the Defence Committee and the War Cabinet on large questions of war strategy and policy … I do not think there has ever been a system in which the professional heads of the fighting services have had a freer hand or a greater or more direct influence or have received more constant and harmonious support from the Prime Minister and the Cabinet under whom they serve.[31]

While Brooke, for one, may have argued about the level of 'harmony', Churchill's statement reflects the overwhelming responsibility of the Joint Chiefs. Unsurprisingly given the weight of their responsibilities, the Portal–Brooke partnership would go through a baptism of fire in 1942, exacerbated by interpersonal tension and operational reverses.

Brooke aptly described the reverses, reflecting on his first year as CIGS in early 1943:

> I cannot help glancing back at Jan 1st last year when I could see nothing but calamities ahead; Hong Kong gone; Singapore going, Java etc very doubtful, even Burma unsafe, would we

30 Eden, Anthony, *The Reckoning; the Memoirs of Anthony Eden, Earl of Avon.* Boston: Houghton Mifflin Co., 1965, 536.
31 Bryant, Arthur and Alanbrooke, Viscount Alan Brooke, The Turn of the Tide: a History of the War Years Based on the Diaries of Field-Marshal Lord Alanbrooke, Chief of the Imperial General Staff. 1st ed. Garden City, N.Y.: Doubleday, 1957, 9–10.

be able to save India and Australia? Horrible doubts, horrible nightmares, which grew larger and larger as the days went on till it felt as if the whole Empire was collapsing round my head. Wherever I looked I could see nothing but trouble. Middle East began to crumble, Egypt was threatened. I felt Russia could never hold, Caucasus was bound to be penetrated, and Abadan (our Achilles Heel) would be captured with the consequent collapse of Middle East, India, etc.[32]

It was a horrifying six months for Britain, only partially ameliorated by the United States' entry into the war. However, America needed to significantly alter Lend-Lease commitments to account for a more direct role in the war, which initially drained rather than bolstered access to wartime materiel. This dearth of resources added to the tension between Portal and Brooke, which at times in 1942 was palpable and girded by the change of character within the COS Committee.

Brooke thought quickly and talked quickly, rarely having to hear anything twice.[33] If nothing else, Portal found the change of pace abrasive compared to dealing with the more easy-going Dill. He was initially unconvinced this was what the COS Committee needed. Brooke's staccato delivery and blunt manner also frustrated dealings with the US JCS, who were somewhat wary of him.[34] However, this was not the primary bone of contention for Portal and Brooke in 1942. Britain needed a coherent and agreed military strategy to take forward to the 1943 conferences, but that agreement would be hard won. Portal and Brooke had differing strategic outlooks that coloured their views. Most disagreements revolved around how the RAF could best support the war.

By 1942 Britain was engaged in a global war with extremely limited assets. Tedder, in the Middle East theatre, suffered the loss of significant numbers of aircraft from North Africa to the Far East. At the same time, both the British Army and Royal Navy respectively demanded better support for Army Co-operation and the Battle of the Atlantic. A final sore point for Brooke was the notion of strategic bombing as a war-winning mechanism. He thought Portal wholly overcommitted to it.[35] These factors all led to strained discussions but, according to John Slessor, it was to Portal's great

---

32 Alanbrooke, *War Diaries*, 355.
33 Portal interview for Broadcast on BBC 17 September 1963, CC/3/A/A5.
34 Ismay, Hastings Lionel, *Memoirs,* New York: Viking Press, 1960, 317.
35 Alanbrooke, *War Diaries*, 332.

credit that they never boiled over. 'Portal was wise and very patient – if I had been in his place, I am sure there would have been a rare bust-up, which of course would have been a mistake.'[36] Disagreements between Portal and Brooke were inevitable; their individual proclivities reflected their formative service experiences.

Brooke's views on Army Co-operation were well established from his time as Commander-in-Chief Home Forces. He lambasted Portal on several occasions in his nightly diary about the lack of air support to the British Army, of great personal concern since he had become CIGS following a tour as Commander of Home Forces. On 11 March 1942, Brooke reported a heated debate that did not lead anywhere. He anticipated further 'stormy passages' in the weeks to come.[37] On 19 May 1942, Brooke reported, 'Difficult COS at which we discussed Army and Navy air requirements. It led in the first place to heated arguments between me and Portal and subsequently between Pound and Portal! ... It is a depressing situation and the Air Ministry is now so divorced from the requirements of the army that I see no solution except an Army Air Arm.'[38]

Portal's belief in the efficacy of strategic bombing was unsurprising; he was both a former AOC Bomber Command and steeped in RAF doctrine and theory that made great claim for the morale effects of strategic bombing. Portal, along with many others, initially believed strategic bombing could be used to destroy the German people's will to fight and obviate the need for victory in the land domain. Portal outlined his views in a 1941 paper:

As our forces increase, we intend to pass to a planned attack on civilian morale with the intensity and continuity which are essential if a final breakdown is to be produced. There is increasing evidence of the effect which even our present limited scale of attack is causing to German life. We have every reason to be confident that if we expand our forces in accordance with our present programme, and if possible beyond it, that effect will be shattering.[39]

---

36 Slessor, John Cotesworth, *The Central Blue; Recollections and Reflections,* London: Cassell, 1956, 419.
37 Alanbrooke, *War Diaries*, 238.
38 Ibid., 258.
39 Terraine, J. (1985), *A Time for Courage: The Royal Air Force in the European War, 1939–1945.* New York, N.Y.: Macmillan, 291.

This belief proved erroneous; it is highly unlikely the strategic bombing of Germany could ever have resulted in the toppling of such a highly oppressive regime as the Nazis. However, in 1942, Portal had not yet been given the chance to prove the viability of the strategy, and he felt it would be premature to abandon it without at least attempting it.

Brooke remained blind to both the capabilities and limitations of airpower, creating a strategic schism between him and Portal. Brooke's perspective was, in fact, somewhat incongruous with his understanding of the overall strategic situation. At the ARCADIA Conference in December 1941–January 1942, the US JCS suggested a possible autumn 1942 invasion of France, which Brooke considered wholly unrealistic. He expressed these views in a COS Committee Meeting on 2 January 1942, responding to a report from the Joint Planning Staff on Operation ROUNDUP, the proposed re-invasion of France. He stated, 'We should prepare to act earlier than the report visualised, even though the opportunity for this might at the moment seem remote.'[40] The report highlighted that OP ROUNDUP would only be possible after severe degradation of both German bomber and fighter forces. It further warned that in the absence of such, delay beyond mid-1943 was inevitable. The primary agent delivering this pre-condition was Bomber Command, through a precipitous escalation of attacks on German industry. Brooke's pessimism regarding strategic bombing clouded his logic. If strategic bombing did not work OP ROUNDUP was a non-starter in any event. Moreover, with prioritisation of assets of paramount strategic importance, Brooke's proposed allocation of support to the land component made little sense. If there was little prospect of ROUNDUP in 1942, elements of Army Co-operation relating to reinvasion of the Continent should not be afforded high strategic priority.

More than once, Brooke equated his fight with that of the Royal Navy in the Battle of the Atlantic. The two were not alike. The Battle of the Atlantic was the Royal Navy's number one priority, whereas ROUNDUP preparations sat below support of both the Middle East and Far East theatres for the British Army at that time. While Pound had some call on the RAF to provide more for the Battle of the Atlantic, Brooke's case was baseless. Delegating such a large percentage of RAF assets would have strategically hamstrung the RAF. Portal would have lost the flexibility to prioritise the use of air power where it was most needed, which was essential given the

---

40 The National Archives, Kew (Hereafter referred to as TNA), CAB/79/17/2.

limited production figures. Brooke's critique also reflected a fundamental deficiency in Army thinking at all levels: if the Army could not see air power, then it was not assisting them. Portal, who fervently believed in the efficacy of bombing the enemy long before its capabilities were able to engage the British Army, found such critique infuriating.

Brooke was also somewhat blinded by his operational commanders, notably General Archie Wavell in India, who continually crowed for supporting aircraft. Wavell, who had inadvertently aided and abetted the firing of Arthur Longmore as Air Commander in the Middle East with incessant calls for more aircraft, maintained his modus operandi in India. Brooke, opposed as he was to the strategic bombing campaign against Germany, lent a friendly ear. 'We are now reaping the full disadvantages of an all-out independent air policy directed towards the bombing of Germany. As a result, we are short of all the suitable types of aircraft for support of the other two services.'[41] Brooke may have been right, with the benefit of hindsight, regarding the inability of strategic bombing to affect the collapse of the German people's will to fight. However, he took mind of neither the tremendous destruction the bombing caused German industry, nor the subsequent dispersal of German factories that assisted effectiveness but at a huge cost to efficiency.

Chronic supply problems followed US entry into the war, bringing ever-louder calls on UK manufacturing. Brooke consistently failed to account for the limited numbers of available aircraft in his disagreements with Portal. Problems with US supply in 1942 changed Portal's calculations, to Brooke's irritation. On 15 September 1942, Brooke went into bat for the airborne forces promised in May. Portal had to report that 89 per cent of the promised transport aircraft from the US were still in the US, necessitating reprioritisation.[42] Brooke described having 'a difference of opinion with CAS,'[43] arguing 'airborne forces would be an essential part of any major operation against the continent.'[44] While factually accurate, operations in France in 1943 were becoming less and less likely, rendering Brooke's commentary irrelevant. Portal's equanimity in dealing with Brooke's ranting was remarkable, as Slessor described. By contrast, Brooke's underestimation of Portal's regard for Army Co-operation stood

41 Bryant, *The Turn of the Tide*, 311.
42 TNA/CAB/79/23/13.
43 Alanbrooke, *War Diaries*, 321.
44 TNA/CAB/79/23/13.

at odds with Portal's own experience; he had spent the best years of the previous war engaged in precisely that role. Where they differed, and would continue to clash, was in the priority it was afforded. Rather smartly, Portal would later point out, 'There has been a tendency in the past to confuse lack of co-operation with lack of means to co-operate.'[45]

Brooke used the term Army Co-operation as a catch-all for a variety of demands. In May 1942 it encompassed: twenty squadrons for Operation SLEDGEHAMMER (the Southern France incursion subordinate to ROUNDUP); fifteen fighter squadrons to exercise and operate with the Army; the build-up of No. 2 Group to twenty squadrons for Army air support; fifteen squadrons for fighter and bomber reconnaissance in the Middle East; the adaptation of other bombers to support airborne forces; air observation post squadrons and ambulance aircraft. The daunting list had a deleterious effect on the materiel and manpower allocated to Bomber Command, which less than two weeks later would deliver the first 1,000 aircraft raid over Cologne. From Portal's perspective, this planned mission was only the beginning for Bomber Command, as it afforded a starting point for proving the efficacy of strategic bombing.

Nevertheless, and despite the CIGS's complaints, Portal agreed to a great deal of Brooke's demands. He supported the provision of twenty squadrons for SLEDGEHAMMER, agreed on the requirements for airborne training, as well as the air observations post squadrons and the air ambulances. Portal would not promise all fifteen squadrons for the Middle East, nor would he subordinate No. 2 Group to Army Co-operation Command (on what was a training and not an operational task), as this would preclude the flexible use of air power as and when most urgently needed. Portal was at pains to point out the reason for the deficiencies:

> The disappointments experienced by Army Co-operation Command are due, not to lack of goodwill on the part of the Air Ministry, but to the hard realities of the aircraft supply position over an acutely difficult period. The freezing of American deliveries, the urgent calls from Libya and the Far East and the necessity for maintaining a punctual monthly quota to Russia have meant shortages all round.[46]

---

45 Richards, *Portal*, 204.
46 TNA/AIR/8/989, 1 April 1942.

Despite their differences over this allocation, both men understood how important it was to emphasise what they could agree on before presentation to Churchill. They sent a joint memorandum to the Defence Committee, drawing attention to the large measure of accord reached, with a cursory mention of the unresolvable.

Portal and Brooke were, in fact, in violent agreement on many strategic principles, despite what the contents of Brooke's diary might indicate. This was crucial in dealing with both the Prime Minister and American allies. In mid-July 1942 the US JCS (General George Marshall and Admiral Ernest King) travelled to London to discuss strategy. They wanted a cross-Channel operation in 1942: Portal and Brooke were vehemently opposed. Their roles in discussions were akin to a sword and shield. Brooke, as Chairman of the British COS Committee, was the primary spokesman. He laid out the proposed British strategy pointedly. Portal then defended the position with cool logic and calm demeanour.

Brooke, having evacuated from France twice already, knew the perils of returning to the Continent without sufficient forces to make it stick. So did Portal. The Americans argued first for a six-division incursion, and then for a bridgehead for a further operation in 1943. Neither course of action reflected the British view, articulated in the 17 July 1942 War Cabinet paper on future strategy: 'Even if Russia holds, Germany may still be able to withdraw to France and the Low Countries sufficient forces to prohibit "Round-up" next spring.'[47] While the German invasion of Russia, Operation BARBAROSSA, had sent enormous numbers of German forces east, their position in France remained extremely strong. In the event, it took Portal and Brooke several days to convince the US delegation of the impossibility of cross-Channel operations in 1942, and to deter Admiral King from trying to divert all effort to the Pacific.

At that time, the US had less sway in strategic discussions because the troop composition would have been largely British. By 24 July 1942, as Brooke noted, 'They all agreed to giving up an immediate assault on the continent, to prepare for attack on North Africa to be carried out if re-entry into Europe was impossible next year.'[48] The attack on North Africa, Operation TORCH, was agreed; the Brooke–Portal 'sword and shield' tactic had worked. They later used this approach to great effect during

---

47 TNA/CAB/79/22/11.
48 Alanbrooke, *War Diaries*, 285.

Allied conferences in 1943–45, but this was its first outing. Keeping the US committed to a 'Europe First' approach was a delicate business, with Admiral King a particularly prickly character. Not only was he constantly ready to exploit any opportunity to promote a 'Pacific First' strategy for the US,[49] he could also be extremely obstinate and rude. Eisenhower once mused that shooting King might assist the war effort.[50] Despite their success, Portal and Brooke remained divided on several matters.

Brooke travelled to Moscow in August to explain to Stalin why there would be no second front in 1942 (though Portal and Harris might have argued that the bombing of Germany was exactly that). On this occasion, Churchill took the straight-talking Brooke to deal with the Russians, perceiving Portal's hallmark compromise and diplomacy as potentially tantamount to weakness in Russian eyes. Brooke left the Russians in no doubt about the probability of the second front, as summarised by Archie Wavell on the plane ride out of Moscow. Brooke guiltily watched on as Wavell worked, seemingly making notes from all the meetings that had taken place. When Brooke saw what Wavell was working on, however, his guilt melted away. It was entitled 'Ballad of the Second Front.'

MOST PERSONAL AND VERY SECRET
BALLADE OF THE SECOND FRONT
P.M. Loquitur
I do not like the job I have to do. I cannot think my views will
    go down well.
Can I convince them of our settled view; will Stalin use
    Caucasian oaths and yell?
Or can I bind him with my midnight spell; I'm really feeling
    rather in a stew.
It's not so hot a thing to have to sell; No Second Front in 1942.
I thought so, things are stickier than glue; they simply hate the
    tale I have to tell.
Stalin and Molotov are looking blue; if they give in an inch
    they'll take an ell.

49 Interview: Portal and M.C. Long, 1952, KCL/AB/11/7.
50 Eisenhower, Dwight D. (Dwight David) and Ferrell, Robert H., *The Eisenhower Diaries,* 1st ed. New York: Norton, 1981, 50.

I wonder if they'll put me in a cell, and deal with me like Hitler
with a Jew.

It's not so hot a thing to have to sell; No Second Front in 1942.

Come, things are taking on a rosier hue; the whole affair has
got a better smell.

I think that after all we'll put it thru; though not as merry as a
wedding bell.

The sound is now less like a funeral knell; another vodka for?
Here's Fortune-Phew!

I've got away with what I came to sell; No Second Front In
1942.

ENVOI

Prince of the Kremlin, here's a fond farewell;

I've had to deal with many worse than you.

You took it though you hated it like hell;

No Second Front in 1942.[51]

COS Committee meetings during the last week of October and first week of November were the forge that tempered British strategy. The planning staffs provided the generic plan; the Joint Chiefs, and primarily Portal and Brooke, honed the plan. During these two weeks they fought out the combined Anglo-American European strategy for the remainder of the war, fine-tuning their proposed plan to be more acceptable to their allies. Brooke and Portal argued over allocation of aircraft to Bomber Command, to airborne forces and to Army Co-operation Command, among other things. On 23 October 1942 Brooke wrote, 'We are getting a little nearer, but the divergence between Portal's outlook and mine is still very great. He is convinced that Germany can be defeated by bombing alone, while I consider that bombing can only be one of the contributory causes toward achieving that end.'[52] In fact, the two men were not quite so far apart as Brooke claimed.

It took Portal some time to visualise the Combined Bomber Offensive (CBO) as merely a precursor to OVERLORD, and Brooke must take the lion's share of praise for him having done so. On 5 October 1942, Portal tabled a paper regarding Allied strategic options. He proposed three options:

---

51 Alanbrooke, *War Diaries*, 307.
52 Ibid., 332.

A. To build up sufficient land and supporting air forces, shipping, landing-craft, etc. to enable us to gain a decision by invasion and the defeat of the German Army on the Continent before German industry and economic power has been broken.

B. To build up a bomber force in the United Kingdom strong enough to shatter German industry and economic power in the face of the strongest defence of which Germany is capable. When this has been achieved [an] army defined ... above [sufficient to restore order in and occupy a defeated Europe] would be launched on the Continent.

C. A compromise under which we attempt to build up simultaneously strong land and air forces on a scale unrelated to any particular task, without any clear indication of attaining a definite object within a definite time ... To me its only merit is that it is largely non-controversial whereas its greatest deficit is the absence of any clear objective. On that basis I believe we should never have either the shipping or the landing-craft to transport and maintain the necessary land forces to defeat an unbroken Germany on the Continent, or a bombing force strong enough to break German industry by bombing. Therefore, we should be condemned to a weak and indecisive middle course relying mainly on the Russian effort, on partial blockade, on German war-weariness, on the cumulative effect of relatively light bombing and land operations in areas where the German army cannot operate in full strength and therefore cannot be decisively defeated. Under these conditions the war may drag on for years; Germany will be enabled to exploit Russian and other occupied territory, expand her U-boat production, shift some of her industry to safer areas and generally to consolidate for a long defensive war.[53]

While Portal's exposition was clear, his assessment that the compromise course was potentially disastrous reflected the pessimism of the first six

---

53 Butler et al, *Grand Strategy Vol. IV*, 198–199.

months of 1942, not the evolving industrial reality of the future. But the paper provided the basis for the discussions of the next month, during which Brooke gradually softened Portal's stance, and a consensus emerged. Portal always knew the contribution the CBO could make to the destruction of Nazi war-making materiel and, by November 1942, he was strategising the CBO as a necessary enabling operation for the liberation of France. That month Portal issued a 'Note by the Chief of the Air Staff – an Estimate of the Effects of an Anglo-American Bomber Offensive against Germany.' In this missive Portal stated:

> I am convinced that an Anglo-American bomber force based in the United Kingdom and building up to a peak of 4,000 to 6,000 heavy bombers by 1944 would be capable of reducing the German war potential well below the level at which an Anglo-American invasion of the Continent would become practical. Indeed, I see every reason to hope that this result would be achieved well before the combined force had built up to peak strength.[54]

Historical critiques of Portal conveniently forget that following the evacuation from Dunkirk, RAF Bomber Command was the only means of striking directly at Germany, and that the bomber offensive accordingly merited high priority.[55] Britain had no offensive alternative until American entry into the war. The critique also ignores the incalculable damage done to German industry by Bomber Command. By late 1942, Portal accepted the sequential nature of the operations to come, and the bomber offensive's essential role in creating conditions for the successful reinvasion of the Continent. Neither Portal nor Brooke was totally infallible. They needed one another; COS meetings were a crucible in which myriad ideas and plans were forged into a coherent military strategy to present to Churchill. Both had to compromise.

Portal wanted a fifty-squadron bomber force. Brooke was worried this would delay the preparation for a continental landing, whereas Portal thought it would assist in destroying German war materiel, bringing the date

---

54 TNA CAB 74/24/19, 18 November 1942. Saward, Dudley, *Bomber Harris: The Story of Marshal of the Royal Air Force, Sir Arthur Harris* ... 1st ed. in the USA ed. Garden City, N.Y.: Doubleday, 1985, 176.
55 Interview Marian C. Long with Sir James Grigg, KCL/AB/11/7.

of invasion forward. As ever, the question was logistical; with limited assets to apportion for victory, everything required prioritisation. Portal expressed his evolving approach to Churchill on 7 November 1942. 'It has always been rightly emphasised that we must do all we can to impose wastage on the G.A.F. [Luftwaffe] in every theatre of war if our preponderance in production is to be used to the best advantage.'[56] Portal went on to describe the importance of mutual Bomber Command and Eighth Air Force efforts in attritting German fighters, which could catastrophically weaken Hitler's forces while affording continuing air superiority for the Allies on all land fronts.[57] Portal also knew, 'Premature opposition to their [the US's] plan may well lead their high authorities to seek other theatres where the virtues of day bombing might be better appreciated.'[58] This was what swayed Brooke.

The Americans generally supported the CBO as an element of the war-winning strategy; they were determined to put into practice what their interwar theorists had postulated. Churchill too was on board. Brooke could do little but accede, though he had lingering doubts. Brooke felt the bombing plan ought to specify nodes of German industry rather than merely naming German towns. He doubted the projected bombing tonnages and worried about the underestimation of German defences.[59] Nevertheless, this element of British strategy was now set in materiel as well as purpose. The other key discussion in late 1942 centred on the best way to sell Britain's preferred Mediterranean strategy at the CASABLANCA Conference in January 1943.

Of course, before they convinced the Americans of their chosen strategy, Brooke and Portal had to get Churchill's agreement. On 3 December 1942 the two men discussed a note from the PM regarding the possible scale of 1943 continental operations. This was referred to the respective planning staffs and, on 8 December 1942, Brooke described the COS meeting as being spent, 'Deciding line of action to adopt in order to influence the PM to abandon ideas of invasion of France in 1943 for more attractive prospects in the Mediterranean.'[60] The final paper was presented to Churchill in

---

56 Portal to Churchill, 7 November, 1942, CC/1/3/26.
57 Ibid.
58 Ibid.
59 TNA/CAB/79/24/19; Overy, R.J., *The Bombing War: Europe 1939–1945*, London: Penguin, 2013, 297–8.
60 Alanbrooke, *War Diaries*, 347.

mid-December. It strongly expounded a robust Mediterranean strategy for 1943 and demonstrated that any invasion of France would be impractical that year. A mere twenty-five Allied divisions would be available in the UK in 1943, but planning estimates for ROUNDUP stated forty-eight were needed.[61]

The aims of the proposed Mediterranean strategy were twofold: to push Italy out of the war, and secondly to bring Turkey into the war and, thereby, relieve the pressure on Russia. The COS Committee painstakingly reviewed the draft memorandum to ensure it reflected their jointly held views on future strategy again and again. Such preparation and detailed work paid off, as on 16 December 1942, Churchill agreed to support amphibious operations in the Mediterranean over a Western Front in France.[62] This ensured a unified British position, which was essential to countermand American proposals. On 11 December 1942, the Washington Staff Mission had sent the COS Committee a note indicating General Marshall's preference for abandoning the Mediterranean once the Germans had been ousted for a 1943 French operation.[63]

Brooke and Portal saw victory in North Africa, followed by an assault on Italy, as vital precursors to re-entering France; US leaders did not. The Americans were culturally inclined to suspicion regarding British imperial ambitions in North Africa and considered the strategy non-essential to winning the war.[64] While British leaders were cautious about operations in France, having been twice ejected, Americans were, in stark contrast, over-confident of success. Moreover, while Britain may have harboured Imperial intentions, the resources of the British Empire, such as the oil fields at Abadan in Iran, were essential to Britain's warfighting capabilities. The two were fundamentally intertwined.

Complicating Allied discussions was Admiral King, who maintained a Pacific preference and was more than willing to abandon the agreed 'Europe First' policy at any sign of British narrow-mindedness.[65] It was important to arrive at accord regarding European strategy, as the CCS had an

61 Butler et al, *Grand Strategy Vol. IV*, 212.
62 Ben-Moshe, *Churchill*, 209.
63 Roberts, *Masters and Commanders*, 306.
64 Pogue, Forrest C., Bradley, Omar Nelson and Brėdli, Omar. *George C. Marshall: Organizer of Victory, 1943–1945*. New York: Penguin Books, 1993, 8–12.
65 Pogue, Forrest C., *George C. Marshall: Ordeal and Hope 1939–1942*, New York: Viking Press, 1963, 323.

ever-present advocate for a fundamental shift in approach that would have been extremely deleterious to British plans. Brooke was the British spokesperson responsible for selling Britain's preferred strategy at CASABLANCA. The process proved less than seamless.

Brooke gave an eloquent opening address on 14 January 1943 to the US JCS. He congratulated them on the 'magnificent work of the U.S. Forces during the last twelve months after the early disasters of the war against Japan.'[66] Brooke also described the changes in the strategic situation, and how Germany was now fundamentally on the defensive while the Allies could switch to the attack. He then got to the heart of the argument that had won over Churchill. 'Italy was becoming more and more shaky; and if she collapsed, Germany would not only have to bolster up Italy by sending troops into the country but would also have to replace the numerous German [*sic*] divisions in Yugoslavia and in Greece.' He continued, 'The British Chiefs of Staff felt that we should first expand the bomber offensive against the Axis to the maximum and that operations in the Mediterranean offered the best chance of compelling Germany to disperse her resources.'[67]

Brooke's statement was an admission of the CBO's importance in strategically destroying German war materiel, and degrading the effectiveness of German fighter aircraft. Portal underpinned this final point, stating, 'They [Germany] are incapable of conducting large scale operations on two fronts and if they are kept fighting through the winter and spring they will have in the summer a shortage from seven hundred to two thousand first-line aircraft below what will be necessary for all fronts ... Our greatest need is to force the Germans to extend the use of their aircraft to as many areas as possible and thus destroy and bleed them.'[68] Though Brooke and Portal had powerfully described the proposed British strategy, both Marshall and King disagreed.

Marshall spoke first, stating US concerns regarding a Mediterranean strategy. He worried the risks proposed would not deliver commensurate advantages, and found an operation launched from the UK more attractive

---

66 Liddell Hart Centre for Military Archives, King's College London (Hereafter referred to as KCL), Alanbrooke Papers (AB), KCL/AB/6/1/1/170.
67 KCL/AB/6/1/1/171–174.
68 KCL/AB/6/1/1/179.

due to the high availability of coalition air support.[69] Following lunch, Admiral King put forth his position.

King was understandably frustrated at the Pacific being a secondary theatre, and requested an upturn from 15 to 30 per cent of the overall war effort for the Pacific.[70] Where Portal was concerned about maintaining the attrition of German forces to keep numbers manageable, King felt similarly about Japan. The 'Europe First' approach meant holding operations in the Pacific, which might allow Japan to re-equip and attack once more. Marshall, though primarily an advocate of a European strategy, was supportive of King. 'We must not allow the Japanese any pause. They fight with no idea of surrendering and they will continue to be aggressive until attrition has defeated them. To accomplish this, we must maintain the initiative and force them to meet us.'[71]

Brooke pointed out his fears that, 'If operations were too extended it would inevitably lead to an all-out war against Japan and it was certain that we had not sufficient resources to undertake this at the same time as a major offensive against Germany.' Portal asked, 'Was it not possible to stand on a line and inflict heavy losses on the Japanese when they tried to break through it? From the very fact that the Japanese continued to attack, it was clear that they had already been pushed back further than they cared to go.'[72] Despite Brooke and Portal's mutual efforts to bring the Americans on board, Brooke's diary entry depicts 'a long and laborious day' in which strategic accord remained elusive.

The following day, King raised another objection to Mediterranean-centric operations. He was concerned that an Allied focus in the region was more likely to lead Germany 'to move into Spain in order to cut our line of communication through the Straits of Gibraltar. An invasion of northern France such as the seizure of the Brest peninsula would not nearly so likely precipitate such an event.'[73] Brooke replied that, 'The British Chiefs of Staff did not consider it was at all probable that Spain would permit free passage to the German forces. It was calculated that some twenty divisions would be necessary to occupy the country if the Spaniards resisted at all.' Portal added:

---

69 KCL/AB/6/1/1/180.
70 KCL/AB/6/1/1/186.
71 KCL/AB/6/1/1/187.
72 KCL/AB/6/1/1/191.
73 KCL/AB/6/1/1/204.

If the Spaniards allowed the Germans free passage, we should declare war on Spain which was depending on us for many of the necessities of life. Even if the Germans did go in, we should be better able to afford aircraft for the protection of shipping through the Straits of Gibraltar than could the Germans for its attack. It would be much more advantageous for the Germans if we built up against France and left the Mediterranean alone. They would then be able to withdraw large numbers of air forces from the Mediterranean and reinforce the Russian Front, relying on the strong defences [sic] of Northern France to resist an invasion. On the other hand, if we kept the Mediterranean active, they would be compelled to keep large air forces there the whole time. This was of the greatest importance since Germany's main shortages were air forces and oil.[74]

The exchange showed the value of the British planning process in determining strategy. Having fully discussed this potentiality, Portal and Brooke provided mutual support in attacking US suppositions.

By the following day, Brooke was more upbeat. 'I think we are beginning to make some progress and that they are getting interested in our proposals.'[75] General Marshall raised many questions regarding the British analysis. In particular, he queried whether the German East–West lines of communication had been severely degraded by bombing; whether a Mediterranean operation might reduce the opportunity of exploiting a break in German strength; what effect such operations would have on Allied concentrations in England; and what the relative merits of attacking Sicily or Sardinia were.[76] General Arnold wondered if operations against Sicily were a means to an end or an end in themselves.[77] There was still much to resolve but the progress achieved largely rested on Portal's defence of Brooke's proposals. His frank and honest assessment elicited trust from the American contingent. In part, this was because he was willing to admit what he did not know. For instance, Portal considered:

It is impossible to map out a detailed plan for winning the war, but Germany's position, if we knocked out Italy, would

---

74 KCL/AB/6/1/1/205.
75 Alanbrooke, *War Diaries*, 360.
76 KCL/AB/6/1/1/209.
77 KCL/AB/6/1/1/210.

undoubtedly be most serious. Her ability to continue the fight depends on (a) the possession of the necessary resources and (b) the will to fight on. As regards resources, her main shortages at present are oil and air power. We have no exact knowledge of her oil position, but if she does not succeed in gaining the Caucasus oil, and if her synthetic oil plants are attacked by precision bombing in daylight, there is little doubt that her forces would rapidly become immobilised from lack of oil.[78]

While there was speculation in what Portal stated, and an admission of a lack of knowledge about the exact German oil situation, his logical reasoning was compelling. Despite Portal's efforts, Brooke was in the doldrums again by 17 January 1943. Faced with lingering US objections, he turned to his diary, decrying a 'desperate day!'[79]

The British COS were, however, successfully pursuing Churchill's tactics for convincing the Americans: 'the dripping of water on a stone.'[80] In keeping with this approach, Portal's slow and deliberate speech patterns proved effective.[81] On 18 January 1943, Portal iterated, 'it was impossible to say exactly where we should stop in the Mediterranean since we hoped to knock Italy out altogether. This action would give the greatest support to Russia and might open the door to an invasion of France.'[82]

Disagreements continued, however, regarding the liberation of Burma and the assets needed for it. When the Committee adjourned, Portal tweaked a paper drafted by John Slessor, which provided a compromise acceptable to all. It ensured a 'Europe First' policy; committed the Allies to Operation HUSKY, the invasion of Sicily, but not to the further invasion of Italy; allowed the initiative to be maintained against Japan; and did not rule out a continental invasion through France should the opportunity arise in 1943.[83] General Dill showed the paper to Marshall before the meeting reconvened, ensuring he was onside and rendering Admiral King's Pacific preference

---

78 KCL/AB/6/1/1/214.
79 Alanbrooke, *War Diaries*, 361.
80 Fraser, *Alanbrooke*, 289.
81 Pogue, *Ordeal and Hope*, 271; Richardson, Charles, *From Churchill's Secret Circle to the BBC: The Biography of Lieutenant General Sir Ian Jacob*, London: Brassey's, 1991, 167; Ismay, *Memoirs*, 318.
82 KCL/AB/6/1/1/239.
83 Fraser, *Alanbrooke*, 292.

an irrelevance.[84] Portal had played a full part in ensuring the Allies would follow the proposed British strategy, at least for the time being. Sometimes, deferring disagreements for later consideration is victory. There was no firm decision about what to do in the Mediterranean following the invasion of Sicily, no final decision on timing for the liberation of Burma, and no agreement to postpone OVERLORD (the liberation of France) to 1944. Before long, these unresolved matters necessitated another conference.

Feelings of betrayal festered in American minds in the months between conferences, leading to acrimony at TRIDENT, the Second Washington Conference.[85] The Americans believed they had been promised a continental incursion in 1943 at CASABLANCA, and it was increasingly clear that this was becoming improbable at best. Delayed progress in the Mediterranean unfortunately made clear that 1944 was the earliest this could take place. The Americans were unconvinced the British were committed to France at all (perhaps unsurprising considering the swathe of historical antipathy between Britain and France) and suspected a plan to continue operations in southern Europe ad infinitum. Arnold summed up American frustration in an internal memo three months after CASABLANCA; 'It is becoming more and more apparent that the British have no intention of invading France and continental Europe.'[86]

The British were, in reality, merely more circumspect about the amphibious assault on France. They believed the ultimate defeat of Italy would tie up many German divisions in Italy (rather than Germany simply abandoning the area). In British minds this was one of the essential precursors for successful landings in France. Once Italy was defeated, German East–West lines of communication would need to be degraded to preclude rapid reinforcement, control of the air had to be taken and maintained, and sufficient landing craft built to get the Allied troops across the Channel. Nothing, in British minds, would be more harmful than an ignominious defeat in France and having to rebuild afresh.[87] Britain agreed the only way to bring the war to a close was through an invasion of France, but the timing and preparations had to be right.

---

84 Alanbrooke, *War Diaries*, 362.
85 Ismay, *Memoirs*, 296–298.
86 Arnold, Henry Harley and Huston, John W., *American Airpower Comes of Age: General Henry H. 'Hap' Arnold's World War II Diaries*, Maxwell Air Force Base, AL: Air University Press, 2001, 274.
87 Ismay, *Memoirs*, 296–297.

The British had other valid strategic reasons for continuing operations in the Mediterranean. In a memo penned on SS *Queen Mary* during the voyage across the Atlantic, the COS argued, 'We cannot afford to keep those forces out of action for a period of nine or ten months before we can launch an offensive from the United Kingdom into northern France. During this time, the battle on the Russian Front will be raging, and Germany will require all the forces that she can muster against the Russians.'[88] The British point was logical: Stalin would have been livid had the Allies sat tight in Sicily. Moreover, Portal and Brooke's strategy for saturating and overcoming German forces depended on the continued application of pressure at as many points as possible. Without an invasion of Italy, which would stretch German resources further, any liberation of France would be threatened.

Portal and Brooke made significant strides toward bringing the Americans on side during TRIDENT. When the US delegation suggested Italy's capitulation could be achieved through bombing alone, Brooke expressed his doubt.[89] Portal backed him up, stating, 'He was doubtful, however, if air alone would achieve the desired results. It had never been claimed that Germany could be knocked out by air alone,[90] but rather that it would reduce her power to such an extent that her forces available against Russia and ourselves would be so weakened as to permit of her defeat.'[91] Portal and Brooke stayed in strategic locked step, evidenced by Portal's subsequent observation: 'The most important point was to decide whether the defeat of Germany would be brought nearer by immediate Mediterranean operations at some expense to Operation BOLERO,[92] or, alternatively, by stopping operations in the Mediterranean in order to build up at the maximum rate for cross-Channel operations.'[93] His advocacy for landings on the Italian mainland was vital, as it came from an airman who might be expected to think bombing alone could get the job done. Portal also had wider strategic reasons to support a land invasion of Italy. The establishment of strategic air assets around Foggia would enable attacks on southern Germany and targets in Eastern Europe. However, the British did not get their way, leaving Washington with an agreement that General

---

88 KCL/AB/6/1/2/46.
89 KCL/AB/6/1/2/324.
90 Harris, among others, had claimed exactly that.
91 KCL/AB/6/1/2/330.
92 The build-up of US forces in Britain.
93 KCL/AB/6/1/2/367.

Eisenhower, the Supreme Commander, should consider further operations following the liberation of Sicily. Churchill boarded a plane for Algiers immediately following the TRIDENT Conference to ensure Eisenhower chose 'correctly.'

A mere ten weeks later, during a conference in which trust was the main issue, Portal's role was once more crucial. The QUADRANT Conference took place at Quebec in Canada. In the interim much had occurred. Churchill and party docked at Halifax on 9 August 1943, by which time Allied operations on Sicily were at an advanced stage. Amid bitter acrimony, Portal's ability to mediate proved unparalleled. For instance, he reassured General Marshall about British air support for China once the war with Germany was over.[94] Portal was also characteristically politic in his effusive praise of American bombing efforts against Ploesti, which he called, 'perhaps the most brilliant and outstanding single air operation of the war.'[95]

Even so, the growing staffs in attendance meant frequent disagreement at meetings, as some of the more bellicose attendees resented losing face in front of subordinates. The Allies reached accord only once Brooke had the room cleared, and the chiefs could talk alone.

Amid waning Italian resistance, Mussolini was arrested on 25 August, the day QUADRANT ended. By this time, the Brooke–Portal nexus had convinced the Americans to continue operations in the Mediterranean following the capture of Sicily, while accepting the American approach to the war in the Pacific. Additionally, Brooke and Portal had to head off more wild Churchillian schemes at the pass. In the Far East, Winston was dead set on an operation against Sumatra, for which he 'shouted … like a small child,' but with no plan for what would follow.[96]

Another of Churchill's pet projects nearly killed Portal. The almost fatal project, code name HABBAKUK (named after a Hebrew prophet), involved icebergs being used as aircraft carriers. The ice was treated with sawdust, making it stronger while slowing the melting process significantly. Lord Mountbatten carried out a demonstration of its strength by firing a revolver at a normal block of ice, then at the reinforced ice, called pykrete. The ordinary ice split instantly, but the pykrete was undamaged, as Mountbatten planned. What he had not foreseen was the bullet ricocheting back among

---

94 KCL/AB/6/1/3/428, 468.
95 KCL/AB/6/1/3/419.
96 Alanbrooke, *War Diaries*, 446.

the Combined Chiefs, nicking the leg of Admiral King's trousers and narrowly missing Portal.[97]

After this brief brush with death, Portal and Brooke proceeded on a fishing break, where they cemented their mutual respect and regard. They also proved their expertise by catching literally dozens each on a day Mary Churchill snagged only one.[98] Dudley Pound, long-time First Sea Lord and also a keen fisherman, did not accompany them. By this stage he was dreadfully ill and died on 21 October 1943, to be replaced by Tedder's sparring partner in the Middle East, Admiral Andrew Cunningham.

While Pound was ailing, Portal and Brooke failed, for once, to deter Churchill's strategic folly. The PM ordered further operations in the Dodecanese Islands following Italy's capitulation, despite Brooke and Portal emphasising that such action was incompatible with the agreed Anglo-American strategy for the Mediterranean.[99] Churchill believed the capture of the Dodecanese to be 'a business of great consequence', and urged for an expedition with increasing insistence.[100] Eventually, exhausted by the conferences that demanded so much energy, and saddened by Pound's absence, Brooke gave grudging assent to the operation.[101] The Germans, on Hitler's insistence, quickly captured Rhodes, making both the support and evacuation of British forces from the remaining islands much more difficult. Eisenhower and his Middle East commanders met on 9 October to discuss the possibilities of operations in both Italy and Rhodes. The Germans had reinforced south of Rome, so the meeting concluded that there was no possibility of achieving both objectives, and that Italy must be the priority.[102] The absence of American support, which the COS knew to be almost inevitable, resulted in an ignominious, and unnecessary, British defeat.

---

97 Richards, *Portal*, 267.

98 TNA/PREM/3/172/1, 27 August 1943.

99 Butler, James Ramsay Montagu, Gwyer, J.M.A., Ehrman, John and Howard, Michael, *Grand Strategy: History of the Second World War Vol. V,* United Kingdom Military Series. London: H.M. Stationery Office, 1956, 86–87.

100 Bryant, Arthur and Alanbrooke, Viscount Alan Francis Brooke, *Triumph in the West: a History of the War Years Based on the Diaries of Field-Marshal Lord Alanbrooke, Chief of the Imperial General Staff.* 1st ed. Garden City, N.Y.: Doubleday, 1959, 30.

101 Fraser, David, *Alanbrooke*. London: Bloomsbury Reader, 2013, 338.

102 Playfair, Ian Stanley Ord, Molony, C.J.C. and Jackson, W.G.F. *The Mediterranean and Middle East: Volume V,* London: Naval & Military Press, 2004, 545 Ismay, *Memoirs,* 546.

The remaining conferences of 1943 concentrated on convincing the Chinese and Russians of the way ahead. Unfortunately, Stalin's insistence on an early Operation OVERLORD, with which Marshall agreed, brought matters to a head once more. Compromise was eventually reached, but not until after Brooke and King had an almighty argument. They disagreed about the relative importance of operations in the Mediterranean and Pacific, and General Stilwell (who was in attendance) reported, 'Brooke got nasty and King got good and sore. King almost climbed over the table at Brooke. God, he was mad! I wish he had socked him.'[103] No single incident in all the Allied conferences more instantly displayed the importance of having a man such as Portal present, who never once lost sight of the aim of all Allied conferences: not to win the argument, but to agree a way forward. Though Brooke and others have awarded most of the credit to Marshall and Dill, Portal played a vital role, evidenced by the Americans' views of him. Averell Harriman, Roosevelt's special advisor, perhaps summed up Portal's contribution best:

> Peter accepted me as a friend and was perfectly frank. Of all the people I knew during the war, I had a personal respect and affection for Peter almost beyond any other. He was utterly honourable, he dealt with the situation as it existed, and he had the knack of getting the best out of other people ... Whenever he intervened it was in a quiet, effective way, and so forthright he always won his point ... He had enormous influence on that Committee – he was ready to take on new ideas and explore them, and very practical in throwing anything out when it was not realistic ... Portal was extremely balanced. Marshall had a high regard for him ... and paid great attention to what Peter had to say ... [Sometimes] he turned to Peter for support [against King]. Peter played a special role – he stepped into the breach when agreements couldn't be reached.[104]

Portal's diplomatic aplomb was on show once more during the SEXTANT Conference towards the end of 1943. Roosevelt had made promises to

---

103 Bryant, *Triumph*, 53.
104 Interview: Denis Richards and Averell Harriman, 18 Jul 73, CC/3/VIII/A.

Chiang Kai-shek, the Chinese leader, regarding a significant amphibious operation to seize the Andaman Islands: Operation BUCCANEER.[105] Brooke and Portal were against the operation, as they worried it would reduce the shipping available for OVERLORD, planned for mid-1944. On 4 December 1943, Portal explained the limited utility of the Andamans for air operations, as there was only one good airfield. The following day he suggested substituting a hit-and-run commando landing in lieu of BUCCANEER to satisfy the Chinese desire for amphibious activity while preserving the shipping required for OVERLORD.[106] He had offered Roosevelt not only a strategic critique of the proposed action, but an escape from the President's dilemma: a middle ground. This was typical of his manner of engagement, and allowed discussions to move forward once more.

With 1943 coming to an end, Portal and Brooke had been to Casablanca, Washington, Quebec, Cairo, Tehran, and Cairo once more, all in the name of alliance. Much had been achieved in terms of strategic agreement, supported by operational successes in the Mediterranean against both Germany and Italy; Italy's capitulation validated at least part of the British strategy. There had been disappointments, such as failure in the Dodecanese, which unfortunately meant Turkey had still not joined the war. However, the Axis was on the back foot, and the Portal–Brooke strategy had proven effective despite American doubts. In 1944 it was Britain's turn to do America's bidding: OVERLORD.

Having set the alliance on a course for success, the major challenge of 1944 was ensuring the path was followed. This necessitated curbing the more outlandish strategic impulses of an incorrigible Prime Minister. In Europe, Churchill fixated on Vienna following the push through northern Italy. The minor geographic inconvenience of the Alps seemed not to worry him. In the Pacific, the COS had great difficulty in weaning Churchill away from ideas about landing on Sumatra. Being of stubborn disposition, it proved a Herculean challenge to get the PM to cede any strategic proposal of his own making. The matter first came to a head in August 1943 at QUADRANT. When Brooke asked, not unreasonably, what the follow-on strategy to Sumatra was to be, Churchill cried, 'I do

---

105 Ismay, *Memoirs*, 336; Richards, *Portal*, 273.
106 KCL/AB/6/1/4/400.

not want any of your long-term projects, they stifle initiative.'[107] The COS penned a paper refuting the Sumatra option and putting forward their preferred Pacific strategy to present to the Americans. Churchill accepted it and the point was won, but only for a time, as the PM was nothing if not persistent.

By spring 1944, Churchill was, once more, insistent on Sumatra as the linchpin of Pacific strategy. On 17 March 1944, Portal reported its unsuitability as a base of air operations while Andrew Cunningham pointed out the huge threat posed by the Japanese fleet at Singapore were the operation carried out.[108] Churchill then proceeded to pen a document on his preferred Pacific strategy, wholly divorced from the COS's views. He cleverly sent it to each of them separately, hoping to divide and conquer. The COS, however, understood that only by standing together could they withstand Churchill's onslaught. Brooke wrote on 21 March, 'It would be better if we all three resigned sooner than accept his solution.'[109] The Committee took more than a week drafting a carefully crafted response to the Prime Minister, making it respectfully clear why he was wrong strategically and that, should he insist, the wholesale resignation of the COS would result. It was a difficult time for Portal and Brooke; Churchill was hard to shift once he got an idea in his head. Eventually, a compromise was broached that dampened tensions. The disagreement, over a period of several months, was not unusual. The unanimity of Portal, Brooke and, latterly, Cunningham was vital in overcoming prime ministerial mulishness.

The events of 1944 validated Brooke and Portal's strategy, but fine-tuning remained essential. Over the objections of Marshall et al, they successfully argued for further operations in Italy to tie up German divisions, while simultaneously continuing the aerial assault on Germany. Such actions reduced Germany's ability to reinforce the Western Front once OVERLORD happened. This action was reinforced by an attack on the German and French railway hubs, termed 'The Transportation Plan,' that degraded east–west lines of communication and prevented rapid reinforcement at the Allied landing sites in Normandy.

---

107 Roberts, *Masters and Commanders,* 405; Alanbrooke, *War Diaries,* 445.
108 Bryant, *Triumph,* 121; Alanbrooke, *War Diaries,* 532.
109 Bryant, *Triumph,* 123; Alanbrooke, *War Diaries,* 533.

Once OVERLORD began, control of the war passed to Eisenhower as Supreme Commander. Though there were some temporary reverses, notably during the December German counter-offensive and the ill-fated Operation MARKET GARDEN, the result was never truly in doubt. Differences in strategy among the COS were no more, though there were some minor disagreements. Montgomery, aggrieved that he was not the overall commander for OVERLORD, vented about what he perceived as Eisenhower's deficiencies. Brooke, who had twice been unofficially offered the command of OVERLORD by Churchill, was more than willing to listen to critique of Eisenhower's performance.[110] Neither Brooke nor Montgomery thought Ike knew what he was doing strategically. Brooke railed against what he considered Eisenhower's mishandling of the command.

Portal was hearing a different story from Tedder, no fan of General Montgomery. Tedder had observed Montgomery's command of the Eighth Army in 1942 and had not been particularly impressed. Freeman, Tedder's mentor had warned him that Montgomery was 'small-minded – and nearly had a mutiny in his regiment when he commanded it. He might do well, for he has energy – but he talks balls – is conceited, a hard worker and a cad.'[111] Tedder immediately noticed an improvement in air-land integration during Montgomery's tenure in North Africa. However, Tedder (and Mary Coningham) considered Montgomery to have been far too passive during the second battle of El Alamein, when a decisive victory was possible.[112] Two years later, Tedder was critical of Montgomery's failure to take Caen, accusing him of literally 'stopping the armour from going further' absent a blanket of air cover.[113] He expressed as much to Portal on 25 July 1944 in a long missive. Tedder wanted Montgomery gone, and had written to Eisenhower on 23 July to say he would support him fully in any action he deemed appropriate.[114] Brooke knew Monty was a tactless egotist, and had hauled him over the coals for it on more than one occasion. Nevertheless, he had chosen Montgomery because he was the British Army's most capable operational commander. Portal

---

110 Orange, *V., Tedder: Quietly in Command (Cass series – studies in air power, 9)*, London; Portland, OR: F. Cass, 2004, 271.

111 Ibid., 184.

112 Tedder, *Arthur William, With Prejudice: The War Memoirs of Marshal of the Royal Air Force, Lord Tedder.* London: Cassell, 1966, 359.

113 Orange, *Quietly in Command*, 269–270.

114 CC/2/C/1.

knew the die was cast and, understanding there was little he could do, left things to run their course.

As victory approached more conferences were needed to decide what to do after the war. Following the Second Quebec Conference, OCTAGON, in September 1944, Portal and Brooke took another fishing trip. On the evening of the fourth day's fishing, they received the following from Churchill:

> GUNFIRE (305)
> Following for CIGS and CAS from Prime Minister.
> Please let me know how many captives were taken by land and air forces respectively in Battle of Snow Lake.

Portal worded the reply:

> CORDITE (420)
> Following for Prime Minister from CIGS and CAS.
> Your gunfire 305 only just received. Battle of Snow Lake began at dawn 19th and finished 2.30 pm on 20th. Enemy forces were aggressive throughout and put up fierce resistance at all familiar strong points particularly Churchill Bay and Brooke Bay. Casualties inflicted by our land and air forces were approximately equal and totalled about 250 dead including the enemy general who surrendered to Land forces on Tuesday afternoon. In a short rear-guard action at Cabane de Montmorency our air forces accounted for the largest submarine yet seen in these waters. We trust that you have had a comfortable journey.[115]

Their joint love of fishing and ornithology brought Portal and Brooke closer together during four long years working for the brilliant and amusing, but extremely taxing, Churchill. The notes above reflected the lessening of tension, echoing the state of the war. With the Anglo-American advance from the west being mirrored by a Russian push from the east, Hitler's months in power were numbered. Victory in Europe arrived on 8 May 1945, and victory over Japan came ahead of schedule, negating the need for

---

115 Richards, *Portal*, 208, Alanbrooke, *War Diaries*, 596.

Britain to head en masse to the Pacific and obviating the need for further discussion about the relative merits of operations in Sumatra. At the end of 1945, Portal called time on his military career, a short six months before Brooke did likewise. On Portal's final day, Brooke wrote:

> I shall miss him badly. We understood each other well, were prepared to have the most heated professional discussions, but these were never allowed to affect our personal relations. I had the greatest admiration for Peter's ability, not only in connections with the air where he was superb but in all the other matters we had to deal with. In debate with the Americans, he was invaluable and had a wonderful way of clarifying complicated problems. The country was indeed fortunate to have had a man of such ability and character at the head of the Air Force throughout the war.[116]

---

116 Bryant, *Triumph*, 403.

Chapter 5

Portal and Tedder

Oh, I think Peter Portal was outstanding. So was Tedder.
They had to understand warfare in three elements, where and
how to use their forces.

Clement Attlee

Portal had never worked directly with Tedder when he proposed him as Longmore's deputy in the Mediterranean and North Africa in 1940. Tedder's former mentor, Wilfrid Freeman, was undoubtedly crucial in pushing Tedder's candidacy with Portal. Freeman knew Tedder extremely well, and was more than willing to sing his praises. Portal saw something; Churchill, who initially refused the appointment, did not. Churchill considered Tedder 'a man of nuts and bolts,'[1] but Portal saw an effective triphibious leader, who had commanded effectively in Singapore. In Portal's eyes, Tedder's belief in the efficacy of joint operations made him ideal for the Mediterranean, where the RAF's strategic reach was a huge force multiplier. Moreover, Tedder was a meticulous organiser, a great co-operator, and shared Portal's broader strategic vision concerning the essential nature of joint operations and the imperative to maintain productive Alliance relationships. Both men were also accomplished writers. This factor enabled them to pursue a frequent and detailed correspondence that Portal enjoyed with no other commander. They also shared the traits of humility, pragmatism, and honesty. It was this last characteristic that later caused Portal significant problems, but not with Tedder per se. Tedder's brutal honesty strained Portal's relationship with Churchill, who retained lingering doubts about Tedder's operational capabilities long after his appointment, and sought his removal.

---

1 Tedder, Arthur William, *With Prejudice: The War Memoirs of Marshal of the RAF, Lord Tedder*. London: Cassell, 1966, 319.

Arthur William 'Tirpitz' Tedder was born in Glenguin, Scotland, in 1890, the son of a civil servant, also named Arthur, and Emily. Little Arthur was the third child, born eleven years after Henry, the eldest, who left home when Arthur was only two, and who died aged only twenty-six in India.[2] Arthur's elder sister Margaret and he were closer in years and became better acquainted during years of family upheaval as Arthur Senior was pulled north and south to meet the needs of the civil service, with the family ever in tow.

From Glenguin, the family went to Edinburgh for four years and then to Lerwick, the most northern of British towns, where the Tedders lived in a villa overlooking the town harbour. It may have been these littoral vistas that first inspired young Arthur to pick up pencils and paints, but painting became both a lifelong passion and a means of escape when the burden of high command was weighing heavily on his narrow shoulders in later years. His early schooling was provided by his mother Emily, who Tedder later described rather harshly as 'a martinet in every sense of the word.'[3] Margaret, more fairly, said that Emily would attempt perfection even if she sometimes failed. Arthur Senior was also meticulous, as he had to be working for the Excise Department. This attention to detail eluded young Tedder, though it would come later and prove a valuable skill, and one that Portal desperately needed.

In 1898 the Tedders began to move south, with a three-year assignment to Elgin where Arthur's formal schooling began at the academy. In 1901 they continued this southern migration moving to Croydon, and the following year Arthur started attending Whitgift School.[4] His attire at Whitgift caused quite a stir with the locals. He wore a kilt in Croydon and became the butt of some juvenile leg pulling, but Tedder dealt with it all calmly, a personality trait many remarked on later in his life. He also developed a penchant for writing, doing so frequently and at length to his family. He described both people and places, especially the panoramas of the local countryside in the changing light.[5] Arthur also proved an able sportsman, playing first XV rugby and breaking five minutes for the mile, but he was especially taken by the challenges of the Officer Training Corps (OTC).

---

2 Owen, R., *Tedder.* London: Collins, 1952, 25.

3 Ibid., 24.

4 Orange, V., *Tedder: Quietly in Command* (Cass series – studies in air power, 9), London; Portland, OR: F. Cass, 2004.

5 Ibid., 5.

Arthur greatly enjoyed being in the OTC and was promoted from private to cyclist-sergeant in quick order. Moreover, he also became sergeant of the Recruiting Section, guiding the younger entrants in their formative experiences. He wrote about OTC camps in the school magazine, describing 'seven shivering mortals in different states of *déshabillé*,' but continued effusively regarding the ten most enjoyable days of his life.[6] Nevertheless, Tedder took a rather circuitous route to a military career.

In 1909 Tedder was awarded a place at Magdalene College, Cambridge, to study history.[7] Having failed to secure a scholarship, he was grateful to both his parents and his Uncle Henry, secretary of the Athenaeum, for financing his further education. Uncle Henry was a huge influence on Arthur's academic career. His early studies met with sporadic success, as application was not yet one of his great qualities. In due course he graduated with a second class, second division degree, despite winning the College Historical Prize and Newton Essay Prize. Perhaps surprisingly, and against the initial judgement of his father, Tedder was selected to study for a fourth year and sought a dissertation topic.

Having found the elusive application when he met and fell in love with an Australian girl, Rosalinde, while in Germany, Tedder set to work.[8] His tutor A.C. Benson remarked, 'What I like about his work, is his independence of thought and his caution in argument and statement, unless he knows his ground.'[9] Tedder's dissertation, initially entitled 'The History of the English Navy from the Death of the Protector to the Restoration' won the Prince Consort Prize, but publication did not come until 1916, by which time Tedder was fully occupied with the First World War.

Tedder arrived in the conflict via a brief sojourn with the Colonial Service in Fiji. When war broke out, he realised he would be needed, as he had followed through his schoolboy interest in the OTC throughout his time at Cambridge and was, therefore, entitled to a regular commission.[10] He initially joined the Dorset Regiment of the British Army, but his time was cut short by a knee injury suffered in February 1915. Tedder's expectations of a rapid recovery were not met and the doctor's prognosis precluded

---

6 Ibid., 33.

7 Ibid., 35.

8 Owen, *Tedder*, 42.

9 Orange, *Quietly in Command*, 9.

10 Owen, *Tedder*, 53.

service in the infantry. Fortunately for Britain, Tedder's incapacity did not disqualify him from service in the Royal Flying Corps (RFC).

After finally freeing himself from the clutches of the British Army after several applications to transfer, Tedder at last joined the RFC in January 1916. By June, and following the birth of his first son, Tedder had found his way to France with No. 25 Squadron flying the F.E.2b, affectionately known as the Johnnie Walker. The squadron's work consisted mainly of aerial photography and bombing in the ever-reliable F.E., and by August Tedder had been appointed flight commander. This presented an opportunity to Tedder as, in September the head of the RFC in France, Major-General Hugh Trenchard, visited No. 25 Squadron while the squadron commander was away. He asked Tedder many questions, and was clearly impressed since, by the year's end, Trenchard had him appointed as a squadron commander.

Tedder was appointed commanding officer (CO) of No. 70 Squadron on 1 January 1917. Lacking the customary array of medals adorning the breast of most other squadron COs, Tedder did not initially impress his charges, being described as 'unimpressive, a wet blanket, not much of a leader.'[11] Tedder transformed this initial impression through his quiet energy, professional approach, and care for the well-being of squadron personnel. He gradually improved squadron morale, decimated by the loss of twenty-seven of the original thirty-six pilots in a little over two months, and made them a fighting force once more. Tedder busied himself with squadron administration, and writing endless letters to his wife, Rosalinde.

Tedder's time with No. 70 Squadron was fraught, due in equal part to Trenchard's policy of constant offensive and the appearance of the German Albatross D.III, yet his steel was developing. Concerned at the attrition rate (No. 70 Squadron lost a shocking seven of eighteen Sopwiths on 24– 25 March 1917) Tedder started to send the aircraft out in packets of nine rather than six.[12] He hoped this would provide better mutual protection and act as a deterrent to German fighters. He also sent the aircraft out with two cameras instead of one, which significantly increased the photographic processing workload at 2nd Brigade. Tedder was husbanding his resources effectively, but was nevertheless summoned to HQ for a 'Presence' and scolded over the large number of photos being supplied. Tedder merely stood there, coolly silent, which encouraged the hearing to begin to present

---

11 Orange, *Quietly in Command*, 42; Owen, *Tedder*, 68.
12 Owen, *Tedder*, 69.

their arguments. Tedder bit back, 'I understand, sir. You're much more worried about the number of photographs than the number of pilots we lose!'[13] Tedder had cut right to the chase, with a heavy dose of acerbic sarcasm, but he had made his point.

In June, following a full year in France, Tedder was posted back to the UK for a training job before being summoned to Egypt in March 1918. He took command of No. 38 Training Wing in Heliopolis, under Brigadier General Philip Herbert, in charge of four training schools. Here Tedder showed the patience, diligence, and diplomacy to wade through the bureaucracy necessary to improve the condition of the schools.[14] Trenchard knew he needed all kinds of airmen to build the new service created on 1 April 1918, and Tedder was an accomplished manager. Any worries about being left behind and forgotten were baseless; Tedder was awarded a permanent commission in Trenchard's new and independent RAF.

During the interwar years, Tedder's organisational competence shone through. He developed squadrons for active duty both at home and abroad, and was sent to the Royal Naval Staff College as a reward in 1923. By this time Tedder was already interested in Joint Operations, which became the subject of several lectures he delivered during the year at Greenwich. As with Portal, Trenchard ensured Tedder was steeped in education and, following another training job, he was sent to the Imperial Defence College in 1927, and later to teach at the RAF Staff College at Andover. Tedder and Portal followed similar paths both intellectually and professionally, but they did not meet until much later.

Tedder's route to high command took an atypical turn when appointed to command of the Armament and Gunnery School at Eastchurch. This proved an important stage in his development. He quickly realised how neglected this element of military aviation was, and instigated much more realistic training, in both daytime and darkness, using moving targets. Eventually he conceded that airborne targets could be towed on a steady course at night 'if only to put the target in some danger.'[15]

Tedder was posted to Singapore to command the Far East Air Force in October 1936, gaining an overseas command shortly after Portal had returned to the UK from Aden.[16] Tedder's position in Singapore was

---

13 Ibid., 70.
14 Ibid., 71–73.
15 Orange, *Quietly in Command*, 83.
16 Tedder, *With Prejudice*, 6.

arguably even more invidious than Portal's had been in Aden. Singapore was the centre point of one of the worst inter-service fights during the interwar period, each service arguing how it alone could defend the base from a potential – and by Tedder's time clearly emerging – Japanese threat. The scale of the problem was enormous, because the 'no war for ten years' rule had set the services many years behind a rapidly growing Japanese military. By 1935, the Japanese Navy had nine battleships, and the British China Fleet none. They also had 102 destroyers compared to 10, and outnumbered the British cruisers four to one.[17] Tedder did manage to fashion an expansion of capability as well as build new airfields. As commander, Tedder bolstered his reputation as a joint leader and thinker, a valuable skill for the future war. However, all Tedder's efforts proved in vain. British strategic priorities remained Europe and the Middle East once war broke out, leaving Singapore dangerously vulnerable. When the Japanese attacked in 1942, they captured the island despite being outnumbered three to one in troop numbers. Absent an effective fleet, for Singapore's defence, and despite Tedder sending hundreds of aircraft from the Middle East, Britain's position in Singapore was doomed.

In 1938 Tedder joined what became the Ministry of Aircraft Production (MAP) as Director-General of Research and Development.[18] At the MAP, Tedder worked for Air Marshal Wilfrid Freeman, Air Member for Research and Development, who had been Tedder's squadron commander back in 1916 and an early supporter of his career. Tedder and Freeman tried to advance the RAF in numerous areas: armour, gun turrets, cannons, engines, navigational aids, undercarriage improvements, bulletproof screens, heating inside bombers, and the like.[19] However, under the threat of a Nazi invasion, Churchill installed Lord Beaverbrook to oversee aircraft production, which helped to win the Battle of Britain, but had adverse longer-term consequences of which Tedder did not approve. Beaverbrook was only interested in shortening the route of aircraft to front-line squadrons, while Tedder remained concerned with solving problems through operational testing at Boscombe Down.[20] Beaverbrook

---

17 Baxter, Christopher J., (1997), 'A Question of Blame? Defending Britain's Position in the South China Sea, the Pacific and South-East Asia, 1919–1941,' *The RUSI Journal*, 142:4, 69.

18 Tedder, *With Prejudice*, 8.

19 Ibid., 108.

20 Owen, *Tedder*, 121.

also streamlined production to only five aircraft types; choosing the Blenheim and Whitley would later cost Bomber Command many lives. Beaverbrook's strategy was correct in the short-term, but ought to have been revisited once the Battle of Britain was won, amid shifting strategic RAF requirements.

Tedder had several disagreements with Beaverbrook, who subsequently sought to have him fired from the MAP. Portal proposed Tedder to go to the Middle East as Arthur Longmore's deputy, but Churchill refused and sent Owen Boyd instead. When Boyd was captured, having been forced to land in Sicily, Portal and Freeman (recently appointed Portal's deputy) ensured Tedder was appointed. Tedder was on the plane to high command in Britain's most significant theatre. Soon, he began a remarkable correspondence with the new Chief of Air Staff, Sir Charles Portal.

Tedder arrived in North Africa during a highpoint for the British. Operation COMPASS, the first British offensive of the desert war, was a stunning success, and 'victory sparkled in the Libyan desert.'[21] The British, led by General Archie Wavell, caught the Italians off guard, due in large part to the RAF suppressing a numerically superior *Regia Aeronautica* and preventing any of their aircraft from taking to the air on the day before the assault began.[22] The British Army, outnumbered four to one, took the fortress of Sidi Barrani in short order, expelled Italian forces from Egypt, and captured 130,000 Italian soldiers in the process.[23] Churchill was thrilled with Wavell's performance, as well as that of Arthur Longmore, Commander-in-Chief, RAF Middle East (C-in-C RAF ME). A delighted Prime Minister wrote to Wavell, 'Pray convey my compliments and congratulations to Longmore on his magnificent handling of the R.A.F. and fine co-operation with the Army.'[24] Longmore's position was, however, less assured in Air Ministry circles, and remaining in Churchill's good graces was entirely results dependent.

Portal and Tedder's relationship developed over time, but it was Freeman who gave Tedder specific instructions for his new role and a warning to

---

21 Churchill, Winston S., *The Second World War, Vol. II, Their Finest Hour*, The Educational Book Company Ltd: London, 1951, 476.

22 Rowan-Robinson, Henry, *Wavell in the Middle East* London: Hutchinson & Co., 1942, 60.

23 Porch, Douglas, *The Path to Victory*, New York: Farrar, Strauss, and Giroux, 2004, 128.

24 Churchill, *Finest Hour*, 467.

Tedder's new commander. Though Longmore had only been in command for six months, his signals back to the Air Ministry were already beginning to irk the powers that be. Freeman described the missives as 'moan, moan, moan;' Freeman instructed Tedder to ameliorate this aspect of Longmore's communication.[25] Tedder warned Longmore that the tone of his communication was considered unhelpful by the Air Ministry, and Longmore agreed to allow Tedder to sanitise his messages before they were sent on.[26] Once or twice, however, Longmore slipped a missive through unchecked. On 30 April 1941 Longmore sent the signal that ended his time in command.

Longmore informed Portal that he was being constantly hounded by his sister services regarding new aircraft types and upgraded armaments, of which desert forces had read much but seen little. The theatre commander, Wavell, and especially his naval counterpart, Andrew Cunningham, were constantly bleating for additional help from the RAF, and Longmore was both too weak to resist their overtures, and unaware of the broader parlous state of RAF logistics. The clamour only became louder once Rommel arrived in North Africa in February 1941, and inflicted a series of reverses upon the British-led forces. Longmore agreed the Middle East was not getting its fair share and requested Portal inform him of his intention to send these new types either operationally or on trial.[27] Longmore unwisely asked Portal to reassure his fellow commanders that any shortage in capability was in no way down to an absence of argumentation from Longmore.[28] This was exactly the type of appeal designed to antagonise Portal, as it demonstrated a lack of both perspective and backbone. Moreover, the Stirling and Manchester – the new aircraft to which Longmore was alluding – were not operationally effective. Tedder could have appraised Longmore of this fact had he asked, as Tedder had observed their uninspiring maiden voyages when serving as Director General of Research and Development in the late 1930s. This signal, which Tedder would never have allowed Longmore to send had he seen it, was the last straw for Churchill and Portal. Longmore was out; Tedder was now C-in-C RAF ME.

Almost immediately Portal reassured Tedder of the confidence he had in him. He wrote that Tedder must feel, 'free to act as you see fit in spite

25 Tedder, *With Prejudice*, 50.
26 Ibid.
27 Furse, Anthony, *Wilfrid Freeman*, Spellmount, 2000, 178; Tedder, *With Prejudice*, 81–82.
28 Tedder, *With Prejudice*, 82.

Viscount Portal, by Oswald Birley (1948). It hangs in the Great Hall of Christ Church College, Oxford.

A poster produced between 1942 and 1945 depicting senior RAF officers. In the centre is Air Chief Marshal, Sir Charles Portal. (All images via Historic Military Press unless stated otherwise)

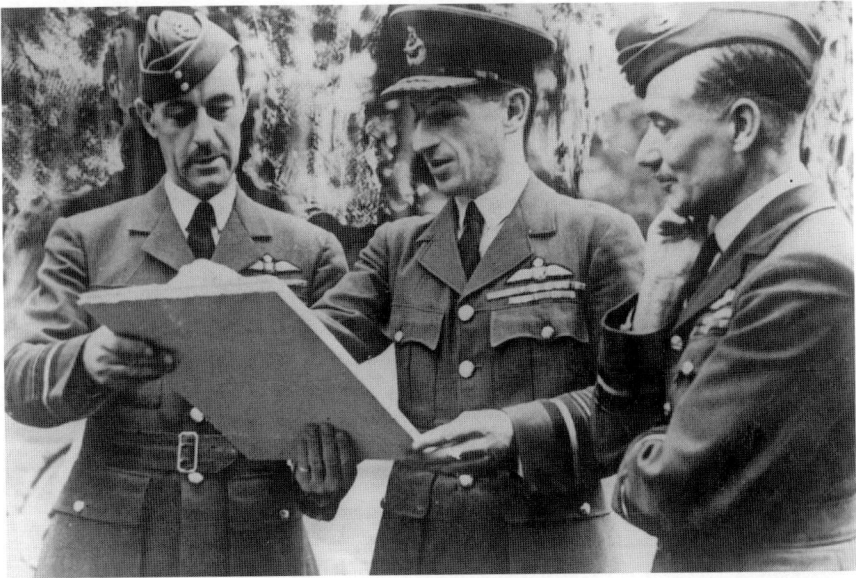

Air Chief Marshal Sir Charles Portal pictured with two members of his staff at the time of his appointment as Chief of the Air Staff, on succeeding Newell, on 25 October 1940.

Air Chief Marshal Sir Charles Portal in the cockpit of a Curtiss Tomahawk at an unidentified RAF airfield circa June 1941. The original caption states: 'Air Chief Marshal Sir Charles Portal KCB, DSO, MC, Chief of the Air Staff, accompanied by General Chaney, United States Air Attaché, visits a Royal Air Force station to inspect newly arrived American-built aircraft which will be put into operational service with the Royal Air Force.' (Historic Military Press)

The CASABLANCA Conference in January 1943. Prime Minister Winston Churchill poses with members of his delegation in the grounds of President Franklin D. Roosevelt's villa at Casablanca, 17 January 1943. Seated are, left to right, Air Chief Marshal Sir Charles Portal, Admiral of the Fleet Sir Dudley Pound, Churchill, Field Marshal Sir John Dill and General Sir Alan Brooke. Standing behind Churchill is Vice Admiral Lord Louis Mountbatten.

Lieutenant General H.H. Arnold, commanding the US Army Air Forces (left), in earnest conversation with Air Chief Marshal Sir Charles Portal, Chief of the Air Staff of Great Britain, at the CASABLANCA Conference, 14–24 January 1943.

The Anglo-American Combined Chiefs of Staff pictured during a meeting held in the Public Health Service building in Washington D.C., in 1943. The American officers, on the left side of the table, are (front to back): Lieutenant General J.T. McNarney, General George C. Marshall, Brigadier General J.R. Deane, Admiral William D. Leahy, Admiral Ernest J. King, and Lieutenant Colonel R.L. Vittrup. The British officers, on the right side of the table, are (front to back): Commander R.D. Coleridge, Brigadier General H. Redman, Field Marshal Sir John Dill, Air Chief Marshal Sir Charles Portal, General Sir Alan Brooke, Admiral Sir Dudley Pound, and Lieutenant General H.L. Ismay.

Three Allied leaders and the Chiefs of Staff gather for the camera on the terrace of the Citadel in Quebec for the First Quebec Conference in 1943. In the front row, left to right, are Mr Mackenzie King, President Roosevelt and Winston Churchill. In the back row, also left to right, are General Arnold, Air Chief Marshal Sir Charles Portal, General Sir Alan Brooke, Admiral King, Field Marshal Sir John Dill, General Marshall, Admiral Sir Dudley Pound and Admiral Leahy.

After attending the Tripartite Conference at Teheran, Persia, Allied service chiefs travelled to Cairo where they went into conference to discuss points arising from the Roosevelt-Stalin-Churchill talks. Pictured at the conference table in this image taken on 4 December 1943, is Air Chief Marshal Sir Charles Portal, with, to his right, General Sir Alan Brooke, Chief of the Imperial General Staff.

The Yalta Conference in February 1945. The 'Big Three' pictured in the courtyard of Livadia Palace, Yalta, during the conference. As well as Churchill, Roosevelt and Stalin, also present are the Soviet Foreign Minister, Vyacheslav Molotov (far left), Admiral of the Fleet Sir Andrew Cunningham and Air Chief Marshal Sir Charles Portal (both standing behind Churchill), and Fleet Admiral William D. Leahy USN, (standing behind Roosevelt).

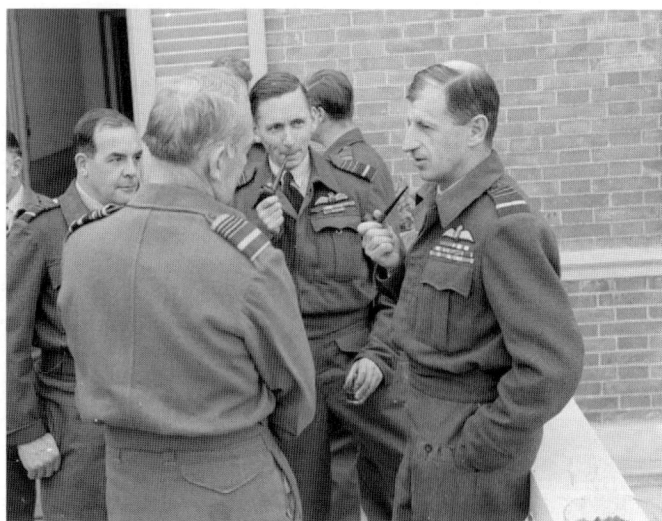

Portal with Tedder, Coningham and Broadhurst in Italy, in December 1943.

Prime Minister, The Right Honourable Winston Churchill, with his Chiefs of Staff in the garden of No.10 Downing Street, London, on 7 May 1945. Seated, left to right, are: Air Chief Marshal Sir Charles Portal; Field Marshal Sir Alan Brooke; Winston Churchill; and Admiral Sir Andrew Cunningham. Standing, left to right, are: Major General L.C Hollis, the Secretary to the Chiefs of Staffs Committee; and General Sir Hastings Ismay, the Chief of Staff to the Minister of Defence.

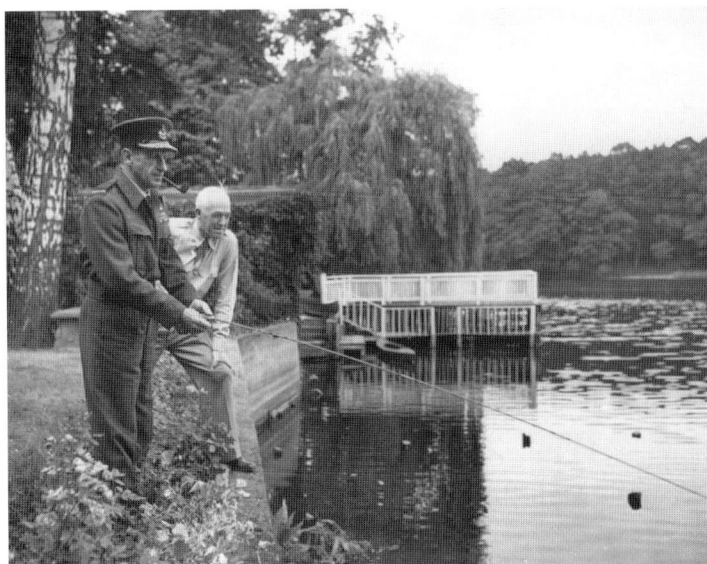

Two senior Allied officers pictured at Potsdam. Air Chief Marshal Sir Charles Portal, left, and General Henry 'Hap' Arnold fishing in a lake in Potsdam, Germany, on 21 July 1945, during their attendance at the Potsdam Conference.

Above: A group of senior American and British military leaders are pictured in a half-track while inspecting the British victory parade held in Berlin on 21 July 1945. Standing in the front row, left to right, are: General Henry H. Arnold; Air Chief Marshal Sir Charles Portal; Field Marshal Sir Harold Alexander; and General of the Army George C. Marshall. Behind General Marshall is Admiral Ernest J. King.

Left: The bronze statue of Portal in the Victoria Embankment Gardens outside the MoD. It was unveiled by Harold Macmillan on 21 May 1975. (Shutterstock)

of any appreciation or directive issued before Longmore's departure.'[29] Noting the enemy's successes through joint action, he recommended, 'bold thrusts against the enemy's communications using land and air forces in a well-co-ordinated plan.' Portal went on to state his, 'complete faith in your judgement, determination and ability to lead the Air Force in the Middle East and you can rely on my not interfering but supporting you in any bold and well-conceived joint operation whatever its results may be. Best wishes to you and Drummond.'[30] With the Battle of Britain over, the Mediterranean and North Africa was Portal's most immediate concern. He needed a capable commander there, and he wanted to know exactly what was going on because the British Army and Royal Navy never missed an opportunity to point an accusing finger at the RAF when things went wrong.

Tedder was the right man for Portal. The air forces in the Middle East needed better organisation and to be more effectively integrated into joint operations. Tedder had the broader strategic perspective to do Portal's bidding, as well as the steel to stand up to his fellow commanders. Tedder was aware Portal's allocation of aircraft in the Middle East was less than ideal, but understood this reality was ubiquitous in all RAF commands. In this regard, Tedder's time in the MAP gave him a perspective Longmore simply did not possess. Tedder could see beyond the selfish desires of his fellow commanders. Recognising that the RAF was not to blame for every failure of the land and maritime components, he refused to kowtow to Wavell and Cunningham. Despite his diminutive stature, Tedder was more than willing to go toe to toe with Cunningham, whose narrow-minded views of air power included what he considered an inalienable right to his own personal air force. Tedder grasped instantly that Cunningham's views on the inadequacy of aircraft numbers in the theatre and his demands for operational control of his own aircraft were incongruent. The paucity of aircraft, and the inherent characteristics of speed and reach, meant Tedder needed the maximum flexibility to task aircraft centrally and ensure air power was decisive at the right time and in the right place.

Portal needed a conduit for reliable information from the theatre. Tedder understood the Mediterranean theatre on a macro level and was able to provide Portal with his own views of the major issues in the theatre,

---

29 Richards, Denis, *Portal of Hungerford: The Life of Marshal of the RAF, Viscount Portal of Hungerford, KG, GCB, OM, DSO, MC.* New York, N.Y.: Holmes & Meier, 1977, 231.
30 Richards, *Portal*, 231; Tedder, *With Prejudice*, 83.

something Portal had specifically requested. Following the confirmation of Tedder's command, Portal wrote to him saying:

> It would help me if you could from time to time send me very private – repeat private – telegrams giving with complete frankness your view of the Middle East picture as it affects all three services. This would not be shown to anyone except possibly the Prime Minister and then only after reference back to you … I feel that whereas the Air Force and to a less extent the Navy have all their available units in constant action which lash out in all directions whenever the chance occurs the Army tends to proceed methodically and unimaginatively along approved text-book lines … The state of Hun supplies in Libya … indicate valuable prizes which might be won by bold and rapid action which cannot be taken by one Service alone but in which I know you would co-operate fiercely if given the chance. Tell me frankly if you think my impressions are wrong.[31]

Portal was wooing Tedder, which was necessary as the two were not well acquainted. Tedder was initially reticent, and told Rosalinde, 'All very well if it were really private to him – but things get round and back.'[32] Tedder's reserve was unsurprising. Despite having both served in the RAF since its formation in 1918, Portal and Tedder had followed different paths. Portal had risen to the top of the Air Force extraordinarily quickly; he was younger than Tedder. He had done so via all the key posts: Air Minister for Personnel (AMP) and Commander-in-Chief of Bomber Command in particular. By contrast, Tedder had followed a rather esoteric route to high command, abjuring the traditional path and taking a succession of training jobs that largely kept him out of the limelight.

Need drove Portal and Tedder together. The pre-war promises of strategic bombing had not been realised and it would have been easy to lay joint operational failures at the RAF's door. Portal needed an insider, because North Africa and the Mediterranean was Britain's primary theatre of operations at that time. He was also acutely aware that the British Army

---

31 Portal to Tedder, 19 May 1941, Portal Papers, Christ Church College, Oxford (Hereafter referred to as CC), CC/2/C/8.
32 Orange, *Quietly in Command*, 133.

had been blaming the Royal Air Force for its own shortcomings ever since France in 1940, while comparing it unfavourably with the Luftwaffe. Tedder needed the support of the Chief of Air Staff both logistically and politically. Despite lingering reservations, Tedder had little choice but to co-operate as Portal desired.

While Portal and Tedder operated at different levels of war, inter-service politics was a game both had to play. In late May 1941 Lord Mountbatten visited Cairo and met Tedder. In keeping with many sister service commanders, Mountbatten derided the RAF's support to the land and maritime components, which Tedder reported to Portal the following day.[33] In fact, Tedder's inability to provide full support was, in part, due to an absence of assets, but this was not the most pressing problem. The British Army had thrived against an enormously inept Italian force during COMPASS.[34] Unfortunately, the Army had 'learnt' many lessons from this operation that would backfire when facing a better trained foe. Some British officers thought they could win through manoeuvre alone, that there was no need for combined arms warfare and that concentration of forces was not a significant requirement for success.[35] Before Operation BATTLEAXE in June 1941, an Allied offensive designed to raise the siege of Tobruk and recapture Eastern Cyrenaica from Axis forces, the British Army did not even allot any time for the infantry and armour to train together.[36] Yet, Rommel's Afrika Korps had already begun ruthlessly exposing British limitations earlier that spring.

For his part, Andrew Cunningham refused to leave his command ship and form a joint headquarters. He continued to insist that the RAF needed to delegate squadrons to his direct control, and went behind Tedder's back to attempt to have this enforced from above.[37] Tedder knew of the problems across all three services before Mountbatten's visit and had written to Portal accordingly:

> One is frankly worried by the situation both as regards the mental and physical inertia which has to be overcome before action is taken and as regards lack of real co-operation between the Services ...

33 Tedder, *With Prejudice*, 107.
34 Porch, *Path to Victory*, 198.
35 French, David, *Raising Churchill's Army*, Oxford: OUP, 2011, 215.
36 Playfair, Ian Stanley Ord, Molony, C.J.C., and Jackson, W.G.F., *The Mediterranean and Middle East: Volume II*, London: Naval & Military Press, 2004, 172–173.
37 Cunningham to Admiralty, 5 June 1941, CC/2/C/8.

> As regards co-operation, the small joint planning Staff has done excellent work though there has recently been an unfortunate change in Army representation ... One main difficulty is that C-in-C., Med. And Staff are afloat and sometimes at sea at critical times. Other is that Army G.H.Q. lack senior staff with real appreciation of meaning of combined operations. Air Force and Navy are merely called on to help out of difficulties ...
>
> Both Cunningham and Wavell appear to think answer to all problems is more aircraft in Middle East. At the moment one squadron of Beaufighters is considered by them the complete answer.[38]

Following this forthright assessment of the problems in the theatre, Tedder finished by assuring Portal, 'I have only made foregoing criticism of outlook and organisation in Middle East after very careful thought and because I feel prospects are grave unless there is change.'[39] While Tedder privately acknowledged the materiel deficiencies in his command, he equally understood there was a great deal more that could be accomplished with the forces he, and his sister service commanders, already had. The fundamental problem in his eyes, as he wrote following Mountbatten's visit was, 'the failure to hold the necessary air bases.'[40] Army commanders were simply not considering the basing needs of the RAF, which limited the support that could be provided. Mountbatten echoed Cunningham's view in believing the British Army should control their own air assets. Tedder rightly refused to spread his forces thinly wherever that could be avoided, because he knew the importance of striking the enemy at the *Schwerpunkt*, the basic principle of concentration, even if his fellow commanders did not.

In the run-up to BATTLEAXE, Portal worried about the optics for the RAF if the operation should fail. He wrote to Tedder on 11 June 1941, four days before the start of the operation:

> Political circles here will be on the lookout for any failure on the part of the R.A.F. to afford close repeat close support to troops in forthcoming operations. Suggestion is being made

---

38 Tedder to Portal, 26 May 1941, CC/2/C/8.
39 Ibid.
40 Tedder to Portal, 31 May 1941, CC/2/C/8.

that we shall pay too much attention to shooting up lines of communication and aerodromes in rear and not enough to dealing with anti-tank guns, tanks and artillery that may be firing on our own troops …

It is essential that you and Collishaw at your respective levels should obtain beforehand complete agreement of Army to your tactical plans. If their requirements appear to you unsound and if persuasion fails to move them you should do your best to act as they require and register your disagreement to them and to me before action starts.[41]

This was an especially shrewd move by Portal, and key in the future relationship between land and air, which had to be on an equal footing. He advised Tedder to acquiesce and form an ineffective command arrangement to prove that the Army's constant criticism of the RAF, and its belief that more 'organic' support would deliver victories, was not only ill-advised but also a shield for the Army's own chronic operational inadequacies. If Tedder provided exactly what the Army wanted, and failure resulted, blame could not be laid at the RAF's door.

Tedder had grave concerns about combined arms warfare and the lack of command and control (C2). Wavell, rather than worrying about the paucity of effective C2 of his land forces, and their own equipment deficiencies, was instead concerned with the relative numbers of aircraft prior to BATTLEAXE. Collishaw (Tedder's subordinate commander) had 105 bombers and 98 fighters, compared to 84 Axis bombers and 130 fighters.[42] A simple numerical comparison could be misleading though, as it ignored serviceability of the aircraft, the skill of the pilots, the capabilities of the aircraft and proximity to the battlespace. This last factor was crucial because long transit times severely affected time on task and the ability to provide continuous and timely air support. This was why control of airfields was crucial in Tedder's mind. Tedder was quietly confident his forces could achieve a degree of superiority.

Portal's congruent analysis, and associated advice to minimise the effects of a possible future smear campaign reassured Tedder, who declared himself, 'Glad to be fore-warned.'[43] Tedder agreed, 'If there is any failure, quite clear

---

41 Portal to Tedder, 11 June 1941, CC/2/C/8.
42 Orange, *Quietly in Command*, 140.
43 Tedder to Portal, 11 June 1941, CC/2/C/8.

that any opportunity of making RAF scapegoat will be seized upon.'[44] He also identified one of the more difficult aspects for the RAF to deal with. The British Army considered any Axis aircraft observed overhead Allied troops to be a disgraceful failure of the Air Force, and not something to be expected in war. The expectation was absolute air supremacy, and anything falling short simply would not do. This may have represented lingering resentment from the evacuation at Dunkirk and the 'Royal Absent Force.' Tedder had little sympathy and wrote poetically, 'Having been given jam and cream, Army now complain they do not always have both.'[45] Already reassured of Portal's support, this mutual understanding of the malign organisational intent of the Army drew the two RAF commanders closer together.

Despite Portal and Tedder's developing bond, Churchill maintained serious reservations about the latter, exacerbated by the fall of Crete in late May 1941. Yet after BATTLEAXE failed, it was Wavell, not Tedder, who was fired and replaced by General Claude Auchinleck in July 1941. Churchill owned at least a part in the operation's failure, having robbed Wavell and Tedder of a significant portion of theatre forces and sent them to intervene in Greece against Portal's advice. So did Beaverbrook, who insisted on maintaining the preponderance of RAF fighter strength in the United Kingdom, where it served little purpose absent the threat of imminent invasion.[46] Portal's foresight precluded any attempted Army broadside aimed at the RAF, and Churchill began to recognise the Army's view of air power as blinkered. Tedder survived BATTLEAXE, the RAF having done sterling work despite Wavell's lukewarm assessment. His time in Churchill's crosshairs lay ahead.

Auchinleck demonstrated a more joint-minded approach than his predecessor and, ahead of the planned autumn assault, Portal was able to offer the Navy some succour, too. Admiral Cunningham signalled the Admiralty on 7 June 1941 (and Tedder a few days later), indicating he wished for an organisation of at least ten squadrons, analogous to Coastal Command in the UK, under the operational control of the Royal Navy.[47] While Tedder was amenable to a force whose primary role would be naval co-operation, he rejected the analogy:

---

44 Ibid.
45 Tedder to Portal, 11 June 1941, CC/2/C/8.
46 Ehlers, Robert, *The Mediterranean Air War: Airpower and Allied Victory in World War II* Lawrence, Kan: University Press of Kansas, 2015, 84.
47 Tedder, *With Prejudice*, 147.

In my view Naval air operations cannot be properly considered as a self-contained activity separate from the main land and air operations in the Middle East … In my opinion, sea, land and air operations in the Middle East Theatre are now so closely inter-related that effective co-ordination will only be possible if the campaign is considered and controlled as a combined operation in the full sense of that term. The enemy has consistently gained his successes by concentration. Not only must we from the defence point of view be able to meet concentration with concentration, but also, if we are ever to regain the initiative, we must be able to concentrate on offence whenever the weak spot appears and opportunity arises.[48]

Portal was unwilling to undercut his operational commander when quizzed by Admiral Dudley Pound, the First Sea Lord:

I could never agree to it as long as Tedder is responsible for the air war in the Mediterranean Theatre as a whole. I am convinced that our only chance of success against the numerical and geographical advantages which the enemy enjoys is to maintain the maximum of versatility and the minimum of specialisation.[49]

Portal understood the inherent joint aspects of the Middle East theatre, and the critical role of air power in such a large battlespace. Moreover, he was equally frustrated with Cunningham, whose 'tactless and stupid remarks … are definitely handicapping our relations with the Navy.'[50] Portal diagnosed the problem in the same way as Tedder: his sister services did not understand that the Mediterranean and North Africa was one huge, combined theatre.[51] After protracted discussions with the Admiralty, Portal did manage to broker a compromise. On 4 October 1941, Portal detailed his agreement to Tedder:

After a series of most exhausting and prolonged discussions with the Chief of Naval Staff we have at length reached

---

48 Ibid., 148.
49 Orange, *Quietly in Command*, 144.
50 Portal to Tedder, 2 September 1941, CC/1/12.
51 Orange, *Quietly in Command*, 147.

agreement ... I gave way on the nomenclature of the Group [No. 201 Group became No. 201 (Naval Co-operation) Group] in order to secure that operational control should be exercised by the RAF (though they would not quite swallow that wording) and that you should be recognised as the authority ultimately responsible for the employment of all the air forces under your command. I hope you will now find the path of co-operation smoother than before ...[52]

This left a few operational details for Tedder to resolve. He was incensed Cunningham wanted the new headquarters sited next to a jetty in Alexandria where his flagship sometimes docked. Tedder pointed out the site was adjacent to timber yards and oil tanks, so thoroughly unsuitable. Cunningham also initially denied Army representation, but Tedder was able to both move the location of the new headquarters and ensure a land presence, for the first time enabling an embryonic joint staff to come into being. Cunningham was somewhat appeased, yet the two men never truly warmed to one another. Tedder's relationship with Auchinleck, Wavell's replacement, proved extremely productive by comparison.

With Operation CRUSADER approaching in the autumn, Portal requested from Tedder, 'a comparison of your own and enemy strengths at different stages, and methods you propose to employ to attain and exploit air superiority.'[53] Operation CRUSADER, designed to relieve the siege of Tobruk and push the German forces back west, was to be the 'big push' for the Allies. Confidence was high due to an increased flow of materiel into the theatre. Tedder replied, with his customary candour, that he was certain of mechanised superiority but expected numerical inferiority in the air.[54] He nevertheless expected to be able to gain air superiority and support the Army. Reasonably, Tedder added, 'Complete immunity from air impossible until enemy air knocked out, but reasonable degree of freedom from air attack should be attainable provided enemy does not send substantial air reinforcements during next three weeks.'[55] Tedder was not too concerned about raw numbers, as he knew that combat experience, realistic training

---

52 The National Archives, Kew, (hereafter referred to as TNA), TNA/AIR 8/593.
53 Orange, *Quietly in Command*, 155.
54 Tedder, *With Prejudice*, 177.
55 Ibid., 178.

and determination were more important factors in achieving victory.[56] The message antagonised Churchill, who largely ignored the detail in it, concentrating instead on the overall numerical inferiority. The timing of Tedder's missive was particularly unfortunate.

Churchill had been experiencing problems with the commitment of the Dominion nations, Australia and New Zealand, to CRUSADER. In particular, the Australian theatre commander, General Thomas Blamey, wanted his forces at Tobruk relieved so he could reconstitute the national contribution holistically in accordance with the agreement with the British Government. For Auchinleck this was highly undesirable, as the replacement forces would then be unable to take part in CRUSADER, denuding the effectiveness of the operation. Both Australian and New Zealand politicians were dealing with delicate domestic political situations, in which no repeat of Dominion losses in Crete and Greece could be allowed to take place. Additionally, the relief of Tobruk was complicated by the need to extract forces using naval destroyers operating in close proximity to Axis air forces. Nevertheless, eventually Churchill capitulated and the Australian forces were relieved, fortunately without too much interference from the Luftwaffe.[57]

The New Zealand prime minister visited London in the run-up to CRUSADER, seeking assurances there would be air superiority for the operation, which Churchill had given.[58] Churchill was still vastly irritated at having caved to Australian demands, and particularly annoyed with Tedder, who had wrongly intimated in a telegram to Portal on 29 September that Blamey no longer desired the relief of Australian forces from Tobruk.[59]

According to Portal, Tedder's Pre-CRUSADER air estimate, 'raised acute political controversy.'[60] Though Tedder's analysis was both accurate and operationally astute, it put Churchill in an awkward position. Tedder's estimate was also much more pessimistic in purely numerical terms than that provided by the Assistant Chief of the Air Staff (Intelligence) on the

56 Orange, Vincent, *Coningham: A Biography of Air Marshal Sir Arthur Coningham, KCB, KBE, DSO, MC, DFC, AFC*. Washington, D.C.: Center for Air Force History, 1992, 83.
57 Cox, Sebastian (1994), '"The Difference between White and Black:' Churchill, Imperial Politics, and Intelligence before the 1941 Crusader Offensive', *Intelligence and National Security*, 9:3, 405–447.
58 Orange, *Quietly in Command*, 157; Furse, *Freeman*, 178.
59 TNA/AIR/23/1395, signal Tedder to Portal, 29 September 1941.
60 Richards, Denis and Saunders, George, *RAF 1939–1945 Vol. II: The Flight Avails*, London: York House, 1954, 170.

same day.[61] Portal responded, 'Your signal has caused me considerable disappointment. No commander could expect to go into battle with all units up to their full establishment, and no squadron should be left out merely because of a shortage of M.T. In a battle of such far-reaching importance, every unit in your command, which by improvisation could be made fit to fight, should be used, and other units should be denuded if necessary.'[62] The signal was copied to Churchill, who wholeheartedly approved. However, Portal sent Tedder another signal shortly afterwards explaining to him that Freeman was heading out to North Africa as Churchill could not be appeased simply through more correspondence. He continued, 'Assure you that this unfortunate development in no way affects my absolute confidence in your ability and determination to win.'[63]

After receiving the first signal, but before getting the second, Tedder penned his forthright reply. He informed Portal (for Churchill's eye) that he was not downbeat, and was ruthlessly stripping other theatres to give all for CRUSADER:

> I am not satisfied I cannot do more, but I will not, repeat will not, promise until I am sure I can effectively keep promise. I will not put dummies in a shop window for D Day. Our battle is joined now, repeat now, and my object is to maintain and increase the pressure to attain air superiority before the Army move.[64]

These were strong words, but Churchill, as Portal alluded, demanded the RAF send out someone senior to find out what was going on. Portal sent Freeman, in whom he had complete trust. Portal had no wish to be pushed around by the Prime Minister so, in sending Tedder's old mentor Freeman, he ensured Tedder would receive a fair hearing. While Portal was assuring Tedder of his continuing confidence in him, and that the current situation in no way affected his support, Churchill was trying to have Tedder removed by writing directly to Auchinleck:

> I thought it very wrong that such mis-statements should be made by the Air authorities in Cairo on the eve of a decisive

61 Cox, *White and Black*, 421.
62 Tedder, *With Prejudice*, 178; Orange, *Quietly in Command*, 157.
63 TNA/AIR/23/1395 signal PUNCH 11, Portal to Tedder, 15 October 1941.
64 Tedder, *With Prejudice*, 180.

battle, and I shall not conceal from you that such conduct has affected my confidence in their quality and judgement.

You will find Freeman an officer of altogether larger calibre, and if you feel he would be a greater help to you and that you would have more confidence in the Air Command if he assumed it, you should not hesitate to tell me so.[65]

Fortunately for Tedder, neither Portal, nor Freeman, nor Auchinleck was interested in removing Tedder at this crucial time. Freeman and Tedder fudged the aircraft numbers for forthcoming operations to send the right political message, and Freeman once more assured Tedder of Portal's support.[66] Auchinleck, in turn, made it clear to Churchill that the Army and RAF were co-operating effectively, and wrote to Churchill on 21 October, stating, 'I earnestly request you not – repeat not – consider any change at this present time.'[67] Freeman refused to betray his former charge, and told Portal a change of commander would be a 'fatal mistake.'[68] Back in London, Portal convinced Archie Sinclair, Minister for Air, that they should both resign if Churchill insisted on Tedder's removal against their wishes; Freeman agreed to follow suit.[69] Yet Portal's support was not unequivocal, and he sought the ground truth from Freeman:

Sinclair and I being pressed to follow course which you suspected and I told you I would oppose to the point of going. Before I consider extreme measures, please answer the following questions: (A) Modesty apart, has your visit led you to think that change would improve Crusader's chances of success? (B) Would you accept job if offered?[70]

Freeman replied (A) No and (B) Certainly not, repeat not.[71] That settled the issue for Portal, and he flatly refused to replace Tedder. Churchill was

---

65 Churchill to Auchinleck, 16 October 1941, Chartwell Papers, Churchill College Cambridge (hereafter referred to as CHAR), CHAR 20/20/40.
66 Furse, *Freeman*, 180.
67 Orange, *Quietly in Command*, 159.
68 Freeman to Portal, 22 October 41, CC/2/C/8.
69 Terraine, J., *A Time for Courage: The Royal Air Force in the European War, 1939–1945.* New York, N.Y.: Macmillan, 1985, 355.
70 Portal to Freeman, 22 October 41, CC/2/C/8.
71 Furse, *Freeman*, 180; Terraine, *A Time for Courage*, 355.

obdurate once set upon a course of action, and only the combined efforts of Portal, Freeman, Sinclair and, not least, Auchinleck saved him. For Portal, it provided an opportunity to have his most trusted deputy carry out an independent assessment of Tedder's performance in command. Freeman reaffirmed Portal's faith in Tedder and their correspondence continued apace.

Tedder regularly informed Portal of unfortunate early developments during CRUSADER. The Army plan called for outflanking Rommel, which was unwise, as it required dispersing British forces. With broad numerical equality of respective forces, the British plan allowed Rommel to counter-attack the British brigades piecemeal.[72] British strategy played to the Germans' primary advantage, their professional tactical competence. Though the British had rough materiel supremacy, the Germans were simply a much more effective fighting force due to superior field command, as Tedder bluntly conveyed to Portal.

When Lieutenant General Alan Cunningham, Auchinleck's field commander (and incidentally, Andrew Cunningham's brother), was fired on 25 November, Tedder reported that the change had come 'in the nick of time, and it was a great relief that the move received such emphatic support from home.'[73] Tedder thought Alan Cunningham a total stranger to armoured warfare, saying once the battle started, 'He fluctuated between wishful optimism and the depths of pessimism.'[74] Moreover, Tedder reported Cunningham's inability or unwillingness to co-operate with Tedder's field commander, Arthur 'Mary' Coningham. Even Tedder knew this communiqué marked a fresh level of forthright honesty, and deliberately handwrote it to Portal in his almost indecipherable scrawl to ensure only Portal would read it. Tedder was delighted to see the back of Admiral Cunningham's brother, as was Coningham. 'Mary tells me that under the previous regime co-operation in the true sense was almost impossible, since (Alan) Cunningham would not discuss his plans or even disclose them except under extreme pressure.'[75]

Unbeknownst to Tedder, Churchill continued to exert considerable pressure on Portal regarding Tedder's position. Portal required an option that would enable him to maintain the exceptional standard of leadership in the theatre, use Tedder in a different way, and get Churchill off his back. He wrote to Auchinleck on 25 November 1941 to determine whether

---

72 Porch, *Path to Victory*, 246.
73 Tedder to Portal 4 December 1941, CC/2/C/8; Orange, *Quietly in Command*, 163.
74 Tedder to Portal 4 December 1941, CC/2/C/8.
75 Ibid.

Auchinleck would consider losing Tedder (with Auchinleck's agreement) to appease Churchill.

Portal's actions reflected the moment of his greatest difficulties during the war, a time when he was under immense pressure. Compounding the highly damaging Butt Report in September, Bomber Command losses rose through the year, from less than 2 per cent in the first half of the year, to 5 per cent in November. Most damaging was the 400-strong bombing raid dispatched on the night of 7 November 1941 that suffered 9 per cent losses and resulted in Churchill ordering Bomber Command to conserve its strength.[76] Amplifying Portal's difficulties were the heavy losses suffered by Fighter Command during the CIRCUS and RODEO missions, flown over France to try to draw German fighters away from the Eastern Front. The fact that the plan, strongly endorsed by Portal, failed to lure German fighters away from the east was another bitter pill to swallow. It was perhaps unsurprising that Portal would try to alleviate pressure from Churchill in one area, though his choice of Richard Peirse to replace Tedder was another misstep. Not only was Peirse the commander responsible for the disastrous bomber raid on 7 November 1941, he had submitted a report attempting to blur the reasons for the failure rather than taking responsibility.

Fortunately, Auchinleck was appalled at the suggestion of having Tedder replaced, and Portal demurred.[77] Portal was willing to be ruthless if required, but it was clear from Auchinleck's fierce defence of Tedder he trusted him implicitly. On reflection, Portal decided to endure Churchill's continuing antics rather than break the air–land bond of co-operation that was, belatedly, developing. This proved the correct decision, not least because Auchinleck and Tedder's joint leadership led to Rommel's first defeat towards the end of the year.

Despite the persistent threat of Rommel's Afrika Corps, Portal had to make some eye-watering decisions in early 1942 due to the growing Japanese menace. Portal's only recourse for rapidly reinforcing the Far East, stripping the Middle East of air assets, contributed to the poor operational showing in North Africa early that year. However, planning entailed dispersing British forces once more, making them operate on divergent lines, which allowed

---

76 Davis, Richard G., *Bombing the European Axis Powers: A Historical Digest of the Combined Bomber Offensive 1939–1945*. Maxwell Air Force Base, AL: Air University Press, 2012, 115.

77 Orange, *Quietly in Command*, 163.

the Germans to pick them off sequentially once more.[78] Other factors exacerbated British problems. The Germans received new tanks in January, tipping the balance against the British Matilda, and Ultra intelligence intercepts proved useless because Rommel never bothered to report his planned operations to higher echelons.[79] Additionally, the British Army was severely disorganised.[80] Tedder's 6 February critique was scathing:

> The original enemy advance up the road ... was literally unopposed, Why, no man knows, but someone blundered pretty badly.
>
> One of our Armoured car Sections which had had some of its cars knocked out by gunfire brought back six perfectly good British tanks which had been left: I believe two walking-back pilots brought one each as well.
>
> Army Divisional and Corps Commanders still seem quite incapable of understanding the importance of their aerodromes ... There are a most unpleasant lot of lessons to be learned out of all this, and I am afraid the main and quite unescapable one is a Root and Branch policy amongst the Army Commanders ... The old school tie and the bran-mash school and the Camberley drag have all got to go.[81]

Portal gained excellent intelligence on theatre problems from Tedder's brutal analysis of the British Army's antiquarian nepotism. It empowered Portal during the daily COS Committee meetings, at which the individual service chiefs discussed broader military strategy. Superbly informed of the British Army's problems, Portal was able to curtail the endless Army and Navy RAF bashing and keep his newest COS Committee colleague, General Sir Alan Brooke, on his toes. With Tedder in his corner, Portal was better equipped to fight both of their professional battles. Auchinleck was unquestionably helpful in this regard, and magnanimous in pointing out the

78 Rommel, Erwin and Liddell Hart, Basil Henry, *The Rommel Papers*. (1st American ed.). New York: Harcourt, Brace, 1953, 184.
79 Playfair, Ian Stanley Ord, Molony, C.J.C., and Jackson, W.G.F., *The Mediterranean and Middle East: Volume III*, London: Naval & Military Press, 2004, 139–140; Warner, Philip. *Auchinleck: The Lonely Soldier*, Barnsley: Pen & Sword, 2006, 149.
80 Warner, *Auchinleck*, 149.
81 Tedder to Portal 6 February 1942, CC/2/C/8.

RAF's exceptional support, yet the Desert Air Force remained deficient, both quantitatively and qualitatively.[82]

The Japanese attack on Pearl Harbor and consequent expansion of the war affected the flow of aircraft to North Africa in several ways. Firstly, the Lend-Lease agreement had to be reworked by Portal and Arnold in 1942 to account for the realities of America's burgeoning need for its own forces.[83] American delivery figures were already seriously shy of those promised in 1941, depressed by Russian demands following entry into the war and US aircraft factory strikes.[84] More problematically, mass production factories, such as Henry Ford's Willow Run bomber plant, underdelivered epically in 1942. While the factory would produce a B-24 Liberator every hour later in the war, it manufactured only fifty-six in 1942.[85] Secondly, as Japan directly threatened the Far East, aircraft had to be sent to bolster British defences. Naturally, these aircraft came from the Middle East because they were the most geographically proximate. Every aircraft that could be spared was sent; Tedder was ordered to dispatch some 450 aircraft in all.[86] Shocked, Tedder wrote, 'Please confirm this is an executive order to despatch reinforcements. Will begin immediately first squadrons ready. The 36 Hurricane IIs will also be sent.'[87] While Tedder could see the situation in the Far East was rapidly deteriorating, losing such a large proportion of his force severely impacted the efficiency of an already overworked Desert Air Force. The reorganisation of supply and salvage in the Middle East in 1941 went some way to amending the situation, but Tedder left Portal in little doubt that the transfer of so many assets compromised his own organisation significantly:

> The effort of sending the aircraft, spares, etc. to the East has
> strained everything to the limit (we should have been completely
> lost if Dawson and his people had not already begun to pay

82 Warner, *Auchinleck*, 154.
83 Slessor, John Cotesworth, *The Central Blue; Recollections and Reflections*, London: Cassell, 1956, 405.
84 Portal to Churchill, 5 December 1941, CC/1/2/29a; Arnold, Henry Harley, *Global Mission*, London: Hutchinson, 1951, 246.
85 Trainor, Tim, 'How Ford's Willow Run Assembly Plant Helped Win World War II,' *Assembly Magazine*, 3 February 2019, found at, How Ford's Willow Run Assembly Plant Helped Win World War II, 2019-01-03, ASSEMBLY (assemblymag.com) accessed on 3 June 2021 at 18.00 Central Time.
86 Furse, *Freeman*, 185.
87 Tedder to Freeman, 29 December 1941, quoted in Furse, *Freeman*, 185.

good dividends from their repair organisation. Even so, it has left us very thin. The trouble has been that it happened just at a time when we needed to put all our efforts on re-bushing the squadrons who were getting part-worn after some two months intensive operations under very hard conditions.[88]

Worse yet (for the Desert Air Force), the increasing German pressure on Malta in spring 1942 meant that Portal, correctly, sent the majority of Spitfire reinforcements there, and not to Coningham. Portal had little choice, but Tedder made him aware of his own debilitating shortages. 'I have today discussed the Western Desert situation with Coningham. There is no doubt that our weakness during the past four or five weeks has allowed the enemy to get his tail up. His tip-and-run tactics with handfuls of 109s have been a nuisance and we have had a number of aircraft shot up on the ground.' He continued, 'I am hoping that our Spitfires will not be too long delayed. There is no doubt that the presence of even a few aircraft with speed comparable to that of the 109 would have a great moral effect on the enemy.'[89] Tedder clarified the operational conditions for Portal, explaining, for example, that attacks on Tripoli could not be carried out because the delivery of American Liberators had been delayed. The inability to strike Tripoli allowed Rommel to unload tanks and vehicles at the port unhindered, as Tedder's other bomber aircraft had insufficient range to reach the target.

The fight for Liberators was fierce; their extended range made them ideal for convoy support in the Battle of the Atlantic. While the Liberator shortage exposed logistical shortfalls, it also gave Portal the ammunition to defend Tedder and the RAF against resurgent political scrutiny. Nevertheless, Tedder pointed out, 'There is no doubt they [the British Army] have grounds for expecting more than they are actually getting [from air power].' Having been quizzed by Auchinleck regarding his dearth of aircraft, Tedder, unlike his predecessor, advised him there was little to be gained by sending a joint missive demanding more assets.[90] He knew why Longmore had been dismissed. Patience was the key; the American industrial machine would deliver in time. The tone of Tedder's discourse

---

88 Tedder to Portal 11 March 1942, CC/2/C/8.
89 Ibid.
90 Ibid.

impressed Portal. This was not the 'moan, moan, moan' of Longmore, but the reasoned assessment of an operational commander who fully grasped the strengths and weaknesses of his forces, and exactly what he needed to turn the tide. Portal also appreciated Tedder's broader understanding of Portal's own difficulties in London. Tedder finished a long March letter, 'You must be having a trying time and one wishes one could do more to help with dividends.'[91]

While Portal spent early 1942 trying to arrest the losses to Japan, Tedder was dealing with rumours and demands from other RAF commanders. When Portal ordered further reinforcements for India, on 15 March, Tedder sent twenty more Hurricane fighters and twenty Blenheim bombers. However, he explained curtly to the Air Commander in India, Air Marshal Richard Peirse, the effects of these demands on the Middle East situation.[92] At the same time, Tedder had to deal with 'three pages of hysterical verbosity' from Air Marshal Arthur Harris, the newly anointed Commander-in-Chief of Bomber Command.[93] Harris waxed lyrical about the immense cost of the nearly 1,000 bomber crews that had been sent to the Middle East and told tall tales of crews kicking their heels in units, when they should be flying for Bomber Command and supporting the strategic assault on Germany.[94] Tedder snapped back, 'Your information is fantastically incorrect,' then wisely wrote to Portal regarding his employment of the 280 Wellington bomber crews sent to the Middle East in the preceding twelve months, of which only eighty-two had actually become part of the establishment. Even if Tedder was playing it straight, Harris was disinterested. There were obviously idle whispers at home, because Air Marshal Sholto Douglas, Commander-in-Chief of Fighter Command, asked Tedder about crews languishing in the desert, while promising him 400 fighter pilots over a period of two months if the men were really needed in Tedder's command.[95] Tedder wrote to Freeman asking that such gossip be scotched.

Despite bleeding away Tedder's assets, the COS Committee pressured Middle East commanders to attack Rommel once more, setting the preliminary date for the next offensive at 15 May 1942. Tedder's numbers in the Desert Air Force would get no better by then, as Portal had other

91 Ibid.
92 Tedder, *With Prejudice*, 252.
93 Tedder, *With Prejudice*, 253; Terraine, *A Time for Courage*, 470.
94 Tedder, *With Prejudice*, 254.
95 Tedder, *With Prejudice*, 255–6.

strategic priorities. Malta desperately needed fighters to fend off continuous German bombing raids attempting to set the conditions for invasion. Fighter Command was also flying thousands of sorties over France and Belgium to draw Luftwaffe assets away from the Eastern Front. Delivering Spitfires to Malta was fraught with danger, and HMS *Eagle* could only transport sixteen aircraft at a time. Churchill enlisted Roosevelt's help, and USS *Wasp*, along with HMS *Eagle*, managed to deliver 126 aircraft to Malta during April and May.[96] The German daylight raids ended, and Malta was saved. Meanwhile, the desert situation deteriorated further and Auchinleck's planned assault backfired, resulting in a retreat all the way to El Alamein by 7 July 1942.[97]

Tedder blamed Auchinleck's field commander for the reverse. 'Ritchie's main pre-occupation was how many tanks of various types he had and would have on various dates. It had become quite an obsession.'[98] Yet again the British Army, and Ritchie in particular, had failed to concentrate its armour, leading to heavy tank losses in the Eighth Army.[99] Tedder was encouraged when Auchinleck took over field command, feeling 'passive bewilderment was being replaced by active command.'[100] He also effusively praised his Air Force's superhuman efforts during the period to Portal:

> Everything possible was done to produce the maximum effort both day and night. The Wellingtons, assisted by Albacores, kept at it from dusk til dawn, and at 7 in the morning the Bostons started an hourly service which went on throughout the day. This was continued the following night with maximum intensity. I have heard squadrons' accounts of these operations and there is no doubt that quite impossible things were done. There were instances in fighter squadrons of fighter aircraft doing as many as seven sorties in the day and pilots doing as much as five sorties. The Boston aircraft did three or even more per day. One of the fighter squadron commanders who

---

96 Churchill, Winston S., *The Second World War, Vol. IV: The Hinge of Fate*, The Educational Book Company Ltd: London, 1951. 233.

97 Moorehead, Alan, *Desert War: The North African Campaign 1940–1943*, Penguin: New York, 2001, 394.

98 Tedder to Portal, 29 June 1942, CC/2/C/8.

99 Warner, *Auchinleck*, 186.

100 Tedder to Portal, 29 June 1942, CC/2/C/8.

had been in the Battle of Britain told me yesterday that the intensity of operations was far greater than anything he had seen during the Battle of Britain.[101]

In so writing, Tedder would have been conscious of both defending his forces from the 'idle gossip' of other commanders-in-chief, as well as the continued RAF bashing that plagued Whitehall and the newspapers. He gave Portal plenty of ammunition to fight the battle at home.

One matter that piqued Portal's interest in Tedder's letters was discussion of Army co-operation:

> I am very far from being satisfied over the working of what is known as air support. We still lack Army support and Army co-operation to a quite deplorable extent. Coningham has had to ram air support down their throats ... The Army still seem quite incapable of knowing the positions and movements of their own forces. The 'bomb line' given by corps, if adhered to, would again and again have completely hamstrung our ability to give effective help in the battle. The complacency with which the Army Staff have frequently said that they really did not have any idea where our advanced forces were has been quite infuriating.[102]

Tedder's analysis provided Portal exactly what he wanted for the developing arguments in Whitehall at the time, and Portal forwarded it to both the Foreign Secretary and the Prime Minister. 'So few people,' Portal replied to Tedder, 'realise that co-operation must be mutual and that subordination is not what is required to achieve it.'[103] Portal's tactful socialisation of Tedder's correspondence to the PM must have had an effect as, when Churchill visited Cairo in August, he took Tedder to one side. 'Tedder, I have an apology to make to you. I was told you were just a man of nuts and bolts. It was not true, and I was not told the truth. I am sorry.'[104] This was a significant victory for Portal. Since Tedder's assumption of command, Portal had acted as a conduit for Tedder's thoughts on the theatre, carefully socialising elements of his

---

101 Ibid.
102 Tedder to Portal, 12 July 1942, CC/1/12.
103 Portal to Tedder, 21 July 1942, CC/2/C/8.
104 Tedder, *With Prejudice*, 319.

analysis to both fellow chiefs and the Prime Minister. More importantly, Portal acted as protector, ensuring Tedder was not unduly criticised for the failures of the other services and refusing to remove him. Stonewalling a Prime Minister who thought Tedder inadequate for his role, while gradually changing Churchill's mind was a delicate task to say the least, but Portal had pulled it off. Churchill's waxing confidence in Tedder was balanced by a waning belief in Auchinleck, who was the final leadership casualty before the Desert War turned inexorably in the Allies' favour.

The arrival of General Harold Alexander as Commander-in-Chief and General Bernard Montgomery as field commander of the Eighth Army coincided with the theatre debut of the Sherman tank with its 75mm cannon, new anti-tank guns, and 900 artillery pieces.[105] Montgomery's appearance heralded a significant change, as he understood that combined arms warfare was essential to battlefield success. 'Tanks alone are never the answer; no one arm, alone and unaided can do any good in battle,' he wrote in August 1942.[106] Montgomery extended this view to air power, enabling the turning of the tide. The Battle of El Alamein was won, due to the maturation of air–land co-operation, and the British advanced 1,500 miles in four months across extremely inhospitable terrain.[107]

With the return of Freeman to MAP in October 1942, and the rapid build-up of US forces, Portal wanted Tedder to become the new Vice Chief of Air Staff, a role Tedder did not relish as he was reluctant to relinquish operational command. Tedder wrote to Portal with characteristic humility, 'I hope you are not expecting too much from me ... I am one of the world's worst staff officers ... But I will do all that is in me to back you and help you – and proud to do it.'[108] In the end Tedder remained *in situ*, as he had the most desert expertise of any senior leader. Once American forces arrived in Africa, General Eisenhower, the overall American commander for Operation TORCH, took an immediate liking to Tedder.

Portal knew this was a critical time for the Alliance. Integrating the disparate forces during the first major combined operation would be a great challenge. He proposed Tedder as the commander of all combined air forces, requesting that Churchill approach Roosevelt with this suggestion. The complex bureaucracy of Allied operations meant Churchill needed the

---

105 Porch, *The Path to Victory*, 311.
106 French, *Raising Churchill's Army*, 262.
107 Moorehead, *Desert War*, 519.
108 Tedder to Portal, 23 November 1942, CC/2/C/8.

agreement of Eisenhower, the CCS, and Roosevelt before anything could be formalised. The decision rumbled on into 1943, with Eisenhower initially preferring General Carl 'Tooey' Spaatz for the job. At Casablanca in January 1943, Tedder was appointed commander of all air forces in the Mediterranean.

Tedder's appointment to a combined command changed the balance of power in the Portal–Tedder relationship. As the predominance of US forces grew, so did Tedder's influence, as he had Eisenhower's ear. The elevation did not go to his head and his first speech to his new charges was one of which Portal would have been proud:

> You know, we British are immensely proud of our Air Force. We think it is the very best in the world, and that it saved England and the world – all of us. We have our own ways of doing things and I suppose we feel we are justified in keeping these ways. But we also know that you Americans are equally proud of your splendid Air Force, and that you feel justified in doing things your way – as well you are. However, it will be the fusion of us, the British, with you, the Americans, that is going to make the very best Air Force in the world.
>
> And now, gentlemen, this is the last time that I shall ever speak of 'us,' the British, and 'you,' the Americans. From now on it is 'we' together who will function as Allies, even better than either of us alone.[109]

Tedder's inclusive approach at the operational level mirrored Portal's behaviour in the CCS Committee, where he sought compromise and co-operation. This commonality allowed the two men to continue their productive dialogue right to the end of the war, despite some differences of opinion. The problems Tedder faced in this new combined organisation were often the same as he had seen developing the joint British organisation in 1941 and 1942. On 26 March 1943, Tedder wrote to Portal about the US attitude to independent air forces:

> They are instinctively antagonistic to it and find it difficult to understand that every General has not a divine right to command his own private air forces, and incidentally a divine

---

109 Tedder, *With Prejudice*, 398.

inspiration by which he knows better than anyone else how those air forces should be employed.[110]

The communication benefitted both men. It kept Portal abreast of problems in the unified command that might go up the US chain and back down through the CCS. For Tedder, it was a way to blow off steam when frustrated with his American counterparts. Doing so allowed him to be more patient. Though he saw many problems and inefficiencies, 'it would be worse than useless to go at it like a bull in a china shop.'[111]

On 20 April 1943, Portal requested that Tedder resume their private correspondence, differentiating them from official views as follows:

> Telegrams to Air Ministry for PM and me should wherever possible be so worded as to allow distribution to other Chiefs of Staff. They should be confined to very hot news or very broad impressions. I should not expect one more often than every week or ten days. Those containing anything Americans or other COS would be better without should be sent to Air Ministry personal to me, and I will use my discretion about wider circulation.[112]

Tedder did just that. He expressed his frustrations with Spaatz, Montgomery, and Alexander in a 5 May 1943 letter. In formal communications, he reported the limitations of the lessons that ought to be learned from the successful attack on Pantellaria, and his proposed strategy for the use of air forces in the continuing attack on Italy.[113]

During 1943, Portal and Tedder both focused on maintaining and strengthening the Alliance. In April 1943, Tedder came down hard on Coningham, who had reacted vociferously to Patton slandering the contribution of the air forces. Though Patton had exaggerated in describing how 'a total lack of air cover for our Units has allowed German Air Forces to operate almost at will,' Tedder still ordered Coningham to withdraw his retort and apologise in person. [114] That same month, Tedder raised

---

110 Tedder, *With Prejudice*, 404.
111 Ibid., 406.
112 Orange, *Quietly in Command*, 216.
113 Tedder to Portal, 14 June 1943 and 16 July 1943, CC/1/12/1 .
114 Orange, *Coningham*, 146–149; Orange, *Quietly in Command*, 214–215.

concerns with Portal about the effectiveness of US ground forces, stating, 'We shall have to be careful to avoid over-stressing British contribution present campaign.'[115] In Whitehall, Portal was thinking along similar lines, highlighting the successes of the Eighth Air Force whenever the chance arose. Later that year, Tedder saw a further opportunity to develop relations, suggesting Brigadier General John Cannon (Coningham's deputy and an American) as head of the Tactical Air Force.[116] Though there were teething troubles, notably in the establishment of HQs, Tedder's organisational skills shone through once more.

Tedder's increasing influence with Eisenhower was due, in no small part, to his objection to further operations in the Aegean, in the hope that Turkey would join the war. The US JCS would not entertain any commitments that diminished OVERLORD preparations, whereas Churchill wanted to expand Mediterranean operations into the Balkans.

Tedder, as well as both Alexander and Cunningham, sided with the Americans. There was a danger of a breach in the Alliance, so much so that Tedder cautioned, 'Sincerely hope there is no question of personal visit [by Churchill] to this theatre, since I feel it would be most dangerous and might have disastrous effect on Anglo-American relations.'[117] Tedder professed that his decision was a military one, echoing Eisenhower's thoughts that, 'when soldiers go in for diplomatic business, then they have a hell of a life.'[118] In reality, it was both a political and a military decision; it was a prickly matter for the Alliance. At any rate, Tedder felt Italy must be the military priority, and allocated appropriately. Starved of the assets that would have been needed for success, to Churchill's significant chagrin, the venture failed.[119] Though he may have blamed Tedder, at least in part, for this failure, his star was rising. With Portal's continuing support and Eisenhower's request that he serve as overall deputy for OVERLORD, Tedder's position was unassailable.

Eisenhower and Tedder moved to London in January 1944, where preparations for OVERLORD began in earnest. The Middle East theatre was relegated to a distant second priority. Unsurprisingly, the first challenges to overcome were organisational. Harris and Spaatz,

115 Tedder to Portal, 17 April 1943, CC/2/C/8.
116 Tedder to Portal 15 October 1943, CC/1/12/3.
117 Tedder, *With Prejudice*, 482; Orange, *Quietly in Command*, 240.
118 Owen, *Tedder*, 232.
119 Tedder, *With Prejudice*, 483–486.

the bomber generals, had had their own way in running the Combined Bomber Offensive (CBO) for almost eighteen months. While Portal was cognisant of the cumulative effects the CBO had on the German ability to prosecute the war, he had long since departed from the view that an overall Allied strategy based purely on strategic bombing would ever be acceptable to joint or Alliance partners. Portal saw the CBO, therefore, as an enabler for OVERLORD, as did Tedder. The bomber generals clearly thought differently. On 22 February 1944, Tedder reported that Spaatz was unwilling to accept orders, or even co-ordination from Leigh-Mallory, the newly installed air commander for OVERLORD.[120] Meanwhile, 'The only sign of activity from Harris's representatives has been a series of adjustments to the record of their past bombing statistics, with the evident intention of demonstrating that they are quite unequipped and untrained to do anything except mass fire raising on very large targets.'[121] Harris had already lodged his objections to supporting OVERLORD earlier, espousing the view that using his strategic bombing force in this manner would:

> commit the irremediable error of diverting our best weapon from the military function for which it has been equipped and trained to tasks which it cannot effectively carry out. Though this might give the specious appearance of supporting the Army, in reality it would be the greatest disservice we could do them. It would lead directly to disaster.[122]

Spaatz's rebellion was at least partially attributable to a personality clash with Leigh-Mallory, whose somewhat dictatorial manner did not suit a subordinate commander who had been fighting his own war up to now; Harris's objections ran even deeper. His obsession with the city bombing campaign would later lead to an extended disagreement with Portal. Churchill's direct intervention resulted in Tedder being appointed the overall air commander for OVERLORD, an arrangement agreeable to the bomber generals. Leigh-Mallory's position was weakened severely, yet Portal chose to leave him in place, complicating the command and control

---

120 Tedder to Portal, 22 February 1944, CC/1/12/1a.
121 Ibid.
122 Quoted in Tedder, *With Prejudice*, 504.

for the invasion unnecessarily. Yet Portal doubtless knew if anyone could make this awkward situation work, it was Tedder.

Portal was more his usual self when faced with Tedder's suggestions regarding pre-OVERLORD bombing strategy. Tedder had employed Professor Zuckerman, an anatomical scholar, to conduct bombing analysis in the Mediterranean. Both men became convinced of the efficacy of a transportation campaign focused on attacking lines of communication, and particularly railways. Well aware of the controversy regarding the preference between the 'oil' and 'transportation' campaigns, Portal professed that he was 'reading all the papers that I can get hold of on this subject. I am trying to keep an open mind until we meet to discuss it and I can assure you that so far I have come to no conclusion, even provisionally.'[123]

Portal organised and chaired a meeting to discuss the relative merits of oil versus transportation on 25 March 1944. Portal had informed Churchill on 14 March that he intended to hold a meeting with the bomber barons, Leigh-Mallory, Tedder and the MEW experts, and he formally told the COS of his intent to do so in a paper dated 19 March. Churchill requested a staff conference to discuss the issue on 22 March but Portal postponed it until after the meeting. Portal wanted the whole picture, and needed all the principal protagonists including Spaatz, Tedder, and the Army transportation experts, as well as the Directorate of Bomber Ops and Ministry of Economic Warfare experts to take part and air their views.

He was, as ever, open-minded and merely wished to choose the approach that would have the most deleterious effect on Germany's ability to reinforce Normandy rapidly. Both Spaatz and Harris opposed the Transportation Plan, preferring to continue the strategic attack on German cities. On the political side, both Churchill and Eden had severe reservations. Eden believed carrying out the plan well in advance of OVERLORD could be a huge gain for enemy propaganda.[124] During the meeting, Spaatz stated that analysis showed attacks on the enemy railway system 'would not affect the course of the initial battle.' His counterpart, General Anderson, conceded that neither would attacks

---

123 Tedder to Portal, 22 February 1944, CC/1/12/2a.

124 Eden, Anthony, *The Reckoning; the Memoirs of Anthony Eden, Earl of Avon.* Boston: Houghton Mifflin Co., 1965, 448–449.

on oil targets.[125] MEW analysis suggested Germany had large reserves of oil such that attacks on oil targets would take three to six months to have an effect. If accurate, this meant attacking oil would be of nugatory value before OVERLORD was launched.[126] Portal stated this analysis, 'showed conclusively that the oil plan would not help OVERLORD in the first few critical weeks.'[127] Eisenhower, as Supreme Commander, owned the decision and concluded that only the Transportation Plan held the possibility of assisting the initial phases of the battle. This ended the meeting, if not the debates.

When the Transportation Plan was discussed at the COS meeting on 21 March, Portal's deputy, Douglas Evill, stated the operation 'would certainly result in heavy casualties to the French population.'[128] Knowing how politically sensitive this would be, Portal devised a mitigation measure to reduce potential civilian casualties. He proposed dropping leaflets within a mile of the attack point to warn citizens to evacuate the area.[129] Portal calculated that if the railways could be so dislocated as to prevent the arrival of nine divisions by around a week, then this would be enough to ensure the success of the Normandy landings.[130] The minute sent to Churchill following the meeting, and with the full approval of the COS (despite Brooke's earlier scepticism), acknowledged the need to 'minimise casualties so far as practicable, without prejudicing the success of the operation.'[131]

Churchill, remembering the French outrage when the British sank their fleet in 1940 was still worried. He asked Cherwell to conduct an independent estimate of casualties, and was aghast at the intelligence estimates of 40,000 deaths and 120,000 grave injuries as well as accompanying

---

125 Rostow, W.W. (Walt Whitman), *Pre-Invasion Bombing Strategy: General Eisenhower's Decision of March 25, 1944*. 1st ed. Austin: University of Texas Press, 1981, 94.
126 Davis, Richard G., United States. Air Force. Office of Air Force History, A.F.C.H.O., and Afcho. *Carl A. Spaatz and the Air War in Europe*. General Histories. Washington, D.C.: Office of Air Force History, US Air Force, 1993, 351.
127 Rostow, *Pre-Invasion Bombing Strategy*, 95; Davis, Richard G., *Bombing the European Axis Powers: A Historical Digest of the Combined Bomber Offensive 1939–1945*. Maxwell Air Force Base, Alabama: Air University Press, 2012, 241.
128 TNA/CAB/79/72/3.
129 Copp, DeWitt S., *Forged in Fire: Strategy and Decisions in the Air War over Europe*, 1940–45. Garden City, N.Y.: Doubleday, 1982, 463.
130 Tedder, *With Prejudice*, 523.
131 TNA/CAB/79/72/14.

opinion that the plan would fail.[132] Churchill then held a series of Defence Committee meetings throughout April in which he decried the choice of the Transportation Plan, trying to wear the COS down. He delayed the full implementation of the plan, enabling Spaatz to dedicate more resources to oil, his preferred target. Churchill also needled Tedder about civilian casualty numbers throughout April and May, on one occasion warning that Tedder would 'smear the good name of the Royal Air Force across the world.'[133]

Churchill also wrote directly to Roosevelt to ask him to reconsider Eisenhower's decision.[134] Roosevelt replied on 11 May that he was unwilling to overrule his military commander if such action might compromise the success of OVERLORD.[135] By the end of May, Tedder had received two caustic minutes from an embittered Churchill on the perils of the Transportation Plan. The French Vichy press were reportedly 'going to town' on the attacks and the casualty numbers.[136]

Despite this prime ministerial onslaught, Portal maintained his firm support for the campaign, which Tedder had proposed and Eisenhower endorsed. Cherwell's casualty estimates turned out to be grossly over-exaggerated, a fact acknowledged by Churchill in his missive to Roosevelt. Yet Churchill had played every card in the deck to try to get his way. On this occasion it took Portal, Eisenhower, Roosevelt, the COS and Tedder to stymie the PM's machinations. History shows the Transportation Plan was a success, and prevented meaningful reinforcement of the German front during the OVERLORD landings, despite continuing objections from both Churchill and Spaatz.

The one downturn in the Portal–Tedder relationship came in January 1945. On the morning of 5 January, 350 bombers attacked the French town of Royan, at the behest of the 1st Tactical Air Force. The action was not cleared with French authorities due to communications problems, and there was a significant loss of civilian life. Portal described the attack, hundreds

132 Butler, James Ramsay Montagu, Gwyer, J.M.A., Ehrman, John and Howard, Michael. *Grand Strategy: History of the Second World War Vol. V,* United Kingdom Military Series. London: H.M. Stationery Office, 1956, 297–298.
133 Orange, *Quietly in Command,* 260.
134 Kimball, Warren F., *Churchill and Roosevelt, Volume 3: The Complete Correspondence – Three Volumes.* Princeton, N.J.: Princeton University Press, 2015, 122–123.
135 Ibid., 127.
136 Tedder to Portal, 22 February 1944, CC/1/12/3g.

of miles from the front, as 'a lamentable affair.' He irked Tedder greatly by continuing, 'It can certainly do nothing but harm to the good name of the RAF, possibly more so than the bombing of the railway centres prior to and during OVERLORD.'[137] This letter came at the same time as word that Tedder was 'to be kicked upstairs' either to the Air Ministry or the Mediterranean. Tedder replied vigorously to Portal, offering his resignation and refusing any other job as, 'the scapegoat has one privilege – he is allowed to go into the wilderness – I think I have at least earned the right to that privilege.'[138]

Portal, despite being extremely busy preparing for the ARGONAUT Conference, the second meeting of Russian, American, and British leaders to discuss the war's progress, wrote back immediately. 'I realise that the alleged innuendo in para. 4 of my letter of the 25th about Royan is only the spark that caused the fire, but I must tell you that it was not intended to bear the construction you have put on it. I plead guilty to signing the letter without carefully checking it.'[139] This was an important admission, as Tedder had taken particular umbrage at Portal's words, who was ordinarily so careful with his use of them. Portal went on to explain that he had been thinking how the Royan attack would be viewed more adversely by history than the pre-OVERLORD attacks on the railways. 'I never gave a thought to the idea that you might think I was regarding the French railway bombing as a bad show. Why should I? I was up to the neck with you in advocating the policy and in answering the allegation that it would smirch the reputation of the R.A.F.'[140] Portal also took the time to assure Tedder that there was, to his knowledge, no Whitehall conspiracy against him, and that he enjoyed the full confidence of the whole COS Committee. Any strategic disagreements that may have arisen with the War Office due to differing conceptions of how to prosecute the war were merely that: differences of opinion. He also said, 'I can assure you that the P.M. has your interests very much at heart in all this.' In typically humble style, Portal finished by stating, 'I cannot tell you how sorry I am that all this should have happened and that the spart [sic] which caused the fire should have been due to my own carelessness in the rush of pre-ARGONAUT

---

137   Portal to Tedder 25 January 1945, C/3/D/9.
138   Tedder to Portal 28 January 1945, C/3/D/9.
139   Portal to Tedder 30 January 1945, C/3/D/9.
140   Ibid.

business ... Ever since 1941 you have had my constant admiration and support in all your work.'[141]

Reassured, Tedder withdrew his imminent threats of resignation and acceded 'to go where and do what one is told.'[142] He remained concerned about the possibility of being replaced by General Alexander, a noted favourite of Churchill. The change never took place, and Tedder remained as Eisenhower's deputy right to the end of the European War, even travelling to Berlin on 8 May 1945 to confirm the surrender of Germany, as the representative of the Western Allies. Never one to miss a trick, Portal wrote to Tedder the following day to thank him, 'from the bottom of my heart, for all the great work you have done during the time I have been CAS. I was so delighted to see that you had a great moment at the end in Berlin – an unforgettable experience and one you had richly earned.'[143] Portal's admiration of Tedder was plain and true. When Portal decided to call time on his military career at the end of 1945, he recommended Tedder replace him.[144] The two men shared many qualities and frequently saw things in the same way. Relations with his counterpart across the Atlantic, Henry 'Hap' Arnold, proved more challenging as, despite a common enemy, much divided them.

---

141 Ibid.
142 Tedder to Portal 3 February 1945, CC/3/D/9.
143 Orange, *Quietly in Command*, 306.
144 Richards, *Portal of Hungerford*, 246.

Chapter 6

Portal and Arnold

*I think Peter Portal has been very underexposed for what he
was, he played a vital role, particularly in
Anglo-American relations.*

Mrs Pamela Harriman

An American airman, and the closest thing to Portal's equivalent, Henry 'Hap'
Arnold was a confirmed Anglophobe. This view had been solidified during
a visit to the UK in 1918, and an enforced stay in a British military hospital.
He described the women as 'having ankles like fence posts. Taking them all
in all they are messes.'[1] He further complained about the British weather
and the arrogance of British troops towards their American counterparts.[2]
This distaste for the British festered after the Second World War began, and
Arnold was ordered to send aircraft across the Atlantic to aid the British fight.
He needed these aircraft to build up his own forces. Later, Arnold frequently
beat a frustrated figure. He was destined to spend the Second World War as
he had the First, behind a desk in Washington D.C., far from the action he
craved. This made him irritable and ill-disposed towards Portal, who was
close to the front line on the other side of the Atlantic. Arnold's Anglophobia,
professional jealousy, and indignation at the perceived misuse of his aircraft
combined to make him arguably Portal's biggest challenge.

Hap Arnold was born in Philadelphia in 1886, the second son of a stern
father who was a local physician and member of the National Guard. The
family was fairly affluent, and Hap had a mostly contented childhood.
When Hap was six, the Arnolds moved to Ardmore, where they became

---

1 Daso, Dik A., *Hap Arnold and the Evolution of American Airpower*. Washington, D.C.:
Smithsonian Institution Press, 2000, 89.
2 Yenne, Bill, *Hap Arnold: The General Who Invented the U.S Air Force*. Washington,
D.C.: Regnery History, 2013, 79.

acquainted with the Pool family, whose daughter Eleanor later became Hap's wife. Of a mischievous disposition, Hap had to be certain, as did the two other Arnold boys, that any antics were carried out beyond the gaze of the humourless doctor. Hap's frustrations with the small town of Ardmore exploded in his junior year when he and eleven of his classmates were suspended for 'gross violations of discipline.'[3]

The Arnold family had a rich military vein running through it. Great-great-grandfathers on both sides of the family had fought in the War of Independence, while Hap's paternal grandfather had served in the Federal Army at Gettysburg during the American Civil War.[4] Doctor Arnold was extremely keen for this family legacy to endure, but his eldest son, Thomas, proved disinterested in a military career. Per his mother's wish, Hap had been slated for the clergy, but West Point offered more exciting opportunities for an adventurous young man. His father had written to their member of Congress to seek patronage, which was still required in those days. Hap was accepted into West Point in 1903, following a nervous wait. He was determined to escape Ardmore.

Arnold's efforts in different pursuits at West Point were directly proportional to his level of interest. Academically he was the 'grey man,' ensuring he passed the most important classes while avoiding any hint of distinction. He finished eighty-second overall in his first year, and sixty-third in his second, right in the middle of the class.[5] Arnold's interests lay outside the classroom; he performed well in military conduct and on the sports field. He represented the academy at football, ran track and threw the shot putt. However, his first love was equestrianism.

Henry Arnold wanted to join the cavalry; this was his main goal in attending West Point. 'It was what we lived for – our whole future!'[6] Hap practised all aspects of the cavalry life, and emulated cavalry stunts such as riding in pyramids, as well as more formal schooling. Moreover, he swaggered, as cavalrymen were wont to do, and chewed tobacco occasionally. One day in Hap's senior year, the senior cavalry instructor ordered him to spit out his tobacco. Arnold quipped back, 'I thought all good cavalrymen chewed tobacco.'[7] He was confined to the area as punishment,

---

3 Daso, *Hap Arnold*, 10–11.

4 Daso, *Hap Arnold*, 7.

5 Ibid., 20.

6 Arnold, Henry Harley, *Global Mission*, London: Hutchinson, 1951. 7.

7 Daso, *Hap Arnold*, 31.

but still graduated sixty-sixth in his class and returned home to await his commission and appointment to the cavalry.

Arnold vividly recalled the morning his commission arrived in *Global Mission*. He was sat with his mother in the kitchen, without a care in the world. He casually tossed the envelope to her to open it, certain of its contents. Inside awaited an unpleasant shock: assignment to the infantry.[8] Subsequent appeals to the Adjutant General proved fruitless, and by November Hap was on the way to Manila as an infantry officer. It appeared his outburst to the senior cavalry instructor at West Point carried graver consequences than Hap's initial restrictions. Missing from Arnold's West Point record was the seemingly innocuous SQ status, which stood for special qualification. Without it, graduating cadets were not eligible for the cavalry.[9] Arnold's indiscretion had cost him his dream of being a cavalry officer, though arguably this was serendipitous, given his future success in the Air Corps.

Arnold spent the formative years of his Army career seeking adventure. In the Philippines, he grasped the chance to traipse through the jungle armed with machete and shotgun, while mapping the local area. During this assignment, Arnold met Captain Arthur Cowan, who became aware of Arnold's dissatisfaction with the infantry. When Cowan was subsequently placed in charge of finding officers willing to transfer to the Signal Corps' embryonic flying programme, he suggested it to Arnold, who willingly applied.[10] Nearly three years later, Arnold was concentrating on passing his exams to transfer to the Ordnance Department (another escape plan), having largely forgotten about his application to the Signal Corps.[11] Then he received a letter requesting he go to Dayton to learn to fly. His commanding officer exclaimed, 'Young man, I know of no better way for a person to commit suicide!'[12] The words failed to deter Arnold, who remained desperate to leave the infantry.

Arnold travelled to Dayton in April 1911, while seventeen-year-old Peter Portal was mastering the intricacies of hawking across the Atlantic Ocean. Hap was one of the first military pilots, instructed by no less than the Wright brothers. Aviation was a hazardous business at the time, and the words of Arnold's previous commanding officer were not entirely wide

---

8 Arnold, *Global Mission*, 9; Daso, *Hap Arnold*, 32.

9 Daso, *Hap Arnold*, 36.

10 Ibid., 37.

11 Yenne, *Arnold*, 17.

12 Arnold, *Global Mission*, 15.

of the mark. Little was understood about flying in those early days, and accidents were common. The pilots were also trained mechanics, as no maintenance personnel existed. This proved useful as, when he graduated from flight school, Hap was assigned to College Park, Maryland, where he had to assemble his own aircraft before flying it.

Arnold and his friend Tommy Milling became the Signal Corps' first two flying instructors, and Arnold became a minor – if unwitting – celebrity. Arnold made the news twice in 1912: once for a near-death experience at altitude in July and once for an impressive Nassau to New York air mail run later that year.[13] He was testing the limits of the possible, though military applications such as bombing proved hazardous with the dearth of power in the aircraft of the day. He also flew as a stuntman in several Hollywood movies. Having won the first Mackay Trophy in September 1912, Arnold was nearly killed in a flying accident in November when he stalled his aircraft and narrowly escaped hitting the ground nose first. Very shaken up, he removed himself from flying duties until 1916.

While grounded, Arnold was sent to Washington D.C. and the War Department. His influence as a famous pilot outweighed his junior rank, and his views were treated seriously. Arnold felt the US was falling further and further behind in aviation development. The lack of funding, coupled with the reported high rate of flying accidents, made him long to escape the Capitol. He felt isolated, in the same way he later would during the CBO.

Arnold was next assigned back to the Philippines, where he met a young lieutenant named George Marshall. The two remained close friends for the rest of their lives, and Marshall was later instrumental in Arnold becoming head of the Army Air Corps in 1938. After two years in the Philippines, Arnold moved back to the Aviation School at Rockwell Island, and then to Panama, to set up the first squadron in the Canal Zone. However, once the US joined the war in 1917, Arnold found himself back in Washington D.C., rapidly jumping ranks from captain to colonel. He became the assistant director of military aeronautics, responsible for the number of pilots trained and aircraft manufactured.[14] The US had fallen much further behind in aviation development after the onset of hostilities in Europe. Arnold had a Herculean task since, in May 1917, the US Army had fifty-five planes and twenty-six qualified pilots. By the following

---

13 Daso, *Hap Arnold*, 50.
14 Ibid., 87.

year, the Army was ordered to have 4,500 aircraft and 5,000 pilots in France.[15] It was a hectic period for Arnold and his team, who visited industry as well as potential airfields for training. Despite the lag in the production of combat aircraft, Arnold achieved a great deal, cementing relationships with industry players who would be key to his task in the future war.

Once the war ended, Arnold left Washington for California, where he was shorn of his elevated rank and returned to the permanent grade of captain. He continued to innovate and find ways to use his aircraft usefully, notably in spotting forest fires. He worked closely with Tooey Spaatz and Ira Eaker, with whom he would remain associated for the duration of his military career. However, his greatest influence was probably Billy Mitchell.

Brigadier General Mitchell was the face of American military aviation, a hero from the First World War. He spent the early 1920s arguing vociferously for an independent air service, but his belligerence delivered self-immolation rather than satisfaction. Arnold had a ringside seat at Mitchell's court martial, but later acknowledged that even if Mitchell was right, America was not ready for an independent air force in the 1920s. High-performance planes, reliable engines and effective navigational aids were all things of the future.[16] Arnold was as keen as his mentor to achieve independence, fiercely advocating for it when he saw fit, despite Mitchell's advice not to follow his path of belligerence.

Arnold faithfully defended Mitchell from the stand during his court martial and was consequentially banished to Fort Riley, Kansas, on a 'punishment tour.' A successful graduation from the US Army Command and General Staff School at Fort Leavenworth in 1929, as well as the publishing of no fewer than five books, demonstrated Arnold's extraordinary professionalism and expertise in his chosen field. Subsequently, Arnold shone as base commander at March Field in California, where he was charged with developing future fighter tactics. His team also worked on cargo airlift and strategic bombing. When the General Headquarters Air Force was formed in 1935, Arnold skipped the rank of colonel and was promoted to brigadier general. He remained at March Field, leading three fighter squadrons and three bombardment groups.[17] There, Arnold oversaw the introduction of modern fighters and

---

15 Yenne, *Hap Arnold*, 32.
16 Arnold, *Global Mission*, 121.
17 DuPre, Flint O., *Hap Arnold: Architect of American Air Power*. Air Force Academy Series. New York: Macmillan, 1972, 70.

bombers; this role offered the perfect preparation for a future chief of staff.

By the time of Arnold's accession to the top post in the US Army Air Corps in September 1938, Mitchell's air power rhetoric of the 1920s was somewhat matched by technological capability. For Arnold, the idea of sending vast numbers of US-produced aircraft to allies was anathema. In fact, he spent two years trying to arrest the flow to Britain, which came at the expense of his own build-up. Time and again Arnold was overruled by the President, which only intensified his ire toward the British.

Post-colonialism, lingering isolationism, and organisational preferences all played a part in Arnold's antipathy towards the United Kingdom. The last dominated Arnold's 1940 thinking, and he testified to Congress in March that the materiel destined for Britain and France directly undermined the Air Corps and its planned expansion.[18] Roosevelt, in no mood to have his policies criticised so publicly, threatened Arnold with exile in Guam, starkly illustrating his diminishing stock. Though Arnold stifled his rhetoric a little, once the Blitz began, Arnold, Marshall, and others questioned how long the British could withstand the Nazi assault. They feared that, in supporting the British and the French, the US would be throwing good money after bad. The prevailing military view held that Hitler was unstoppable.[19] Both the US Ambassador in London, Joseph Kennedy, and the US War Plans Division remained downbeat regarding Britain's prospects.[20]

Aware of the President's resolve, Arnold sought what advantage he could from the situation, sending Army Air Corps observers to bring back lessons from the war in Europe. Nevertheless, his doubts remained and in January 1941, he feared that the US was 'leaning over backwards to give everything to the British,' to the detriment of his own force.[21] Henry Stimson, Secretary of War and more sympathetic to Britain's predicament than Arnold, determined to send Arnold to England 'to get a birds eye view

---

18 Huston, *American Airpower*, 49.
19 Arnold, Henry Harley and Huston, John W., *American Airpower Comes of Age: General Henry H. 'Hap' Arnold's World War II Diaries Vol. 1*, Maxwell Air Force Base, AL.: Air University Press, 2001, 52.
20 Furse, Anthony, *Wilfrid Freeman*, Spellmount, 2000, 212.
21 Huston, *American Airpower*, 69.

of the situation and a first-hand feeling of the atmosphere.'[22] Arnold had historical, military, organisational and personal reasons to limit assistance to the UK. For Portal, winning Arnold over during his first trip to the UK, in April 1941, was a tall order.

The US Administration and Henry Arnold had grossly divergent perceptions of the reasons behind Arnold's visit to London. Harry Hopkins, a close presidential advisor, sent Arnold to 'receive the red-carpet treatment' from the British and muster sufficient credibility with Roosevelt to avoid forced retirement.[23] This second point was a significant concern. Roosevelt had refused to send Arnold's nomination for substantive promotion to major general forward due to personal objections, arising from his continued public obstinacy regarding assistance to the British. Any critique was particularly damaging to Roosevelt, as Lend-Lease was going through the final stages of congressional approval in early 1941.

Arnold was unaware of his continuing low standing with the President, and described his wishes for the trip to Portal as: 'Firstly to see Europe through your eyes and those of the senior members of your staff and of the commanders-in-chief of Bomber Command, Fighter Command and Coastal Command. Secondly to discuss training and thirdly to see from long range point of view how the US Air Corps could best help RAF in an active manner.'[24] In the end, both sets of objectives were achieved.

Arnold was equal parts surprised and delighted by the VIP treatment from the RAF, but it was inevitable. The British were well accustomed to doing such for any American they viewed as useful in assisting the war effort. Hopkins reinforced Arnold's importance, describing him as 'one of our ablest military men' who 'has a tendency to resist efforts to give adequate aid to England' in a letter to Churchill.[25] Arnold was very keen to meet Portal, but expected little fuss because, 'in the United States, I was definitely in the minor leagues. I had not reached the major league status in the military set-up.'[26] It was, therefore, with some astonishment that he faced a welcome delegation of three RAF officers, who had flown to

---

22 Henry L. Stimson Diaries, Yale University Library, New Haven, Connecticut, held at The Air Force Historical Research Agency, Maxwell AFB, Montgomery AL, (hereafter referred to as Stimson Diaries), 21 March 1941.
23 Huston, *American Airpower*, 70.
24 The National Archives, Kew, (hereafter referred to as TNA), TNA/AIR/8/487, 26 March 1941.
25 Huston, *American Airpower*, 71.
26 Arnold, *Global Mission*, 214.

Portugal to meet Arnold in advance of his arrival in London. This seeded a more favourable 'second impression' of the British.

On 12 April 1941, Arnold flew on to Hendon, where he and Portal met for the first time. They shared a drink together and then went on to the Dorchester for dinner, the hotel where Portal lived during the war. Arnold was immediately drawn to Portal, commenting in his diary, 'Portal a very savvy man.'[27] The two men had a great deal to discuss and each, for one reason or another, envied the other. Arnold was jealous of Portal's command of an independent air service, while Portal was green-eyed about the astounding industrial capabilities at Arnold's fingertips.[28] Portal's admission regarding US industry softened Arnold's stance, and the men found they had much in common after all. Arnold was a reasonable man. His route to the top, like Portal's, had been characterised by 'transparent honesty' and 'an ability to put his finger on the big issues.'[29] This common approach formed the basis of a strong bond, founded on mutual respect. This was important because, as in any alliance, bones of contention lay in wait.

At this early stage, there were several disagreements between the UK and the US regarding the air war, but two dominated the discussion. The first, which would remain unresolved for some time, related to differences in respective bombing doctrine. The RAF, having attempted daylight bombing early in the war, rapidly concluded it was unfeasible in Europe. By 1940, unescorted bombers were vulnerable to modern monoplane fighters, enabled by several independent interwar technological developments: high-octane fuels, retractable undercarriages, metal construction, engine improvements and wing-mounted guns. The British also ignored precision bombing in the belief that adverse weather and the inability to maintain level flight once engaged by enemy fighters or *Fliegerabwehrkanone* (flak) precluded precision.

US bombing doctrine, developed by the Air Corps Tactical School in the 1920s and 1930s, was centred on the viability of high-altitude, unescorted, precision, daylight bombing.[30] The advancements in fighter technology did not result in a doctrinal rethink on either side of the Atlantic prior to war. The USAAF would learn their own hard-won lessons in 1942 and 1943.

---

27 Huston, *American Airpower*, 74.

28 Yenne, *Hap Arnold*, 78–79.

29 Huston, *American Airpower*, 33.

30 Crane, Conrad C., *Bombs, Cities, and Civilians: American Airpower Strategy in World War II*. Lawrence [Kan.]: University Press of Kansas, 1993, 28–30.

The second bone was direct American involvement in the war. The Japanese would settle the matter, but Pearl Harbor complicated rather than simplified matters between Portal and Arnold. However, in the absence of foresight, Portal and Churchill courted Arnold, primarily during a sojourn at Ditchley Park, Churchill's unofficial weekend retreat.

Arnold recalled dinner on the second night at Ditchley, during which Portal and Churchill dominated the conversation. Once more, Arnold was impressed by Portal, who 'handled himself brilliantly, in spite of the many quips the Prime Minister made, either joking, or in a serious manner, about the Air Force.'[31] Later in the evening, both Portal and Churchill started working on Arnold, to try to convince him that America needed to come into the fight. The weekend clearly made an indelible impression on Arnold, who noted, 'Portal is a brilliant man who does things, is capable and knows his job. Prime Minister a huge personality and has a most wonderful mind.'[32] The first stage in turning Arnold's pre-trip views around was complete; he liked both Portal and Churchill. Portal further endeared himself to Arnold, an arch technophile, by making the Whittle jet engine technology available to him.[33] Though Arnold remained wedded to US bombing doctrine, and could do nothing about direct US involvement in the war, his attitude to Britain was softening.

One of Arnold's concerns about the British, prior to his visit, was their ability to withstand the German Blitz of London. On the way to Portal's office in the Air Ministry, Arnold commented to Arthur Harris, DCAS at the time, 'It's extraordinary Bert. Nobody seems to be moving. Everyone's working away happily in their offices. Don't you people realise you've lost the war?' 'Good God no, we haven't started the ruddy war yet,' Harris rejoindered.[34] This was a vastly different view to the one that Arnold had formed from across the Atlantic. In discussions with Averell Harriman prior to Arnold's trip, Hopkins suggested experiencing an air raid might be useful in altering Arnold's stance. The British people would alleviate Arnold's doubts. On 14 April 1941, Arnold remarked in his diary, 'Am amazed at calm and peaceful attitude of office personnel, no hurry or excitement anywhere. Sandbags on all streets, bomb

31 Arnold, *Global Mission*, 232.
32 Huston, *American Airpower*, 80.
33 Daso, *Hap Arnold*, 166.
34 Saward, Dudley, *Bomber Harris: The Story of Marshal of the Royal Air Force, Sir Arthur Harris* … 1st ed. in the USA ed. Garden City, N.Y.: Doubleday, 1985, 96.

holes and craters almost everywhere but business goes on just the same.'[35] True to the advertising campaign, the British would 'keep calm and carry on.' On 15 April, Arnold experienced an air raid first hand:

> After sitting about a bit and waiting for others to go home, I started. Then the sirens started, searchlights flashing everywhere, AA guns crackling, AA shells bursting. Still far away, for the guns across the street have not started firing. Several br-umps some distance away, fires, the lights cross closer, the AA guns firing is closer and their shells bursting. They seem to be all around London, bursting bombs on all sides with their br-ump. The AA guns across the street start firing, the planes are overhead, the noise is deafening. It recedes, all is silent again. Another at 12:00 – the searchlights the starlike shells bursting, the incessant cracking of the guns always getting closer and louder. A fire here, another there, they seem to cover as much as a city block closer and closer br-r-rump. Flames high in the sky, two, three city blocks on fire. The noise again recedes the night becomes silent, but the fires burn on. The raid is over; I leave the window and go to bed.[36]

The following day, Arnold saw the after-effects of the raid. There was glass everywhere, windows and doors were blown out, and workers were ubiquitous, fixing all that was broken. Despite the evidence of widespread damage, Britain was back at work, and in a determined manner.[37] The resolve of the British general public was proven. If Arnold's experiences thus far had warmed his heart to the British, an unexpected visit with the king cemented his new feelings. He was getting the full treatment! Arnold returned to America with a modicum of faith in both Britain and the British; it would be essential for the success of the Alliance and for Arnold to maintain what remained a tenuous hold on his job. Portal, sensing Arnold's lingering doubts, quickly wrote to him expressing, 'deep appreciation for your keenness to help us,' and for Arnold's, 'readiness to bear sacrifices

---

35 Huston, *American Airpower*, 75.
36 Ibid., 76.
37 Ibid., 78.

in the equipment of your own service.'[38] If Portal's words did not heal old wounds, they at least soothed them a little.

Arnold's visit improved both the standing of the British in his eyes and his own credibility with the President. Arnold spoke warmly of the resolve of the British people to the New York press upon landing stateside, and then gave what FDR regarded as the best account yet of the situation in Great Britain.[39] What set Arnold's report apart from others, much like Portal's work, was the depth and breadth of strategic nous he showed the White House. He addressed many topics, including:

(1) the inability of the British to extend their destroyer and airplane convoy protection any farther to the west; the ever-increasing range of the German submarines, and the ability of the German submarine packs to hit convoys almost within gunfire of the American shores;

(2) the British solution to this problem, which was for the United States to establish bases in Greenland, Labrador, Newfoundland, and Iceland for air ferrying, air patrol, and destroyers;

(3) the necessity for, and the possibility of our taking over such patrols;

(4) the probability of our assuming responsibility for ferrying all airplanes across the North Atlantic along the then partially created ferry route;

(5) the need for us to get airplanes to the R.A.F. as fast as possible;

(6) the need to establish air and sea bases in the South Atlantic for the protection of convoys making the South Atlantic crossing.[40]

Arnold further recommended the military chiefs of the Allied nations get to know one another, as Churchill and Roosevelt had. Arnold's position was strengthened later by further public declarations of support for the British.

---

38 Portal to Arnold 23 April 1941, TNA/AIR/4/487.

39 Huston, *American Airpower*, 91.

40 Arnold, *Global Mission*, 241.

Consequentially, by the end of May, Roosevelt had approved Arnold's promotion and invited him back to the generals' top table.

This newfound presidential approbation resulted in Arnold joining the US JCS and CCS Committees. While Portal's position on the equivalent joint committee, as the head of an independent air force, was assured, for Arnold it demonstrated both a burgeoning faith in him and a recognition of the growing importance of the air weapon in the future of the war. It also ensured Arnold's attendance at a series of Allied conferences over the following years, beginning in Argentia, Newfoundland, in August 1941.

Portal did not attend the ARGENTIA Conference because Churchill needed him to 'stay behind and mind the shop.' Portal's deputy, Air Chief Marshal Wilfrid Freeman, went in his stead.[41] Freeman was a long-time friend and colleague of Portal, having instructed him at Staff College in 1922 and had dutifully, but willingly, taken a step down the RAF ladder to become Vice Chief of Air Staff. More pertinently for the British war effort, Freeman had arrived at the Air Ministry fresh from the Ministry of Aircraft Production (MAP), so was intimately versed in the exact needs of the RAF.

Though Arnold had warmed to the British position, he still considered his primary role was to arm the USAAF for the war to come, not the British. Arnold saw his priorities as: firstly, development of the US Army, Navy and USAAF; and secondly, to supply foreign governments military equipment that they could use effectively and efficiently.[42] Arnold believed himself accountable to the American people, and wished to ensure the judicious spending of the money thus far allocated for American preparedness. He also wanted to examine the requirements of the other nations requesting assistance, soon to include the Soviet Union and the Philippines, to make sure their requests met his effectiveness and efficiency tests. This posed a particular problem for Britain, where opinions regarding urgent requirements were divergent.

Essentially, there was a split between the MAP, headed by Lord Beaverbrook, and the Air Ministry, headed by Portal. Portal, under severe pressure from Churchill to produce an effective bombing force, prioritised heavy bombers. Beaverbrook considered fighters to be more important. Once Lend-Lease went live, and Roosevelt sent Averell Harriman across

41 Churchill, Winston S., *The Second World War, Vol. III, The Grand Alliance*, The Educational Book Company Ltd: London, 1951, 380.
42 Arnold, *Global Mission*, 248.

the Atlantic to implement it, the divisions became immediately apparent. Beaverbrook, not above circumventing normal channels, had sent MAP's proposed programme to Washington in March 1941. It included 3,000 medium bombers, 4,000 light bombers, 1,400 dive bombers, 6,500 single-engine fighters and 1,000 twin-engine fighters.[43] Very few of these aircraft were of operational utility to the RAF, which had already won the Battle of Britain, and had need of long-range fighters and bombers for strategic operations over Germany and for the war in North Africa and the Mediterranean. From a US perspective, the major problem was that other requests were also received, and it was unclear which orders to push through. As one American officer quipped, 'We can't take seriously requests that come late in the evening over a bottle of port.'[44]

At ARGENTIA, Freeman made it abundantly clear where RAF priorities lay. In fact, the RAF had a capable fighter production line in 1941, but heavy bomber production lagged far behind. The RAF still lacked a four-engine bomber, precluding strategic bombing deep into the heart of Germany; Portal wanted 6,000 in total. Freeman immediately requested 4,000 heavy bombers. However, the US allocation for the British was, at that time, only 250 per month. While US intentions were to double production to 500 per month, even at this rate the request would have taken eight months to fulfil. The large request reflected Arnold's previous over-optimistic assertions of US production capability, as well as Portal and Bomber Command's belief that large-scale bombing raids would instigate an 'airborne second front.' 'My God, what a list,' was Arnold's bewildered response to Freeman's list of production requests.[45]

Had Arnold acceded to the British, the entirety of US bomber production for 1941 would have gone across the Atlantic, leaving nothing for the US, Dutch, Chinese or Russians.[46] This was, of course, unacceptable. It led to a litany of 'helpful' suggestions for aircraft use by Admiral Stark, General Marshall and Admiral Turner, among others, who all opposed strategic bombing and argued heavy bomber production would affect

43 Furse, *Freeman*, 214.

44 Harriman, W. Averell and Abel, Elie, *Special Envoy to Churchill and Stalin, 1941–1946* (New York: Random House), 1975, 15.

45 Wilson, Theodore A., *The First Summit; Roosevelt and Churchill at Placentia Bay 1941*. Boston: Houghton Mifflin, 1969, 152.

46 Arnold, *Global Mission*, 253.

numbers of tanks and ships that could be built.[47] In their post-conference report to Cabinet, the British COS noted, 'a most distressing revelation is the reduction in heavy bomber and Catalina allocation to us.'[48] Despite this disappointment, there was a clear path forward for the RAF. When Freeman left the conference on 11 August 1941, he remarked to Arnold, 'When Portal comes over, I am going to insist that he sees just two people; the President and you.'[49] Portal and Arnold would become the centralised point of contact for British aircraft requests, later formalised through the Arnold–Portal Agreement.

The British wasted no time in simplifying their request process to the US. On 3 September 1941, Portal wrote to Arnold to explain how American concerns would be alleviated. He outlined the primary issues the US had, in that requests came from various channels, these requests were sometimes in conflict, and that there was sometimes no indication of strategic priority given.[50] From that point on, the British Supply Council would be responsible for co-ordinating needs and would then forward these requests to the Joint Staff Mission in Washington D.C., who would represent to the Navy and War Departments the strategic aspects of British materiel requirements. Portal went on to assure Arnold that he would personally address any questions Arnold had regarding strategic needs and for Arnold to let him know at once if the system presented any difficulties.[51]

Portal knew the vital importance of Arnold's role in supplying the RAF, and desperately needed to stay in his good graces because Arnold was in an increasingly unenviable position, juggling many competing priorities. While Arnold wanted to develop his own forces, he also understood the vital importance of the European theatre of operations, where the war was being fought. Moreover, though Arnold was broadly supportive of the British 'General Strategy Review' presented at ARGENTIA, the other US JCS members had significant doubts. The British strategic approach hinged on the effectiveness of strategic bombing to destroy not only the Nazi war machine, but also 'the economy that feeds it, the morale which sustains it,

---

47 TNA/AIR 8/591, Freeman's notes 10 August 1941.
48 Richardson, Charles, *From Churchill's Secret Circle to the BBC: The Biography of Lieutenant General Sir Ian Jacob*, London: Brassey's, 1991, 78.
49 Huston, *American Airpower*, 123.
50 Portal to Arnold, 3 September 1941, AP.
51 Ibid.

the supplies which nourish it … and the hopes of victory which inspire it.'[52] It seemed far-fetched to some. This approach ignored the military defeat of Germany and even the invasion of the European continent, reflecting the British military position accurately but running contrary to US thoughts of total victory. Only through full US participation in the war would total victory become possible.

Both General Marshall and Admiral Stark doubted Germany could be defeated without a reinvasion of the European mainland.[53] These concerns were explicitly stated in the US JCS response to the British Strategy Review, sent to London seven weeks after the conference. The covering letter stated, 'It should be recognised as an almost invariable rule that wars cannot be finally won without the use of land armies.'[54]

Further complicating Arnold's thinking was Roosevelt's intention to support the Russians through Lend-Lease, following Hitler's summer incursion to the east. The Russians had requested some $2 billion in materiel aid, and Roosevelt had requested as much as possible to be shipped by 1 October 1941.[55] Needless to say, the allocation had to come from either the build-up of US forces or the materiel allocated to Great Britain. It was a case of robbing Peter to pay Paul, and none of the ravenous appetites would be fully sated, least of all Portal's.

Arnold responded to Portal later that month, sandwiching the headlining bad news with morsels of cold comfort. Arnold opened by applauding the meeting of both the leaders of their respective governments and the CCS, heralding the, 'more complete understanding … of vital interests to both of us.'[56] However, the meat of the note was the news that the British demand for heavy bombers could not yet be met. Arnold lamented America's inability to provide more assistance to Great Britain, describing 'a period of doldrums in heavy bomber production' due to the order not having been placed eighteen months previously.[57] While Arnold did expect US

---

52 British General Strategy Review, 31 July 1941, AP.

53 Pogue, Forrest C., George C. Marshall: Ordeal and Hope 1939–1942, New York: Viking Press, 1963 144; Bercuson, David Jay and Herwig, Holger H. *One Christmas in Washington: Churchill and Roosevelt Forge the Grand Alliance*. Toronto: McArthur, 2005, 26.

54 Wilson, *The First Summit*, 217.

55 Pogue, *Ordeal and Hope*, 72.

56 Arnold to Portal, 23 September 1941, AP.

57 Ibid.

bomber production to exceed 500 per month by spring 1942, only half of that production was currently allocated to Britain. Portal's desired force of 4,000 heavy bombers was slipping away. Arnold's news arrived at possibly the most difficult point in Portal's tenure as Chief of Air Staff.

On 3 September 1941, Portal received a missive from Churchill demanding his response to the damning Butt Report. 'This is a very serious paper, and seems to require your most urgent attention,' the Prime Minister warned.[58] The report, presented to Churchill by his scientific advisor, Lord Cherwell, cast significant doubt on the RAF's bombing effectiveness during summer 1941. In particular, it described how 'two-thirds of the crews believed they had found their targets whereas actually one-fifth had actually dropped their bombs within five miles thereof.'[59] The Butt Report went on to depict adverse weather effects that exacerbated extremely poor results in the Ruhr, where only one in ten crews had dropped its bombs within 5 miles of the target. Portal was already under extreme pressure from the Prime Minister to improve Bomber Command numbers, both to up the ante against Germany strategically and to begin to answer Stalin's calls for a Second Front in Europe. Portal now had a qualitative as well as a quantitative bombing problem to solve. Events at Pearl Harbor would conspire to exacerbate British difficulties in 1942.

On 7 December 1941, Japan attacked Pearl Harbor, destroying a significant portion of the US Navy, any lingering hopes Americans harboured of neutrality, and all previous agreements regarding the distribution of US-produced war materiel. Churchill was worried. Though Britain was very keen to see America join the war, the manner of the Japanese attack outraged the American public, who demanded an immediate response focused in the Pacific. In Churchill's mind, the attack threatened the 'Europe First' policy, agreed in March 1941 following a series of secret discussions in Washington D.C.[60]

In fact, Churchill need not have been concerned about this fundamental aspect of Allied strategy moving forward. Six months before the clandestine discussions in Washington, Admiral Harold Stark, Chief of Naval Operations, had spent the week considering America's

---

58 Churchill to Portal, 3 September 1941, Sir Charles Portal Papers, Archive 1, Folder 3, Minute 24 Christ Church College, Oxford, herein after referred to as CC. CC/1/3/24.
59 Ibid.
60 Slessor, John Cotesworth, *The Central Blue; Recollections and Reflections,* London: Cassell, 1956, 344.

strategic options moving forward, and concluded 'Europe First' was the only sure way to deliver American long-term security. In his co-called 'Plan Dog' memorandum, Stark explained, 'If Britain wins decisively against Germany, we could win everywhere; but ... if she loses the problem confronting us would be very great; and while we may not *lose everywhere*, we might, possibly, not *win anywhere*.'[61] Stark convinced Marshall of the veracity of his analysis, then persuaded the President to start the talks leading to the agreement of 'Europe First', long before America joined the war.

This fundamental aspect of strategy was not at question during ARCADIA; the US JCS were united in support for it. This would change once Stark was replaced by Admiral Ernest King in March 1942. However, the allocation of war materiel could not stand now that America was a combatant, which put Portal firmly in the crosshairs. Churchill determined to resolve matters as soon as possible. 'I have formed the conviction that it is my duty to visit Washington without delay, provided such a course is agreeable to President Roosevelt, as I have little doubt it will be,' Churchill wrote to the King.[62] Following the King's assent, Churchill requested to Roosevelt that they meet in person as soon as possible. Roosevelt, in a diplomatic attempt to decline, expressed his worries about the dangers of the return journey. Churchill, undeterred, pressed his case that he, and his military entourage, visit the White House for Christmas.

The First Washington Conference, code-named ARCADIA, yielded affirmation of the 'Europe First' strategy but left Marshall worried about some of the finer details of British strategy. George Marshall was a firm believer in a head-on military approach, suspicious of both the strategic bombing of Germany and the British desire to attack the Axis powers in North Africa and the Mediterranean. Concerned about how the respective military leaders would co-operate, Marshall arranged the first meeting of the respective militaries to be between Portal and Arnold, two men who already knew and liked one another. The two met while Roosevelt and Churchill were enjoying the first of many dinners together, on 22 December 1941.

61 Simpson, B. Mitchell, *Admiral Harold R. Stark: Architect of Victory, 1939–1945*. 1st ed. Columbia, S.C.: University of South Carolina Press, 1989, 68.
62 Churchill, *The Grand Alliance*, 1951, 475.

As Marshall had hoped, the meeting between the air chiefs was extremely productive.[63] Portal described the huge advantages Britain would gain if the whole North African shore and the Mediterranean could be controlled. This was an area of concern for some American planners, who considered North Africa to be a British Imperial campaign outside the national interest of the United States. However, Portal explained it would reduce shipping routes from the colonies from 12,000 to 3,000 miles, and thus improve British logistics enormously.[64] Portal's gambit may have paid off, as Arnold became this strategy's strongest American advocate.

Portal in turn agreed in principle to the US War Department's general intention to prepare a strategic plan, assess the forces necessary to implement it, discuss available forces and facilities, and allocate appropriately the forces and facilities to enact the plan. Noting Bomber Command's gap to full strength, he stated that he 'looked forward to the time when US bombers could be stationed in England to help out their bombing effort.'[65] The following day Roosevelt agreed with Churchill that American bombers would begin to operate from England as soon as possible. Later in the evening, Portal asked Arnold what this meant in terms of timing and numbers. Arnold responded he would send at least one group by March, as it was the smallest self-sustaining unit.[66] On Christmas Eve Arnold stated, during a meeting of the CCS Committee, that American heavy bombers would from then on be manned by American pilots, and that some would go as units. Portal queried the points, which were not in alignment with the agreement. Arnold assured Portal that Britain would not be denied any

---

63 *One Christmas in Washington* characterizes this meeting as having antagonised Arnold and been a precursor for further acrimony. There is no indication in either *Global Mission* nor in Arnold's own notes from the meeting that he felt this way. Moreover, the conference talks that took place at ARCADIA were much less adversarial than presented, largely because the Combined Staffs' two most acerbic members had not yet attained a full seat at the table. Ernest King was not yet CNO and General Alan Brooke had been left behind in London, having just taken over from General Sir John Dill as Chief of the Imperial General Staff.

64 United States Department of State, *Foreign Relations of the United States: The Conferences at Washington, 1941–1942, and Casablanca, 1943*, Washington, D.C.: US Government Printing Office, 1941–1943, 223; Arnold, *Global Mission*, 277.

65 US DoS, *The Conferences at Washington*, 223–224.

66 Arnold, *Global Mission*, 278.

heavy bombers previously agreed to. However, as the Conference advanced so too did world events.[67]

While Britain and America formalised the Grand Alliance, Japan seized Wake Island, Hong Kong and Manila. Their forces also landed in Borneo, Mindanao, Luzon and the Dutch East Indies.[68] Despite this Pacific onslaught, the Europe First strategy endured, and other fundamental arrangements were made. Particularly important was the formation of the CCS Committee as the central body to decide upon UK–US strategy during the war. Portal's part in this was key, as Marshall favoured unity of command in each theatre and had not given thought to the co-ordination of broader strategy. Portal opined, 'The experience in London has been that the highest authority is the only one that can decide as to allocation of forces; and when the allocation is decided upon, the directive has been formulated, and the forces allotted, everything else runs smoothly.'[69] Stated logically and concisely, Portal's argument won out. Only at the highest level could logistical priority between theatres of operation be determined. By the end of ARCADIA, Portal had also arrived at a new agreement for the allocation of aircraft from US industry, the first Arnold–Portal Agreement. The shifting tides of the Pacific balance of power during spring 1942 would, however, cause Arnold to have a fundamental rethink.

To the British in Washington, led by Sir John Dill, it was apparent from early March 1942 that the Arnold–Portal arrangements were unlikely to survive. General Arnold was under significant pressure for several reasons. First was America's inability to meet Roosevelt's ambitious production target of 60,000 aircraft in 1942. Second was the deteriorating situation in the Pacific that had to be stopped, and in which air power must play a key role. Third was the presidential desire, encouraged by Arnold, to man American planes with American pilots. Last, but by no means least, was the increasing demand for Lend-Lease materiel from Russia, China, and the British Dominions. Even within the Arnold–Portal Agreement, Britain and America interpreted the numbers differently.

Churchill laid out the British position, in a speech prepared by Portal, in his opening address to Arnold during his second visit to the UK in May 1942. Britain's overriding consideration was, 'to bring into action against

---

67 US DoS, *The Conferences at Washington*, 255–256.
68 Buell, Thomas B., *Master of Sea Power: A Biography of Fleet Admiral Ernest J. King*. 1st ed. Boston: Little, Brown, 1980, 163.
69 US DoS, *The Conferences at Washington*, 272.

the enemy as quickly as possible in the appropriate theatre the greatest strength in fully trained air forces that is possible with the combined aircraft production, trained manpower and shipping available to the United Nations.'[70] While Churchill conceded, 'as many United States aircraft as possible, operated by U.S. crews, should take their place in active theatres at the earliest possible moment,' this was conditional on both the opening provision and limited by the fact that some of the British and Dominion Air Forces could only be equipped from US production.[71] The increasingly reified American position, which had been overtly stated by Roosevelt to Churchill, was that American crews were going to be 'assigned to American-made planes far more greatly than at present.'[72] Churchill had, slightly peevishly, asked Roosevelt how the 100 squadrons currently planned to operate American aircraft would be replaced.[73] There was an impasse at the top level, and it was the job of Portal and Arnold to find a compromise the two countries' leaders would accept.

Prior to his visit to Great Britain, Arnold had reduced the allocation of aircraft to Britain in 1942 from 5,500 to 1,000. A compromise was reached during the Conference whereby the number rose back up to around 2,500.[74] Neither Arnold nor Portal found themselves in an ideal position. Arnold had given ground, and more of the capacity of the Army Air Forces (AAF) would now go to Great Britain, forestalling the growth of Arnold's organic forces, and the Eighth Air Force in Britain. Portal's position was equally difficult, since Churchill was adamant in his adherence to the principle of attacking Germany as heavily as possible regardless of who was flying the aircraft. Portal was taking flak from below, too. His newly installed Bomber Command chief, Arthur Harris, was desperately trying to build up his force for massed attacks on German industrial cities.

Britain did enjoy a notable success in this field during Arnold's sojourn in England. On the evening of 30 May 1942, while Arnold dined with Churchill, Portal, Eisenhower and others at Chequers, Bomber Command was executing the largest bombing raid in history. Harris had planned the first 'thousand-aircraft raid' attack on the German city of Cologne. Arnold

---

70 Arnold-Towers Conference, Draft for Opening Speech, 22 May 1942, CC/1/3/35a.

71 Ibid.

72 Kimball, Warren F., *Churchill and Roosevelt, Volume 3: The Complete Correspondence – Three Volumes*. Princeton, N.J.: Princeton University Press, 2015, 486–487.

73 Ibid., 487–488.

74 Portal to Churchill, 16 June 1942, CC/1/3/35d.

described his tendency, with uncanny luck, to be present at historical turning points. On this case he considered his luck to have been mixed.[75] Arnold spent the evening attempting to convince Portal et al of the superiority of US doctrine, which favoured high-altitude precision daylight bombing, but his timing could not have been more ironic. The RAF's raid on Cologne was a fantastic success. Only 39 aircraft were lost, an acceptable loss rate from the initial 1,047 aircraft taking part. Arnold later noted, 'Of all the moments in history when I might have tried to sell Mr Churchill and his RAF advisors on the future of American precision bombardment by daylight, I had picked the night when they were selling their own kind of bombardment to the world.'[76] This raid may have left an indelible impression on Arnold as, prior to his return to the United States, he sent the following message to Roosevelt. 'England is the place to win the war. Get planes and troops over here as soon as possible.'[77]

Arnold was under pressure from both Churchill and Roosevelt to deliver American bombs, flown on American planes and piloted by American pilots, but he reached too far too soon. Upon his return stateside, Arnold sent a note to Churchill, promising, 'We will be fighting with you on July 4th.'[78] Unwise though it was to make such a protestation, Arnold felt he had little choice but to live up to it as best he could. What resulted was an inglorious beginning to the Combined Bomber Offensive.

On 28 June 1942, Arnold directed General Carl Spaatz, commander of the Eighth Air Force in England, to begin combat operations on Independence Day.[79] Both Spaatz and his bomber chief, General Ira Eaker, protested in the strongest terms, because the Eighth Air Force had no planes and was not ready to join the fight in earnest. These views were not new, as Spaatz had given repeated warnings against premature combat operations during his final briefings before crossing the Atlantic.[80] Arnold, however, would not

---

75 Arnold, *Global Mission*, 315.

76 Coffey, Thomas M., HAP: *The Story of the U.S. Air Force and the Man Who Built It*, General Henry 'Hap' Arnold, New York: Viking Press, 1982, 275.

77 Arnold, *Global Mission*, 318; Overy, R.J., *The Bombing War: Europe 1939–1945*, London: Penguin, 2013, 296.

78 Huston, *American Airpower*, 165.

79 Parton, James and Air Force Historical Foundation, *'Air Force Spoken Here': General Ira Eaker and the Command of the Air.* 1st ed. Bethesda, M.D.: Adler & Adler, 1986, 166.

80 Mets, David R., *Master of Airpower: General Carl A. Spaatz.* Novato, C.A.: Presidio Press, 1988, 132.

relent because of his promise to Churchill, and because the AAF needed a publicity success.

The US Navy air arm had won the Battle of Midway, but the AAF was still being called into question for its actions at Pearl Harbor and Clark Field in the Philippines.[81] Portal agreed to loan the Eighth Air Force six British twin-engine Douglas A-20s and even had them repainted in American colours. He also provided a British fighter escort, but the raid, an attack on Dutch airfields, was an operational failure. At its end eight Americans were missing, including seven dead, and four of the six bombers had dropped their bombs miles from the target area.[82] Eaker and Spaatz considered the mission a debacle, but it did receive positive press on both sides of the Atlantic, the *Express* headlining, 'U.S. Bombers in Action – First Raid from England' and the *Washington Post* [83]stating, 'Yanks Raid Nazis in Holland.' Regardless, the raid showed that, despite the differences in bombing doctrine, Portal was willing to go above and beyond to try and see the American bombing effort succeed.

Portal lent immediate support as the Eighth Air Force tried to develop its nascent capabilities, despite his reservations about the viability of daylight bombing. Portal had 75 aerodromes allocated to the Eighth Air Force, and a total of 127 installations.[84] There was a three-phased approach to the Eighth Air Force's operational build-up, the first of which involved short-range raids with British fighter escort. The first B-17 raid, with a dozen aircraft, took place on 17 August 1942. As for the eighteen other raids the Eighth Air Force completed in 1942, all were accompanied by RAF fighters acting as escort. This first mission was safeguarded by no fewer than seventy-five RAF aircraft, some flown by Eagle Squadron American pilots. The fighter pilots were instructed to 'guard those B-17s with your lives.'[85] Portal was doing his best to ensure the political and military success of the American contingent with materiel support. He was

---

81 Davis, Richard G., United States. Air Force. Office of Air Force History, A.F.C.H.O., and Afcho. *Carl A. Spaatz and the Air War in Europe.* General Histories. Washington, D.C.: Office of Air Force History, US Air Force, 1993, 90.

82 Parton, *Eaker*, 166–167.

83 Ibid., 167.

84 Copp, DeWitt S., *Forged in Fire: Strategy and Decisions in the Air War over Europe, 1940–45.* Garden City, N.Y.: Doubleday, 1982, 257.

85 Copp, *Forged in Fire*, 308.

keen to back their efforts in public, small though they may have been in comparison to Bomber Command. Privately, he maintained reservations.

By the end of October, the Eighth Air Force had only flown eleven missions, and Churchill queried the efforts. Portal shared some of Churchill's doubts, but expressed logically, 'I do not think we can decide what to do until we have balanced the probability of success, which may not be very high but it is not negligible, against the results of success if it is achieved.' He continued, 'If success could only amount to a tour de force having no real military value, I should be entirely with you in trying to ride the Americans off the attempt altogether. Actually, however, success would have tremendous consequences.'[86] Portal was also diplomatically aware to note that 'premature opposition to their plan may well lead their higher authorities to seek other theatres where the virtues of day bombing might be better appreciated.'[87] This last point was a clear warning regarding American priorities and the threat that aircraft could easily be redirected to the Pacific instead of Europe. One of the other factors Portal mentioned for the low tonnage of American bombs, along with adverse weather, was the reallocation of aircraft to the proposed attack on North Africa: Operation TORCH. This was causing Arnold some angst across the Atlantic.

When Admiral Harold Stark resigned as CNO in March 1942, and Ernest King acceded, opinion on the Europe First strategy among the US JCS switched instantly from unanimous to divided. King was a 'Pacific First' man, unsurprising given the disposition of the US Navy. General Marshall favoured Europe First, but strongly believed in a continental invasion of France in 1942: Operation SLEDGEHAMMER. When this was postponed, and replaced with an Allied thrust in North Africa, Marshall's enthusiasm evaporated. For support in the North Africa endeavours, Portal and the British relied on General Arnold. He did not disappoint, despite his reservations about TORCH, which reallocated resources from his build-up for the strategic attack on Germany. As Spaatz commented in an Eighth Air Force Commanders' Meeting on 10 November 1942, 'What is left of the Eighth Air Force after the impact of TORCH? We find we haven't much left.'[88] Nevertheless, Arnold encouraged Spaatz to continue the Eighth Air Force's offensive operations as far as practicably possible while providing

---

86 Portal to Churchill 7 November 1942, CC/1/3/26.
87 Ibid.
88 Davis, *Spaatz*, 109.

full support to TORCH. Arnold bemoaned the dispersion of his forces, complaining to Harry Hopkins that it had sapped AWPD/1 (the production numbers needed to win the war). He considered its reinstitution vital for attacking enemy number one: Germany.[89]

Despite the impact of TORCH, Arnold primarily laid the problems of the Eighth Air Force's slow build-up on the Pacific theatre. He suggested to Marshall that the US 'should be moving planes from the Pacific to the North African and European theatres' in the immediate aftermath of the Guadalcanal invasion in August 1942.[90] By September, Arnold had adopted Portal's position that, 'TORCH should be recognised as the beginning of the offensive against Germany and that it should be accepted as a "basic principle" that operations both in the Middle East and from the United Kingdom were complementary to TORCH.'[91] He put the matter beyond any doubt in a paper stating, 'No diversion of air forces be made to other areas except those necessary to secure our essential positions elsewhere, until the needs for TORCH, the Middle East and the United Kingdom are met.'[92] All objections from Admiral King were stonewalled, which may have contributed to King describing Arnold rather ungraciously as a 'yes man for Marshall.'[93] In fact, Arnold was playing Portal's and not Marshall's tune.

The first combined land offensive against Axis forces was launched on 8 November 1942, when British and American forces landed on the North African coast. Eight days later, Arnold underlined his strategic views in a memo entitled, 'Strategic Policy for 1943.' Arnold, mistrustful of potential results in North Africa, pointed out that 'Allied successes in North Africa, combined with two indecisive campaigns in Russia and aerial bombardment from the United Kingdom, had considerably weakened the German position and presented an opportunity which might not again exist. The only way they could maintain it under existing conditions was by intensive bombing both from the United Kingdom and from the newly acquired African bases.'[94] Importantly, this paper did not rule out a continental invasion in 1943 (Operation ROUNDUP), something the other US JCS were worried about.

---

89 Ibid., 112.
90 Huston, *American Airpower*, 202.
91 Hayes, Grace P., *The History of the Joint Chiefs of Staff in World War II: The War against Japan*. Annapolis: Naval Institute Press, 1981, 185.
92 Hayes, *Joint Chiefs*, 185.
93 Buell, *King*, 404.
94 Hayes, *Joint Chiefs*, 257.

Arnold's argument about the linkage of the North African theatre with the liberation of France directly mirrored the British COS' view. It again provided a common (though certainly not unanimous) frame of strategic reference ahead of the January 1943 Combined Chiefs meeting at CASABLANCA.

Portal and Arnold set out their respective strategic stalls in written form long before CASABLANCA began. Portal presented his paper to the British COS on 5 October 1942, suggesting three potential ways of winning against Germany. COA A was to build up air, land and sea forces to invade the Continent and defeat the German Army before German industry and economic power had been broken. COA B involved the build-up of a massive bomber force to shatter German industry and economic power, then sending in the Army to restore order. COA C was an amalgam of the two, which Portal considered indecisive at that time.[95] In the end, Portal and Brooke agreed to take a strategy to CASABLANCA that contained elements of all three proposed strategies. Arnold was still dead set on strategic bombing, and complained to Harry Hopkins that air assets had been frittered away to different theatres, scuppering AWPD/1's chance of success.[96] The subsequent air plan, AWPD/42, once more marginalised the Pacific theatre, allocating 2,225 Army Air Forces heavy bombers to the European theatre to work in tandem with the RAF's Bomber Command.

The opening topic of discussion at the first CCS Meeting at CASABLANCA on 14 January 1943 was the allocation of resources between theatres. Admiral King argued only 15 per cent of total resources were currently being used in the Pacific, which was insufficient.[97] The wily Portal managed to broker an agreement whereby the minimum requirements for the war in Japan were specified, and all the remainder of the production programme went to Europe. He explained this to British colleagues, 'We are in the position of a testator who wishes to leave the bulk of his fortune to his mistress. He must, however, leave something to his wife and the problem is how little

---

95 Butler, James Ramsay Montagu, Gwyer, J.M.A., Ehrman, John and Howard, Michael, *Grand Strategy: History of the Second World War Vol IV*; United Kingdom Military Series. London: H.M. Stationery Office, 1956, 198–200; Richards, Denis, *Portal of Hungerford: The Life of Marshal of the Royal Air Force, Viscount Portal of Hungerford, KG, GCB, OM, DSO, MC*. New York, N.Y.: Holmes & Meier, 1977, 253–254.

96 Davis, *Spaatz*, 112.

97 Alanbrooke Papers, King's College London (hereafter referred to as KCL/AB), KCL/AB/6/1/1, 170.

in decency he can set apart for her.'[98] Admiral King was dissatisfied, but this was not an uncommon situation, as the Pacific theatre was a secondary consideration for both political leaders and all the other CCS Committee members. With Europe firmly established as the priority, there remained two major areas of discussion to resolve. The first was between the air chiefs and Churchill, the second between the UK and US.

Churchill remained sceptical about American daylight bombing, despite attempts by Portal and the Secretary of State for Air Archie Sinclair to convince him otherwise. Portal and Arnold arranged for Ira Eaker to argue the case for daylight bombing with Churchill. Eaker was a charismatic speaker and Spaatz often used him to deal with the press. Eaker presented Churchill with a single page memo extolling the advantages of 'round-the-clock bombing,' a phrase Churchill found appealing, perhaps considering it for use in a speech.[99] Churchill generously described Eaker as having argued his case with skill and tenacity: 'Young man, you have not convinced me you are right, but you have persuaded me that you should have further opportunity to prove your contention.'[100] The Prime Minister removed his objections to America's daylight bombing with the B-17 Flying Fortresses, and the Casablanca Directive at the end of the Conference marked the beginning of the formal Combined Bomber Offensive.[101] With this matter settled, what remained was the resolution of American and British strategic views on how far to take the war in the Mediterranean. This rumbled on through 1943, causing considerable transatlantic acrimony.

Arnold's views regarding the Mediterranean War vacillated considerably. Having argued that TORCH would contribute to Germany's overall military destruction in his 'Strategic Policy for 1943' paper, he had re-joined Marshall in uncertainty by CASABLANCA. Marshall still favoured the invasion of France as the sole route to victory and knew that an extended campaign into Italy would remove the possibility of this happening in 1943. The British recommendation for follow-on action was Operation HUSKY, the capture of Sicily. Arnold queried whether an attack on Sicily would be 'a means to an end or an end in itself, and what relation such an attack would have

---

98 Pogue, Forrest C., Bradley, Omar Nelson, and Brédli, Omar, *George C. Marshall: Organizer of Victory, 1943–1945*. New York: Penguin Books, 1993, 27.

99 Parton, *Eaker*, 221; Overy, *The Bombing War*, 306.

100 Parton, *Eaker*, 221.

101 Churchill, Winston S., *The Second World War, Vol. IV: The Hinge of Fate*, The Educational Book Company Ltd: London, 1951, 527.

on the whole strategic conception.'[102] Portal pointed out the urgency of the action since, if the Germans were to be able to reinforce the island strongly during the year, the attack would become much more difficult. By contrast, a near future attack would make it hard for the Axis to retake Sicily.[103]

Agreement was reached on HUSKY, but a further incursion into Italy, that threatened any possibility of ROUNDUP in 1943, was beyond even Portal's powers of persuasion. One further decision made at CASABLANCA changed the character of the Arnold–Portal relationship in 1943. Portal was appointed the de facto commander of the Combined Bomber Offensive, in charge of both the Eighth Air Force and RAF's Bomber Command. This organisational change had repercussions throughout the year.

Having previously privately critiqued the Eighth Air Force, Portal became, in 1943, its strongest public advocate. Being made responsible for the CBO, Portal naturally came to better comprehend the problems Eaker was having in building up his forces. Portal both understood the frustrations and shared in their successes throughout the year, while Arnold felt isolated and out of touch across the Atlantic. In particular, Portal was the strongest defender of the CBO, and the Eighth Air Force specifically, at the conferences in Washington, Quebec and Cairo that took place during the remainder of 1943. Arnold was absent from TRIDENT, because he was hospitalised following his second heart attack.[104] The 'Eaker Plan' was approved at TRIDENT, and Portal declared himself, 'one hundred percent behind the plan.'[105] This was a far cry from his sceptical views of daylight bombing in 1942. Both Eaker and Portal were upbeat about the progress of the Eighth Air Force, but for Arnold it would be a summer and autumn of discontent.

In early summer 1943, Hap Arnold was fighting grave personal health issues and had lost direct control of his bomber force in England. It is unclear which caused him greater frustration but, as summer neared, he became additionally irked by the direction of Allied strategy in Europe. The 'British have no intention of invading Northern Europe,' he asserted in an internal memo on 1 May 1943.[106] Arnold's natural inclinations toward Anglophobia were returning, though Portal may have lessened them

---

102 KCL/AB/6/1/1, 210.

103 Ibid., 213.

104 The first occurred in March 1943.

105 Parton, *Eaker*, 262–263; Copp, *Forged in Fire*, 399.

106 Huston, *American Airpower, Vol. 2*, 20.

somewhat when he took the trouble to visit Arnold in Walter Reed Hospital during the TRIDENT Conference.[107]

Nevertheless, Arnold remained uncomfortable with what he saw as British domination of the direction of Allied strategy. He was frustrated that the North Africa campaign was taking much longer than anticipated to finish. Portal's assertion at TRIDENT that ground forces would be needed to knock Italy out of the war (rather than just air forces) contrasted Arnold's own views.[108] But, through enforced absence, he could not present them and support Marshall, who desperately wanted to build up for the invasion of France. The invasion, now called OVERLORD, was scheduled at TRIDENT for 1 May 1944, much later than Arnold or Marshall wanted, but Portal and Brooke better understood how difficult the operation would be without significantly reducing Germany's available combat power. Detached from the decision-making hub, and despite Portal's kind visit, Arnold's resentment burned, with pressure from all directions in Washington fanning the flames.

Arnold's summer critique of the Eighth Air Force conflicted sharply with Portal's eloquent defence of its performance. When he returned to work in June, Arnold was on the war path. He bluntly wrote to Eaker demanding why, having been given the aircraft and aircrew requested, that Eaker was failing to use them.[109] This was the beginning of a very testy exchange between the two friends. Eaker bit back, not only because many of his crews were new and needed training time, but also because shipping problems had delayed the arrival of ground equipment.[110] Moreover, the Eighth had been steadily increasing its bombing throughout the year. After a series of rebukes, Eaker finished the exchange stating, 'I shall always gladly accept and in the proper spirit, any advice counsel or criticism from you. I do not feel, however, that my past service ... indicates that I am a horse which needs to be ridden with spurs.'[111]

Portal, who was in constant contact with Eaker, grasped the problems (many of which were Arnold's responsibility to resolve), and spoke up for the Eighth and its commander. During the opening meeting of QUADRANT, Portal charitably described the 'extraordinarily effective'

---

107 Arnold, *Global Mission*, 442.

108 Copp, *Forged in Fire*, 398.

109 Copp, *Forged in Fire*, 400.

110 Parton, *Eaker*, 272.

111 Ibid., 276.

daylight bombing.[112] In a cushioned blow directed at Arnold he went on, 'The forces available to the Eighth Air Force have done remarkable work, but the program is behind schedule for reasons, however, which are quite understandable.' Two days later Portal urged that, 'Diversions from the 8th Air Force should be stopped, loans of aircraft ... to other theatres must be returned, and the bomber command of the 8th Air Force must be built up and reinforced to the maximum possible.'[113] While Arnold may have agreed with this statement, it did not stop his written assault, which lasted well into autumn.

During September 1943 Arnold continued to needle Eaker about the absence of mass assaults over Germany; by October, Portal was also in the crosshairs. Arnold complained about, 'Not employing our forces in adequate numbers ... I am pressing Eaker to get a much higher proportion of his force off the ground and put them where they will hurt the enemy.' Arnold's aim, according to Lawrence Kuter, his assistant chief, was to get under Portal's skin.[114] One of Arnold's chief complaints was that Portal's 'thousands of fighters' were being under-utilised.[115] He further railed against the RAF's failure to put long-range tanks on the Spitfire to protect the Eighth Air Force's B-17s. This was a little disingenuous, to say the least. Robert Lovett, Assistant Secretary of War for Air, later observed, 'It was clear from the start that Hap had been making wild statements about what the B-17 could do. It couldn't do everything. It needed a nose turret above everything ... Another thing it needed was fighter escort in deep penetrations ... His hands were tied by his mouth. He said our only need was Flying Fortresses, that's all; very few fighters could keep up with them ... The Messerschmitts had no difficulty at all.'[116]

Arnold had been hoisted on his own petard, but now needed to backtrack. Had he written with any magnanimity, it is likely Portal would have been more receptive to the communiqué. As Arnold had not, Portal rejoindered, calling Arnold's note 'detached' and pointing out that the RAF had fewer than half the number of fighters Arnold thought, adding that in the previous quarter a third of all RAF Fighter Command missions had been flown in direct protection of the Eighth Air Force.[117] Portal was, however, not

---

112 KCL/AB/6/1/3, 413.

113 Huston, *American Airpower Vol. 2*, 32.

114 Parton, *Eaker*, 319.

115 Huston, *American Airpower Vol. 2*, 48.

116 Parton, *Eaker*, 279.

117 Huston, *American Airpower Vol. 2*, 49.

entirely blameless in this exchange; his foresight had been as poor as his opposite number's.

Portal had persistently contended that long-range fighter escort was an impossibility, which may have blinded him to its possibilities. Portal thought the best escort would be another bomber armed with guns instead of bombs. This was manifested in the unfortunate YB-40, a gun-armed and heavily armoured B-17. It was a complete operational failure, as it could not keep up with the other B-17s once the payload had been delivered.[118] Both Arnold and Portal were wrong in their initial assessments, but if Arnold now had the right idea, he was not presenting it in a way Portal considered palatable. Nevertheless, Portal did promise more support for the CBO from Fighter Command, which was duly delivered.

For Arnold's part, he had already realised how overblown his B-17 claims were. In June 1943 Arnold told his deputy, Barney M. Giles, 'You have got to get a fighter to protect our bombers. Whether you use an existing type or have to start from scratch is your problem.'[119] Arnold was, understandably, impatient for results and his lack of control over events caused him to try and wring more assistance from Portal. Arnold did manage to get his message across by having Portal ship three Spitfires to the US to have extra tanks fitted. Within two months, the Spitfires had been returned to the UK, with an extended range of 1,300 miles. In a rare light-hearted note of the period, Arnold quipped to Portal, 'The Spitfires you sent me by ship have landed at London after crossing the Atlantic under their own steam.'[120] Portal was, customarily, sanguine in his judgments and it remains surprising that he did not make a greater attempt to improve long-range fighter escort through this means. It may be that Portal deemed the modification timeframe impossible at such a crucial time, when he wanted to exert maximum pressure on Germany on all fronts.

The urgency of the fighter escort situation was highlighted by the second raid on Schweinfurt on 14 October 1943, during which sixty-four bomber aircraft were lost. This raid, arguably both the high point and low point of Eighth Air Force operations thus far, drew a line under the acerbic period of correspondence between Portal and Arnold. As Arnold summarised, 'In mid-October the weather shut down foggily on Southeast Germany for

---

118 Copp, *Forged in Fire*, 422.
119 Ibid., 413–414.
120 Arnold, *Global Mission*, 495–496.

most of the remainder of the year.'[121] The weather dampened everything, including the argument between the two men. It also conveniently allowed Arnold to ignore the real reason for the halt in operations: unsustainable losses. By the time the weather cleared fully in 1944, Arnold's prayers had been answered with the arrival of the P-51 Mustang.

Two other issues had also been resolved by the end of 1943: one to Portal's satisfaction and the other to Arnold's. Since QUADRANT, Arnold had been seeking to establish a single strategic overall commander for the CBO. Portal, Brooke, and the other British leaders were content with the status quo, which left them in control of the strategic bombing forces that would be vital in preparing the battlefield for OVERLORD.[122] The issue was settled in Cairo in December 1943 when the US abandoned its push. The British did, though, sweeten the pot by giving the top air post in the Mediterranean, vacated by Arthur Tedder, to the US. This allowed Arnold to gain his win by removing Eaker from his command of the Eighth Air Force in Britain. Though Portal attempted a stout defence of Eaker, as he had seen everything Eaker had accomplished at close quarters, Arnold was not to be denied.[123] With most of their issues resolved, Arnold's remaining antipathy evaporated once it was clear command of the bomber forces would pass to Eisenhower. Any jealousy Arnold harboured about Portal's proximity to the war was ameliorated by Portal losing direct command of the bomber forces.

With both men's influences lessened, at least for a time, a quieter period in their correspondence began, though their forces were making more noise than ever over Germany. Once victory in Europe was assured, differences emerged once again.

Portal was keen for the RAF to contribute to the war in the Pacific; Arnold was, at best, indifferent. While Portal felt a moral obligation to assist in Britain's subordinate theatre of operations, Arnold was again keen for the AAF to get the credit for air power's contribution; he didn't want an RAF presence to muddy the waters. Despite Portal's stated intent to have a 'Tiger Force' of 600 and 800 bombers available to attack the Japanese homeland, Marshall and Arnold demurred.[124] Arnold was non-committal, stating RAF

121 Ibid., 495.
122 Davis, Richard G., *Bombing the European Axis Powers: A Historical Digest of the Combined Bomber Offensive 1939–1945*. Maxwell Air Force Base, AL: Air University Press, 2012, 204–205.
123 Davis, *Bombing Axis Powers*, 211.
124 Richards, *Portal*, 278.

participation would depend on 'development of suitable facilities,' though Portal was asked to submit a general estimate of proposed contributions.[125] There were also practical considerations at hand, including a lack of basing for the glut of RAF strategic aircraft. The American delaying tactics broadly reflected what the British had done to ensure the Mediterranean and Italian campaigns went ahead, but now the boot was on the other foot. Though Portal received renewed assurance regarding the RAF's future role against Japan, the abrupt end to hostilities on 2 September 1945 shut the door on this possibility.

The end of the war put a full stop to both men's military careers. Their last meeting occurred during the POTSDAM Conference in July 1945. The day before the conference began, Portal called Arnold's attention to a bet they had made in 1942 during the ARCADIA Conference. Standing together on the roof of the White House, Portal noticed some anti-aircraft guns on nearby rooftops. Arnold opined his worries about the potential bombing of east coast factories. Portal playfully offered Arnold a dollar for every bomb that fell on Washington during the war and, if none fell, Arnold was to pay Portal ten dollars when the war ended. A framed $10 bill with an explanatory note later hung in Portal's house proving the result of the wager.[126]

Portal and Arnold left their respective roles as military leaders within a day of one another on 31 December 1945 and 1 January 1946. Thus ended a long and fruitful relationship, one of co-operation and competition, envy and respect, and the building of enormous military airborne armadas unprecedented in world history. Arnold and Portal were fuelled by a joint desire to defeat the Axis powers, and to see air power proven as a decisive military instrument, though for different reasons. In this last endeavour Arnold was, at last, successful. The advent of the atomic weapon provided, for Arnold, the final proof of the legitimacy he had long sought for the USAAF, though he retired before service independence was achieved. Arnold left active service to retire to his farm in California. A mere eleven days after leaving the military, Portal was asked to serve once more, as head of what would become the British Atomic Energy Agency. Though Portal had an open invitation to visit California following Arnold's retirement, his new duties kept him busy, and he was unable to make the long trip before Arnold died in 1950.

---

125 Huston, *American Airpower*, 194.
126 Richards, *Portal*, 249.

Chapter 7

Portal and Harris

*The fighters are our salvation but the bombers alone provide
the means of victory.*
Winston Spencer Churchill (1940)

When they first met at Worthy Down as fellow squadron commanders in the 1920s, Portal and Harris quickly developed a healthy mutual respect. The two men laboured separately in the corridors of the Air Ministry during the 1930s, as they endeavoured to save the RAF from the scheming of the other services. However, it was only once Portal was appointed head of Bomber Command in April 1940 that the two men really worked closely together. Harris was Portal's direct subordinate, in charge of No. 5 Group. During this short six months the two men developed parallel views about bombing and military strategy, the beginning of a long and close working relationship lasting right until the end of the war. From March 1942, Harris was Air Officer Commanding in Chief of Bomber Command, directly responsible to Portal, Chief of the Air Staff, for the execution of the bombing war. Though Harris could be stubborn and occasionally petulant, he was Britain's foremost expert on bombing, a true pioneer in the art and science of an underdeveloped military capability.

Arthur Travers Harris was born on 13 April 1892 in Cheltenham. His father was a civil servant, working in India. The Harris family had a broad military stripe running through it, with the majority of Harris's uncles being colonels of one regiment or another. His father, excluded from the military due to extreme deafness, nevertheless chose a life of service in the ailing British Empire. Arthur returned to the UK aged only five, to begin his formal education. It was not 'the done thing' for a family of the Harrises' social level to have their child schooled in India. Early separation from his parents imbued young Arthur with an adventurous streak, evidenced by his decision to fly the nest at a young age.[1]

Harris's father retired in 1909 and the threesome were briefly reunited. Harris, though, had wanderlust and, inspired by a play he saw during his last year at school, decided to travel to Rhodesia and seek his fortune. His father was distinctly unamused that Harris had turned down a place at the RMA Woolwich, but generously paid Arthur's passage out. Aged just seventeen, Harris was setting out to make his own life, on his own terms, self-reliant and thoroughly determined.

Following a five-week voyage and three months of language training at the British South Africa Company's Premier Estate, Harris sought work. He took on a number of jobs in those first three years in Rhodesia: building a house for a farmer, working on agricultural and livestock farms, growing tobacco, and going on shooting expeditions to supply meat to miners. Having dogsbodied his way around Rhodesia, and following a tip from a friend, Arthur found a permanent position as a farm manager outside Salisbury. The farm owners, the Crofton Townsends, left Harris in charge of the farm when they returned to Dublin for a year in 1914. Still only twenty-one, Harris had to demonstrate the resourcefulness to run a small business. He could shoot, was a mechanic, and could negotiate, cook, and cope with the unexpected. Harris was a boon to the Crofton Townsends. They were, therefore, understandably perturbed to receive a telegram in August informing them that they needed to return to Rhodesia because Arthur was joining up.[2] Harris had heard the call to service.[3]

Amidst a stampede of young idealists, Harris took up one of the two remaining spots in the 1st Rhodesian Regiment, as the regimental bugler. The second spot was for a machine-gunner, but Harris singularly failed to persuade the adjutant he could tell one end of a machine gun from the other! The bugle did not last long either as, 'I must admit that I got fed up with the thing banging around my knees, so I buried it in the end in the trenches outside Swakopmund – after all, they were never used in serious

1 Saward, Dudley, *Bomber Harris: The Story of Marshal of the Royal Air Force, Sir Arthur Harris ...* 1st ed. in the USA ed. Garden City, N.Y.: Doubleday, 1985, 3–6.

2 Probert, Henry, *Bomber Harris: His Life and times: The Biography of Marshal of the Royal Air Force Sir Arthur Harris, the Wartime Chief of Bomber Command.* London: Greenhill, 2006, 31.

3 Saward, *Bomber Harris,* 8–9.

warfare.'[4] Harris and the new cohort were given rudimentary training in drill, then let loose with five live rounds and proceeded on their first active duty in the British military. It was an underwhelming experience.

Though Harris was involved in a brief skirmish on 26 April 1915, his principal recollection of his time as an infantryman was of marching. 'And how we marched! We marched and we marched and we marched, and, God knows, as far as I was concerned, I'd already marched too far.'[5] The combination of African heat rations of biscuits and bully beef, and the endless marching, left an indelible impression on Harris, who later stated, 'To this day I never walk a step if I can get any sort of vehicle to carry me.'[6] The experience was not a total loss though, as Harris did observe aerial bombardment for the first time.

There was only one German aircraft in South-West Africa and, rather serendipitously, it chose Harris's regiment as its target. The aircraft dropped artillery shells on them, to little effect, but Harris never forgot the experience.[7] Once the Germans were ousted from the region, Harris had the option to return to the farm, but decided to travel to England, amid a worsening European situation. Harris was determined to go to war, but preferably not on foot.

Using the nepotistic but invaluable contact of one of the surfeit of colonels in his extended family, Harris was able to circumvent the 6,000-man waiting list and join the Royal Flying Corps. Following successful completion of flying training in January 1916, Harris was sent to No. 39 Squadron, RAF Northolt, charged with defending London against the Zeppelin attacks. This required night flying, for which there was no formal training. The hazards of this activity were highlighted on Harris's first night at Northolt, when the commanding officer crashed on take-off and was promptly killed.[8] Harris, following his own scare, decided to teach himself to night fly by taking off in the evenings and landing repeatedly as it got darker and darker. Once the assets of No. 39 Squadron were concentrated at Hornchurch, Harris, the new training officer, rolled out his ideas about practise night flying to his new flight. These early experiences cemented the

---

4 Ibid., 9.

5 Ibid., 10.

6 Harris, Arthur Travers, *Bomber Offensive*, London: Novato, CA: Greenhill; Presidio Press, 1990, 16.

7 Probert, *Bomber Harris*, 35.

8 Saward, *Bomber Harris*, 14–15.

value of proper training in Harris's mind, and sowed the seeds about night flying's wartime potential.

Following the war, Harris was awarded a permanent commission as a major. By 1922, he was a squadron commander, with No. 45 Troop Carrying Squadron in Mesopotamia, aiding in the conduct of Air Control in the British Empire. The squadron was equipped with Vickers Vernon aircraft, which Harris quickly realised were well-suited to bombing. In fact, the Vernon had significantly more lift capacity than the chosen theatre bomber, the DH.9A.[9] Harris and his trusty flight commanders, Saundby and Cochrane, converted the Vernons into long-range heavy bombers (of the day) by sawing a sighting hole in the nose of the aircraft and making their own bomb racks.[10] The bomb aimer would lie prone and watch the target approaching, using an automatic release mechanism fashioned from shock absorber cord and a trigger, to release the load.

Harris also pondered the morale impact of night flying on the superstitious locals. He began training the squadron in night flying, discovering that targeting was greatly aided by marker bombs, delivered by the best crew in the squadron.[11] In short order, Harris was able to significantly improve bombing accuracy. He continued to apply his acumen for problem solving and innovation to improving aerial bombing during the interwar period.

Following several commands and a stint at staff college, Harris was posted to the Air Ministry in 1934, where he was instrumental in gradually altering Britain's future bomber requirements. Economic necessity had undermined any revolutionary progress, with the largest bomber specifications in 1934 being medium-range Whitleys, Hampdens and Wellingtons. As the Nazi shadow grew, Harris's more ambitious ideas began to permeate the Air Ministry, and notions of a strategic bomber became the subject of serious discussion. A strategy of attacking Germany from home bases would only be possible with larger and longer-range bombers than any previously envisaged. In 1936, the Air Ministry drew up specifications that led to the Avro Manchester (which would later become the Lancaster), the Handley Page Halifax, and the Short Stirling, aircraft that would form the backbone of Harris's future command.

After listening to what he described as Chamberlain's 'lifeless call to the blood and tears, the toil and sweat of war' on 3 September 1939, Harris

---

9 Ibid., 29.
10 Harris, *Bomber Offensive*, 22.
11 Saward, *Bomber Harris*, 31.

rang Portal up and requested gainful employment.[12] Portal, Air Member for Personnel at the time, called Ludlow-Hewitt, then Commander-in-Chief of Bomber Command, and had Harris appointed as Officer Commanding No. 5 Group at Grantham. Harris estimated it would take five years to train and equip Bomber Command to defeat Germany. He had faith in the bomber offensive, but Britain was in no position to carry one out in 1939, armed as it was with aircraft that were obsolete even as they came off the production line. The 'heavies' had not yet arrived. The 'Phoney War' arrived at a good time for Bomber Command, which lacked both the crews and hardware needed for success.

Harris and Portal soon found opportunity to work more closely together. The head of Bomber Command, Ludlow-Hewitt, was overly vociferous in demanding operational training units (OTUs) and escort fighters to bolster Bomber Command's capabilities. Ludlow-Hewitt's pragmatism was particularly jarring to an Air Staff still unwisely enamoured with Hugh Trenchard's vision of what strategic bombers could achieve while operating without fighter cover.[13] Ludlow-Hewitt was swiftly replaced by Portal, who nevertheless faced exactly the same challenges as his predecessor. Harris was devastated by the loss of a man he regarded as possibly the most capable commander the RAF then possessed.[14] Ludlow-Hewitt gracefully stepped aside, penning a note to Harris maligning the relinquishing of command, yet extolling Portal's virtues. 'I have known my successor for 25 years and have the very highest opinion of his great ability and exceptional qualities of leadership.'[15]

Portal faced myriad problems as he assumed the mantle of Bomber Command, including deficiencies in navigational aids, bomber max loadout, self-defence and escort fighter range. Then, there was the fundamental issue of the Battles and the Blenheims that were lightweight, slow, and virtually defenceless, and which Portal considered utterly unsuited to their role as daylight bombers. This view was proven on 17 May 1940 when only a single aircraft of No. 82 Squadron, piloted by Sergeant Morrison, returned from a raid on Gembloux in France.[16] Big changes were needed.

---

12 Harris, *Bomber Offensive*, 10–11.
13 Wakelam, Randall T., *The Science of Bombing: Operational Research in RAF Bomber Command* Toronto: University of Toronto Press, 2009, 14.
14 Harris, *Bomber Offensive*, 35–36.
15 Saward, *Bomber Harris*, 78.
16 Hastings, Max, *Bomber Command*, (New York: Dial Press/J. Wade, 1979), 59–61.

During his brief months in command, Portal made best use of the imaginative Harris, empowering him to implement several improvements. Portal used Harris's No. 5 Group as a test bed for Bomber Command. In early July 1940, for example, Harris read an intelligence report suggesting the Germans were looking to develop bombs in the order of 4,000lb in size. This sparked Harris's ruminations for future requirements, and he wrote to Portal to suggest a 2,000lb bomb.[17] Portal readily agreed to this proposal, which would be important in the later development of the huge 'Blockbuster' 8,000lb bomb and the 12,000lb 'Tallboy' responsible for the sinking of the *Tirpitz*.

No. 5 Group was also given the go ahead by Portal to conduct the laying of magnetic sea-mines, a capability the Germans introduced in 1939. Portal was an enthusiastic advocate for this action, defending it robustly when critique came from on high. Weather sometimes precluded the correct laying of the mines, something the Admiralty sensibly insisted upon, so some aircraft returned with their mines on board; others were lost to enemy action.[18] As a 'bomber man,' Portal understood the difficulties, and defended the force's actions while reinforcing the benefits of the GARDENING programme.

The two men shared concerns regarding the RAF's future bomber programme. Portal sent Harris to Boscombe Down to see the first Manchester prototype in September 1940, and the latter penned a damning appraisal of its suitability for future operations. Harris critiqued the parachute exits, the bomb aimer's view and the rear turret, mostly because they were unsuitable for night bombing, which both Harris and Portal viewed as the future of strategic bombing. In this, Harris was the perfect underling, providing the devil in the detail Portal sometimes did not have time to attend to with his broader responsibilities. Harris's criticisms were timely, as his proposed improvements could be applied to the ill-fated Manchester, as well as the Stirling and the Halifax, part of the RAF's future heavy bombing force. Moreover, the Manchester, though itself 'a busted flush,' would precipitate the development of the Lancaster, Britain's premier strategic bomber of the war.

The collaboration between Portal and Harris during these six months was extremely productive. They viewed the war through similar lenses, welcoming a future in which the bomber would play a decisive role. Bomber Command was the only available means of directly attacking Germany at

---

17 Saward, *Bomber Harris*, 81.
18 Probert, *Bomber Harris*, 101.

that time. Portal needed a vast bombing force to destroy the German will to fight. When the Senior Air Staff Officer from Fighter Command visited Portal to request some of his force to act as a target for RAF fighters to improve their night-time interception capabilities, Portal remarked, 'The Germans won't win the war by dribbling bombs on London.'[19] Portal knew the vast expansion needed to make bombing decisive in the war. Neither Harris nor Portal would witness this expansion in their current RAF roles. After only six short months at the helm of Bomber Command, Portal moved to the top job. He brought Harris in tow shortly thereafter.

Within the limited confines of Bomber Command, Portal and Harris had a symbiotic approach, but in the Air Ministry their portfolios were much broader and differences gradually emerged. Portal took Harris to the Air Ministry because Harris was a man of action. In the words of Ludlow-Hewitt, Portal's predecessor at Bomber Command, Harris had, 'a … creative and enterprising mind, balanced by long practical experience together with energy and force of character to give his ideas practical shape.'[20] Ludlow-Hewitt's assessment was accurate, but omitted Harris's tendencies toward parochialism, defensiveness, confrontation, truculence and exaggeration. In fairness, these characteristics may have been a benefit to Ludlow-Hewitt at Bomber Command. However, they made Harris's appointment as Deputy Chief of Air Staff (DCAS) a double-edged sword for Portal.

Harris was an operator through and through, mercilessly tackling the inefficiencies of the Air Ministry. Early in his new command, Portal needed an agent for change. Harris began by culling numbers in the 'fantastically bloated' Air Ministry, instigating 'an enormous and very suitable clear-out.'[21] Harris also changed the way the Air Staff communicated with RAF operational commands, insisting that they treat them as responsible and functional commands rather than ineffective organisations requiring staff direction. This closely mirrored the manner in which Portal dealt with subordinate commands, bringing the Air Staff in line with its new chief's modus operandi. Harris tightened security by insisting on reduced distribution of secret minutes, and improved the welfare of the airwomen who worked at night and subsisted almost exclusively on sandwiches.

---

19 Letter from Sir Gerald Gibbs to Denis Richards, 16 October 1972, in Portal Papers, Christ Church College, Oxford (Hereafter referred to as CC), CC/3/XV/XVI/7.
20 Probert, *Bomber Harris*, 95.
21 Harris, *Bomber Offensive*, 50.

Despite this broader activity, Harris's primary concern remained Bomber Command, and its development into a war-winning capability.

Portal needed an advocate for Bomber Command in the Air Ministry because Churchill was impatient about the lack of progress in developing the force. Oblivious to the fact the new CAS was just getting his feet under the table, Churchill penned three separate minutes to Portal on 1 November 1940. In the first he expressed, 'my extreme regret that you do not see your way at all to meet my wish for an expansion of the Bomber Command.'[22] In a separate minute he bemoaned the bombing effort against Germany 'as lamentably small, and it constitutes a serious reproach to the organisation of the RAF.'[23] In his final diatribe the PM exclaimed, 'It is a scandal that so little use is made of the immense masses of material provided.'[24] Churchill's critique was a quantitative one, and he received an answer in kind.

Portal responded to Churchill, describing the two limiting factors on the quantity of bombs dropped by Bomber Command on Germany. The first was the number of trained crews and the second the rate at which they flew.[25] The diversion of large numbers of pilots to both Fighter Command and the Middle East had adversely affected the first factor. Portal estimated British bomber crews were flying 14 per cent more sorties than their Luftwaffe counterparts, and over much longer distances.[26] He detailed possible remedies as follows: replacement of medium bombers with heavy bombers, use of OTU aircraft and crews, reduction in the standard of training, and employment of Coastal Command and Army Co-operation Command squadrons for the bombing of Germany. The first of these measures was already being carried out, and Portal rejected the others for various reasons. He, nevertheless, left Churchill in no doubt he was 'far from being content with the present bomb delivery on Germany and Italy.'[27]

Harris's arrival as DCAS provided some relief against the Churchillian barrage, because of both his well of ideas and his vocal advocacy for them. It took the heat off Portal. Harris also had a direct line to the PM, and was a regular guest at Chequers, where he waxed lyrical about the potential of

---

22 CC/1/1/9, Churchill to Portal, 1 November 1940.
23 CC/1/1/9A, Churchill to Portal, 1 November 1940.
24 CC/1/1/9B, Churchill to Portal, 1 November 1940.
25 CC/1/1/9C, Portal to Churchill, 1 November 1940.
26 Ibid.
27 Ibid.

the bomber to Churchill.[28] Harris wasted no time in voicing his beliefs to all and sundry.

Harris assessed both Britain's industrial priorities and use of the bomber force to be all wrong. He railed against the 2:1 production of fighters to bombers in the UK, and the 8:1 ratio in purchases from the United States.[29] He decried diversions of bombers to Coastal Command, Army Co-operation Command and the Mediterranean. Harris also clashed with the Admiralty about support to the Battle of the Atlantic, arguing for sea-mining versus airborne patrols. Harris studied the statistics of the Whitley aircraft in its sub-hunting role. Between October 1940 and March 1941, No. 502 Squadron conducted 144 sorties and only sighted six submarines, sinking one or two for the loss of eleven aircraft.[30] Harris thought it a total waste of resources, describing it later in the war as 'frightening cod-fish with heavy bombers.'[31] His forthright defence of the bomber force proved useful to Portal, who was very keen to ensure a rapid uptick in the output of his former command. Harris called Portal up to the roof of the Air Ministry in December 1940, during one of the Blitz raids. Observing the German bombers, Harris remarked, 'They are sowing the wind.' Portal agreed, adding that the Germans would get the same and more in return.[32]

Despite his merits, Harris also posed challenges for Portal. Harris was a fierce champion for bombing, even as DCAS, but sometimes he overstepped the mark. His relationship with the Ministry for Economic Warfare (MEW) was particularly acrimonious. The MEW, Harris believed, stressed bombing failures while ignoring its successes, belittling its overall effects. He protested their ignorance of factors that made certain targets, notably Gelsenkirchen, extremely challenging both to find and to hit.[33] Unfortunately, Harris grossly exaggerated successes to counter this rhetoric, which did nothing for his credibility in Whitehall. Blasé statements such as, 'What the writer still has to learn is that far more damage always exists than will or can appear in a

---

28 Interview: Denis Richards with Sir Ian Jacob, 19 October 1972, CC/3/VIII/A; WF, 3:79.
29 Probert, *Bomber Harris*, 111.
30 Saward, *Harris*, 88.
31 Harris to Portal, 24 April 1942, in Harris Papers, Royal Air Force Museum, Hendon, (hereafter referred to as RAFM), RAFM/H81/46.
32 Harris, *Bomber Offensive*, 52; Terraine, John, *A Time for Courage: The Royal Air Force in the European War, 1939–1945*. New York, N.Y.: Macmillan, 1985, 480.
33 Harris to Portal, 9 April 1941, RAFM/H115.

photograph,' made Harris sound like a blind zealot.[34] It did not provide his young chief the support he required.

Portal attempted to educate Harris in his own, more diplomatic approach, but with little success. When Portal received Churchill's acerbic minute critiquing the seventy-seven airmen needed to support each aircraft in the Middle East, Harris advised Portal of the fifty-six soldiers needed to man each field gun.[35] Portal, though he doubtless laughed at the comparison, decided on reflection not to antagonise the British Army. Instead, he cited a favourable comparison with the number of support staff needed in the Royal Flying Corps during the First World War, demonstrating his point that current levels were neither outrageous nor historically anomalous.[36] While Portal chose diplomacy, Harris favoured confrontation, which made him a useful but dangerous actor in the Air Ministry. Before long, Portal decided to move Harris along.

Harris had his heart set on an operational command, but Portal saw the need for an interim posting. He sent Harris to Washington D.C. as the head of the RAF delegation there. Portal hoped Harris would influence the Americans in reallocating more production to bombers instead of fighters. By moving Harris from a position where he was undeniably controversial, especially in his critique of the Army, to one where he could demonstrate his technical expertise to a developing force, Portal could cultivate vital close relationships with future allies. Harris already knew many influential Americans from a previous post in the US, and he could now cement these ties. Nevertheless, this represented a calculated risk by Portal, as Harris was not the RAF's foremost diplomat, and was prone to the 'occasional' acerbic comment or note. Portal's decision became all the more important following Japan's attack on Pearl Harbor, and Germany's consequent declaration of war on America.

During Harris's posting in the US, the requirements of the Middle East and the Battle of the Atlantic severely hampered the numerical build-up of Bomber Command.[37] Following a debilitating attack on Germany in November 1941, when over 9 per cent of assets were lost, the bomber force was mothballed for the winter. Portal reviewed Richard Peirse's position as

---

34 Ibid.

35 Probert, *Harris*, 115.

36 Portal to Churchill, 1 December 1940, CC/1/1/14G.

37 Richards, Denis, *Portal of Hungerford: The Life of Marshal of the Royal Air Force, Viscount Portal of Hungerford, KG, GCB, OM, DSO, MC*, New York, N.Y.: Holmes & Meier, 1977, 301.

AOC Bomber Command, as he needed someone who would work well with the inbound American Eighth Air Force; Harris was the best candidate to helm Bomber Command.

The choice was not, however, without risk. Portal was well aware that Harris could be emotional, defensive and outrageous. He was also passionate, intelligent and inventive. Portal needed transformation at Bomber Command, and Harris was the only appropriate option. Portal had endured a barrage of criticism from Churchill following the Butt Report, and needed a vociferous advocate at Bomber Command as well a catalyst for rapid improvement. Harris was all these things and more. Harris's passion could not fail to impress Churchill, whose needling at Portal about Bomber Command abated. However, Portal knew he would also have to deal with the darker side of Harris. He may not have been the commander Portal wanted in an ideal world, yet Portal was wise enough to realise that Harris was exactly what he needed, warts and all.

Harris's appointment as AOC Bomber Command had an immediate pay-off for Portal. The US Eighth Air Force was in the throes of moving to the UK wholesale. When the Harris family moved into their new official residence at Springfields in Buckinghamshire, the Eighth Air Force Commander Brigadier General Ira Eaker moved in with them.[38] The two were already well acquainted and firm friends; Eaker worked and lived side by side with Harris while familiarising himself with his new duties. Despite Harris introducing the Eighth Air Force staff to every element of Bomber Command, the US was not ready to conduct bombing of its own for some months. The American raid on Rouen in August was a rare high spot in an otherwise frustrating year. Unable to solve the Eighth Air Force's problems, Harris redoubled his focus on Bomber Command.

While Portal tried to ensure Bomber Command would receive the pilots and aircraft it needed, Harris focused on qualitative improvement. The damning Butt Report, instigated by Lord Cherwell in August 1941, concluded 'that of all the aircraft recorded as having attacked their targets, only one-third had got within five miles of them'.[39] This showed unequivocally that navigation was the most immediate problem facing Bomber Command. Portal bore the brunt of the broadside from this report

---

38 Saward, *Bomber Harris*, 133.

39 Webster, Charles Kingsley and Frankland, Noble, *The Strategic Air Offensive against Germany, 1939–1945. History of the Second World War Vol. 1*; United Kingdom Military Series. London: H.M. Stationery Office, 1961, 178..

from Churchill, as earlier described, and dealt with the PM in a masterly manner. Harris's job was to improve Bomber Command's qualitative output, which required hard science rather than Trenchardian romanticism.

The Butt Report illustrated the dearth of analysis taking place in Bomber Command. Harris's predecessor, Richard Peirse, had attempted to rectify the problem in autumn 1941, requesting the establishment of an Operational Research Section (ORS). By the time Harris took command, the ORS was firmly established. Basil Dickens was the head boffin, who described the Command's challenges: improving bombing accuracy, minimising losses, and discerning the major causes of losses.[40] The ORS needed access to accurate data regarding bombing missions to conduct meaningful analysis of the Command's tactics, equipment and training.[41] Detail was crucial in individual mission reports, because if the aircrew chose not to use some new equipment, or could not operate it properly, it was impossible to know if the equipment might assist in solving one of the problems. The close working relationship of the ORS scientists and the Bomber Command crews was, therefore, essential.

Harris recognised the issues 'that could only be surmounted by intensive research, continual experiment, and unshakeable resolve.'[42] He also accepted the data and recommendations from the ORS, which delivered gradual improvements. In this, of course, Harris had much to be thankful for. His task would have been impossible if not for a Prime Minister searching for better results, a Chief of Air Staff who gave him the operational room to fail before succeeding, and the personnel of Bomber Command who risked their lives every day.

It rapidly became apparent that one of the Command's main problems, losses, could be ameliorated through concentration. Electronic separation through 'Gee' provided the way. Gee enabled any number of appropriately equipped aircraft to fix their position accurately by measuring the time difference of arrival between pulses from one master and two slave ground stations.[43] Harris thought concentrating raids would saturate defences, yielding fewer losses in percentage terms. He said, 'I was convinced that a force of 250 to 300 aircraft would be totally inadequate. But if we attacked with a much larger force – supposing we had it – could we put many hundreds of aircraft over the target to achieve the desired concentration

40 Wakelam, *The Science of Bombing*, 44.
41 Ibid., 48.
42 Ibid., 68.
43 Probert, *Harris*, 225.

without danger of collision and chaos in the air – say 600 an hour which was six times greater than concentrations achieved up to the end of 1941?'[44] The scale of bombing improved markedly in late spring, to the relief of Portal and the satisfaction of Churchill. Harris saturated the defences of Lubeck with 234 aircraft. The attack included 144 tons of incendiaries on the built-up area, causing the first firestorm.[45] The following month, the RAF attacked Rostock on four consecutive nights, following which Goebbels remarked that 'community life there is practically at an end.'[46] Flushed with success, Harris decided to up the ante and hit a major industrial town in the Ruhr. He set his sights on Cologne.[47]

If Portal was going to solve the numbers problem, he had to ensure the majority of bombers were flying for Bomber Command. He needed a standout success from Harris to prove the concept of strategic bombing was more than just hyperbole. While Portal accepted the operational necessity of sending reinforcements to the Middle East, the continual bleeding of bomber assets to Army Co-operation Command (ACC) and Coastal Command (CC) had to be stopped. Harris proposed a grandiose, Gee-enabled, thousand aircraft attack on a German industrial city. Harris had wisely listened to the counsel of his ORS, who insisted the raid be carried out against a target within Gee range.[48]

Despite the obvious risks, both Portal and Harris considered the upside to be huge; the damage would be much greater, but the attrition of Bomber Command aircraft would be significantly reduced due to the saturation of the defences. With Portal's encouragement, Harris sought Churchill's support for the planned attack during another weekend at Chequers.[49] Harris expressed such enthusiasm for the proposed raid on Cologne that Portal was able to convince the PM to stop the bleeding of bomber assets to other commands. Portal wrote to Harris on 13 May 1942 to advise him that ACC and CC had been told they now had to provide from their own resources.[50] This was a massive win for both Portal and Harris, advancing their hopes of achieving the much larger bomber force mooted earlier in

---

44 Saward, *Bomber Harris*, 138.
45 Terraine, *A Time for Courage*, 477.
46 Quoted in Webster and Frankland, *The Strategic Air Offensive, Vol 1*, 485.
47 Harris, *Bomber Offensive*, 105–107.
48 Wakelam, *The Science of Bombing*, 227.
49 Harris, *Bomber Offensive*, 109.
50 Portal to Harris, 13 May 1942, RAFM/H81/55.

the war. Harris's planning for the big raid began in earnest, with support promised from both ACC and CC.

On the night of 30 May 1942, 1,046 bomber aircraft took off bound for Cologne on Operation MILLENNIUM. Harris had scrimped and scavenged within his own command, because the Admiralty forbade Coastal Command from providing the 250 aircraft promised for the raid.[51] Harris's decision constituted a considerable risk, as a disastrous raid would have destroyed Bomber Command's training capability as well as its operational output. It was the work of 'a commander endowed with exceptional courage and resolution.'[52] The attack took place in three waves, led by No. 3 Group Wellingtons. The spectacle was one none of the crews forgot, with Gee enabling the aircraft to concentrate in two and a half hours what would previously have taken over seven.[53] Some thought it a great forest fire; the reality was a baptism of fire for Cologne.[54] In little more than an hour and a half, 3,300 houses were destroyed and 9,000 more damaged, thirty-six factories were totally destroyed and seventy more took severe damage. A total of 469 people were killed and 45,000 lost their homes.[55] The German reaction was one of stunned disbelief.

Albert Speer, the German Minister for War Production, was summoned to see Goering the following morning. Goering was equal parts raging and incredulous. 'Impossible, that many bombs cannot be dropped in a single night,' he snapped at his adjutant before demanding to speak to the Gauleiter of Cologne.[56] When connected with the Gauleiter, Goering refused to believe the reports claiming, 'The report from your Police Commissioner is a stinking lie!' He went on to insist such fantasies must not be reported to Hitler and demanded a new report with accurate figures. Three days later, Speer visited headquarters and asked Hitler about the raid, assuming he believed Goering's report of events. Hitler, however, had read the reports from Cologne and the foreign newspapers, whose figures were even higher. He was furious with Goering for the cover-up. The Germans were rattled for the first time.

---

51 Terraine, *A Time for Courage*, 483.

52 FW, 1:404, Terraine, *A Time for Courage*, 485.

53 Verrier, Anthony, *The Bomber Offensive*. London: Batsford, 1968, 146.

54 Hastings, Max, *Bomber Command,* New York: Dial Press/J. Wade, 1979, 152.

55 Hastings, *Bomber Command*, 152.

56 Speer, Albert, *Inside the Third Reich: Memoirs*, New York: Macmillan, 1970, 279.

Harris and Portal had scored a huge win both tactically and strategically. Hap Arnold, dining at Ditchley, wryly recalled the event, as it thoroughly undercut his attempts to convince Portal and Churchill of the superiority of daylight bombing. Politically, the raid on Cologne was a roaring success for Churchill. For Portal, it provided much-needed ammunition in the fight for the prioritisation of bomber aircraft. Of the accolades Harris received following the raid, perhaps the most important came from Russia, and the Commander of the Red Army's Long-Range Bombing Force. It read:

> In the name of the personnel of the Long-Range Bombing Command of the Red Army, I beg you to accept congratulations on the outstandingly successful initiation of massed blows on Hitlerite Germany by the British Bomber Command under your personal direction.
>
> The precision and effectiveness of this immense operation and the valour and skill of the men who took part are highly appreciated by our pilots who beg me to send battle greetings to their British brothers in arms.
>
> A. Golovanov
> Lieutenant General
> Commander of the Long-Range Bomber
> Aviation of the Red Army[57]

With the beleaguered Russians screaming for Western assistance, the Cologne raid was the tonic Churchill needed. It was an airborne second front. Bomber Command was now on the strategic map, in line with Portal's strategic paper of autumn 1941, which proposed bombing as the war-winning weapon.

Unfortunately, the attack on Cologne proved to be the apex of the Allied effort during 1942. Despite Churchill's edict that Bomber Command would get what it needed, strategic reality quickly reasserted itself. The goal of building up Bomber Command to a force of 4,000 aircraft remained distant, as the resolution of crises elsewhere required improved air support. Bomber aircraft were in constant demand, as they were crucial to the Battle of the Atlantic, the Mediterranean and North Africa, Far East efforts, and Army Co-operation Command training. Portal met these challenges with

---

57 Saward, *Bomber Harris*, 146.

equanimity; Harris's elation quickly turned to frustration. In June he wrote to Portal lamenting that he would only be able to replicate the large raids on a regular basis 'in a dim and distant future, subject to successful defence against the depredations of other interests.'[58] While Portal may have privately acknowledged that Harris was correct, his broader perspective precluded satisfying Harris's materiel desires. Harris simply wanted to build up his force to win the war; Portal was more concerned in 1942 with ensuring the war was not lost. Their disparity of views, which only became wider as time went on, led to some difficult exchanges that Portal, with his enormous responsibilities, could probably have done without.

Portal could not deny the greater needs of the war, as he grappled with higher strategic priorities on a daily basis. Ensconced in his ivory tower, Harris was simmering. In August, Harris wrote to Portal on no fewer than three separate occasions about the 'state of Bomber Command'. He first complained, 'There is little hope of expansion while we go on pouring Bomber trained pilots down the sink in this fashion.'[59] Later that month, he explained that a small force meant the raids could not saturate the defences, because the attrition of bomber aircraft would remain high.[60] While Portal still needed a large bomber force, and was prepared to push Churchill to build it, the purpose of that future force was shifting. Portal's day-to-day discussions with Dudley Pound, and particularly Alan Brooke, gave him a broader appreciation for how the bomber force might be used. As 1942 elapsed, Portal increasingly saw the bomber force as a part of a larger joint effort rather than a separate war-winning capability. This broader perspective eluded Harris, whose frustration occasionally boiled over.

The object of Harris's ire in autumn 1942 was the Canadian Group, which was being re-equipped with Harris's beloved Lancasters. What irked the Bomber Command chief was that the Canadian Group was unlikely to bomb Germany, and Harris needed Lancasters to do so most effectively. 'I fail to see why we should give these people, who are determined to huddle into a corner by themselves on purely political grounds, the best of our equipment at the expense of British and other Dominion crews.'[61] He went on to complain about a previous decision that resulted in the Eighth Air Force being given 'the whole of the best flying country in England ...

58 Harris to Portal, 20 June 1942, RAFM/H81/81
59 Harris to Portal, 12 August 1942, RAFM/H81/107.
60 Harris to Portal, 29 August 1942, RAFM/H81/114.
61 Harris to Portal, 26 September 1942, RAFM/H81/126.

utterly regardless of my protests,' before suggesting the Canadians ought to get no more Lancasters than they could produce themselves. Portal told Freeman, by then back at MAP, to instigate this solution, meeting Harris's major complaint.[62] However, further acrimony followed.

Portal's legendary patience evaporated when Harris overstepped the mark and took his complaints into the public domain. Harris wanted every heavy bomber for strategic operations over Germany, yet there were obviously other needs. Portal understood, for example, the critical strategic importance of the Middle East theatre. When Harris complained once more about the loss of bomber assets to North Africa, this time both disparagingly and in public, Portal had had enough. 'I do not regard it as either a credit to your intelligence or a contribution to the winning of the war. It is in my opinion wrong in both tone and substance and calculated to promote unnecessary and useless friction between your Headquarters, the Air Ministry, and Headquarters Middle East.'[63] While Portal was prepared to endure Harris's occasional pettiness in private, he was furious Harris would decry the efforts of others in public. 'I am sure that great benefit would be gained if you could manage to take a rather broader view of the problems and difficulties confronting the Air Ministry and the other Commands and if this could be reflected in the tone and substance of your letters in future.'[64] In Portal's strategic view, the Middle East was the most important theatre of Allied operations at the time, particularly in light of the planning for Operation TORCH, the first real Anglo-American operation of the war.

Having experienced his subordinate's penchant for overclaiming the effects of bombing as DCAS, Portal had to rein in Harris again once he took operational command. In June 1942, Harris wrote to Portal about the bombing of the Emden dockyards and submarine works. He noted, 'About sixty to seventy-five percent of the town and suburban dwelling areas can be described as "devastated,"'[65] Portal immediately called this analysis into question stating, 'Intelligence here tell me that they have seen no photographs to justify the above quotations.'[66] The difference of opinion came down to estimating the damage that could not be seen from photographs. While

---

62 Portal to Harris, 26 September 1942, RAFM/H81/127.
63 Portal to Harris, 10 October 1942, RAFM/H81/139.
64 Ibid.
65 Harris to Portal, 26 June 1942, RAFM/H81/83a.
66 Portal to Harris, 28 June 1942, RAFM/H81/86.

Harris was keen to advertise the maximum damage, Portal warned against this. 'I think it is dangerous to send to Ministers detailed estimates of total damage and photographs demonstrating them, which would involve using such a formula.'[67] He asked Harris to limit the Bomber Command Digest, 'in so far as it assesses bomb damage by photographs, to be confined to statements of what can be seen, as distinct from what can be estimated, unless definite information is available from other sources to confirm the latter.'[68] While Harris was sometimes a thorn in Portal's side, Portal knew his intentions were good. Harris delivered enormous improvements in a short time in command, and pacified Churchillian critique with his impassioned advocacy for the bomber. He also retained many other redeeming features as a commander.

Harris cared deeply about the bombing campaign, yet even more deeply for the sacrifices of his crews. He was determined to get them the credit he felt they deserved. Beginning in 1942, he sought appropriate recognition for Bomber Command's GARDENING operations, which imposed significantly deleterious effects on the German Navy. In a spat with the Royal Navy, Harris haughtily dismissed their reluctance to issue communiqués acknowledging the work of Bomber Command as 'childish and churlish.'[69] He believed the Admiralty's stated purpose to 'deny the enemy knowledge of our mine-laying' to be merely an excuse to eschew giving Bomber Command due recognition. He went on to describe how his 'spies in the Admiralty' have seen 'a deliberate crying down of Air Force credit amongst those higher up. It is time for this contemptible conduct to be brought to a show down.'[70] With this behaviour, Harris simultaneously displayed his best and worst to Portal. He wanted the recognition his crews deserved, but automatically assumed the worst of the sister services.

In September Harris wrote to Portal regarding the awards process. He believed the attrition suffered by Bomber Command crews warranted a huge increase in their awards, 'in order to bring the scale more into keeping with the comparative risks run by them and by crews in other commands at home and abroad.'[71] Harris went on to describe how only three in ten crews would complete their thirty missions if the loss rate was 4 per cent. He

---

67 Portal to Harris, 4 July 1942, RAFM/H81/91.

68 Ibid.

69 Harris to Portal, 24 April 1942, RAFM/H81/46.

70 Ibid.

71 Harris to Portal, 19 September 1942, RAFM/H81/119.

felt, not unreasonably, this should be factored into the allocation of awards, rather than merely using the number of flying hours. Portal, sympathetic, but cognisant of the bureaucratic chain involved, advised Harris to speak to AMP about changing the allocation.

Despite his grumbling and grousing, Harris improved Bomber Command significantly as an organisation, with a meticulous eye for technical detail, and a determination to improve output. His drive, determination and expertise in bombing were second to none. Yet the promise of early summer 1942 had not been fulfilled and the Eighth Air Force had failed to contribute significantly to the bombing effort. Harris was focused entirely on the bombing war; his aperture was small. Portal worried not only about British grand strategy writ large, but how to sell this strategy to reluctant allies at the forthcoming CASABLANCA Conference. While both men understood the criticality of building up Bomber Command, Portal viewed strategic bombing as merely one element of the war-winning solution; Harris thought it was the silver bullet. By the end of the year the perspectives of Portal and Harris stood in stark contrast.[72]

The CASABLANCA Conference, held in January 1943, set the conditions for the Allied forces' ultimate success. Following the advice of both Portal, Slessor, and Secretary of State for War Archie Sinclair, Churchill abandoned his erstwhile objections to the American daylight effort. The Casablanca Agreement was a partial vindication of both countries' approaches to strategic bombing. The primary purpose of POINTBLANK would be 'the progressive destruction and dislocation of the German military, industrial and economic system, and the undermining of the morale of the German people to a point where their capacity for armed resistance is fatally weakened.'[73] The directive reflected Portal's emerging belief that the unconditional surrender of Germany, defined at CASABLANCA as the Allies' mutual goal, could only be achieved by exerting maximum pressure in the land, sea and air domains. Target prioritisation also reflected this reality, with submarine construction yards being the first priority, followed

---

72 See Terraine, *A Time for Courage*, 471 for further discussion of Harris's errant point of view.

73 CASABLANCA Conference Papers and Minutes of Meetings, Alanbrooke Papers, Liddell Hart Centre for Military Archives, King's College London (Hereafter referred to as KCL/AB), KCL/AB/6/1/1/86.

by aircraft plants, transportation, oil installations, and other enemy war industry targets.[74]

By March 1943, Harris was in an acceptable position to exploit these new target sets, commanding thirty-seven four-engine bomber squadrons capable of penetration deep into Germany. More significantly, Bomber Command optimised raids through fitting H2S and Oboe to the aircraft, which electronically assisted navigation and targeting, reducing the adverse effects of weather on Bomber Command accuracy at a stroke. A larger, more durable, and more accurate force could begin to deliver the results Portal and Harris had promised Churchill. Bomber Command's first target was Essen, which was attacked on 5–6 March, 12–13 March, 3–4 April and 30 April–1 May. The massive Krupps works, the supposed hub of the German armament industry, was repeatedly attacked despite being heavily defended by a wall of flak and German fighters.[75] Harris later described the city as having been 'smashed out of recognition.'[76] He planned to 'Essenise' another six cities by September 1943. The burgeoning capabilities of Bomber Command were plain to Nazi propaganda minister Josef Goebbels, who visited the city on 10 April 1943:

> We arrived in Essen before 7 a.m. Deputy Gauleiter Schlessmann and a large staff called for us at the railway station. We went to the hotel on foot because driving is quite impossible in many parts of Essen. This walk enabled us to make a first-hand estimate of the damage inflicted by the last three raids. It is colossal and indeed ghastly. This city must, for the most part, be written off completely. The city's building experts estimate that it will take twelve years to repair the damage … Nobody can tell how Krupps can go on. Everyone wants to avoid transplanting Krupps from Essen. There would be no purpose in doing so, for the moment Essen is no longer an industrial centre the English will pounce upon the next city, Bochum, Dortmund or Düsseldorf.[77]

---

74 Arnold, Henry Harley and Huston, John W., *American Airpower Comes of Age: General Henry H. 'Hap' Arnold's World War II Diaries Vol. 1*, Maxwell Air Force Base, AL: Air University Press, 2001, 186.

75 Hastings, *Bomber Command*, 197, 227.

76 Overy, R.J., *The Bombing War: Europe 1939–1945*, London: Penguin, 2013, 309.

77 Goebbels, Joseph and Louis Paul Lochner, *The Goebbels Diaries, 1942–1943.* (1st ed.). Garden City, N.Y.: Doubleday, 1948, 321–322; Saward, *Bomber Harris*, 196.

Subsequently, Harris became preoccupied with the 'Essenisation' of Hamburg. Hamburg was an enticing target. It was a coastal city, which meant Bomber Command did not have to fly for hours over German-controlled territory. Hamburg was also the second largest city in Germany and one of the hubs for both U-boat construction and shipbuilding in general.[78] Operation GOMORRAH took place over ten days from 24–25 July to 2–3 August. The first operational use of chaff, callsign WINDOW, aided the survivability of RAF assets. This highly secret capability, its use much debated, deployed foil strips to provide a profusion of confusing information to German radar operators.[79] During the first raid, in little more than an hour, 2,284 tonnes of bombs were dropped and 17,000 incendiaries per kilometre, which led to enormous destruction. Fire swept through the city, killing over 10,000 people. Damage to German industry was prodigious. Speer reported to Hitler in August 1943, 'Six more attacks as successful as the attack on Hamburg would bring armament production to a standstill.'[80] Harris now had grand plans for the destruction of all German industrial cities. Portal had largely allowed Harris to prosecute his bombing war as he saw fit following CASABLANCA, and to great effect. Yet Harris's operational genius was marred by his narrowmindedness and a pathology that approached paranoia. He increasingly disparaged any idea that distracted him from his lofty goal. Convinced as he was of the efficacy of his approach, Harris resorted once more to hyperbole.

In March 1943, Harris became irritated by gaps in British intelligence records that precluded, by his estimation, proper recognition of the destructive achievements of the bombing campaign. Convinced of the other services' continued dismissal of the bombing effort, he resorted to exaggeration as a compensatory measure. 'I am afraid we must assume that the Admiralty and other interested parties will continue indefinitely to say that the Bomber Offensive is a futile waste of effort which had much better be employed in chasing U-boats, bombing concrete emplacements or anything else which at the moment seems a good idea to somebody.'[81] Harris enclosed a paper to Portal, containing data on German cities that had either been 'devastated' or 'badly hit.' Portal could immediately see these

---

78 O'Brien, Phillips Payson, *How the War Was Won: Air-sea Power and Allied Victory in World War II*, Cambridge Military Histories. 2015, 279.

79 Overy, *The Bombing War*, 333.

80 O'Brien, *How the War was Won*, 279.

81 Harris to Portal, 30 March 1943, RAFM/H82/XX, (Minute number too faded to decipher.)

terms were unscientific, and not supported by any more evidence than Harris had presented the previous year. When Harris asked for an intelligence organisation to collate all the damage caused to different aspects of German industry to date, Portal pointed out the futility of doing so. There was no intelligence staff large enough for the task, and the requisite information was unavailable.[82] While Harris wanted recognition, Portal was cognisant of the practical limitations in trying to provide it. Harris continued to try to secure Bomber Command's prioritisation and recognition at every turn; Portal remained more concerned with grand strategy than recognition.

The Bomber Command chief continued to display his lack of greater strategic understanding, despite Portal's best efforts to broaden Harris's strategic horizons. Harris railed against the loss of aircraft to the Middle East in March. 'I must protest against the sending of the three Wellington squadrons to North Africa ... There can surely be no justification for devoting further air resources to over-insurance in what is admittedly a secondary theatre of war.'[83] The Middle East was the primary theatre at the time and, with the Battle of the Atlantic at a pivotal stage, Harris's bomber offensive was a distant third. Portal struggled to make Harris comprehend his greater role of 'balancing conflicting claims to the available resources.'[84] The broader Allied strategy in North Africa was designed to soak up German resources, relieve pressure on the Soviets, and to enable an eventual reinvasion of Europe. This was either unapparent or unimportant to Harris, who remained laser focused on the CBO. Portal went on to explain how the Allied commitment to the Mediterranean was diverting German defences that might otherwise be protecting German cities against Harris's bombers. Yet Portal's logical argumentation held no sway with the Bomber Command chief.

Harris determined, entirely incorrectly, that Berlin was Germany's strategic centre of gravity. He resolved to attack the enemy capital mercilessly, even though it fell outside Oboe's range, making it the hardest target of all. Harris assessed that a continuous series of attacks on Berlin would destroy the German people's morale and make them force the government to concede defeat. He optimistically estimated the attacks would yield losses of 400–500 Allied aircraft but 'cost Germany the war.'[85]

---

82 Portal to Harris, 27 April 1943, RAFM/H82/314.
83 Harris to Portal, 26 April 1943, RAFM/H82/313.
84 Portal to Harris, 29 April 1943, RAFM/H82/315.
85 Webster and Frankland, The Strategic Air Offensive, Vol 2, 190.

Harris predicted his assault would produce 'a state of devastation in which surrender is inevitable.'[86] He considered neither the nature of the Nazi regime nor its vicious hold on the German populace, both of which rendered Harris's theory of victory highly improbable. Likewise, Harris gave little thought to the respite his change of focus afforded German industry, which suffered mightily during the autumn 1943 'nightmare of Hamburg.'[87] He only thought of optimising his force to realise his great victory, seeding further differences of opinion with Portal.

As the Allies gradually wrestled North Africa from Germany, Portal determined to squeeze Germany everywhere. His priority for Bomber Command was, therefore, to attack in as many ways and places as possible, to maximise the overall weight of effort. This was why, despite their strategic agreements, Portal largely let Harris carry out his bombing campaign as he saw fit. However, before long, the two men clashed.

Harris understandably sought to minimise Bomber Command losses, so requested a force composed of as high a proportion of Lancasters as possible. He believed them to be more survivable than other bombers. With this in mind, Harris petitioned Portal to have Stirling and Halifax production switched over to Lancasters in autumn 1943. He noted their respective loss rates during attacks on Berlin: 4.6 per cent for the Lancaster; 8 per cent for the Halifax and 9.4 per cent for the Stirling. He fatalistically observed, 'I hope, but I much doubt, that everything possible is being done to switch all available capacity on to Lancasters at the expense of Halifaxes and Stirlings.'[88] From Harris's perspective, which centred on winning the war with bombers, his request made perfect sense. From Portal's viewpoint, it did not. The Allied landings in France were now planned for May 1944, the decisive year for the war. Portal could ill afford the reduction in bomber output caused by retooling factories to make Lancasters. He needed as many bombers as possible to attrit German forces, as well as their lines of communication prior to the landings and support to ground forces afterward. To that end, he proposed repurposing Stirlings from deep penetration missions in Germany to less demanding but strategically useful activities.[89] Harris complained bitterly, culminating in a December meeting,

---

86 Overy, *The Bombing War*, 340.
87 Tooze, Adam, *The Wages of Destruction: The Making and Breaking of the Nazi Economy*. Penguin: New York, 2006, 625.
88 Harris to Portal 7 September 1943, RAFM/H82/366.
89 Portal to Harris, 14 September 1943, RAFM/82/367.

during which Portal reiterated his reluctance 'to do anything which would lighten the blow on Germany in 1944, even though the continued use of the Halifax meant heavier casualties than with the Lancasters.'[90]

As the new year dawned, even Harris's reluctant gaze turned to OVERLORD, and more direct support to the invasion forces. At the beginning of 1944 Harris wrote to Portal, conceding, 'OVERLORD must now presumably be regarded as an inescapable commitment.'[91]

In March 1944, Portal met with Eisenhower, Tedder, Harris, Spaatz, and Leigh-Mallory to determine targeting priorities ahead of OVERLORD. Tedder's Transportation Plan was a logical extension of discussions from the CCS conferences during 1943. One of the primary American objections to continued Mediterranean operations and the occupation of Italy was that the Germans could still move their forces to defend France faster than the Allies could remove divisions from Italy and redeploy them to Britain. This was due both to sea transportation's relative slowness compared to rail and the Germans' ability to operate on interior lines. The destruction of east–west lines of communication would impede Germany's ability to reinforce and redeploy divisions along the French coastline; it would also enable the Allies' establishment and maintenance of a bridgehead in Normandy. Harris gave the Transportation Plan his lukewarm support, primarily because he had greater objections to the Americans' proposed oil plan, which he viewed as more of an unrealistic panacea target.

The Transportation Plan did not, in reality, result in widespread changes for Bomber Command; OVERLORD targets were attacked on moonlit nights unsuitable for deep penetration into Germany. Despite this convenient operational factor, the growing divide between Bomber Command and the Air Ministry regarding the operational capabilities of Bomber Command was abundantly clear. Portal and the Air Staff were upbeat about the improved accuracy of Bomber Command's attacks, aided by Oboe, H2S and the Pathfinder force. Harris remained utterly unconvinced of the efficacy of targeting single nodes of industry, and claimed Bomber Command incapable of accurate attacks despite a growing body of evidence to the contrary.

Portal, increasingly sceptical about Harris's claims, ordered some experimental attacks against 'precision' railway targets. This was a test to determine the validity of Harris's objections to the role proposed to Bomber

90 Meeting held on 21 December 1943, RAFM/H82/397.
91 TNA, AIR 20/3223, Richards, *Portal of Hungerford*, 315; Saward, *Bomber Harris*, 246.

Command by Leigh-Mallory, the Air Commander for OVERLORD.[92] In March 1944, attacks on Vaires, Trappes, Amiens and Courtrai caused significant damage, stopping operations altogether. Only Lyon escaped wholesale destruction, demonstrating the enormous strides Bomber Command had taken since 1942. The Transportation Plan went into full effect and thirty-seven more targets were allocated to Bomber Command. They shredded the German rail infrastructure, bringing the railway network in France to a standstill prior to D-Day, and playing a vital supporting role in the invasion's success.[93] Harris's bombers had completely disproven their commander's assertions of inaccuracy, delivering stunning results. This displayed the enigma that was Arthur Harris, who initially railed against the tasking, then strained every sinew in his command to ensure that it was carried out to the best of Bomber Command's abilities.

Following the Allied breakout from Normandy Harris turned once more to crushing German cities. He had forgotten the failure of his five-month long campaign against Berlin, which had been called off on 1 April 1944 following an unsustainable loss of 1,047 bombers. Portal's view, supported by intelligence, was to concentrate attacks against oil, something Harris considered a panacea target. June raids in the Ruhr on synthetic plants had not improved Harris's view of this target set, as losses were an eyewatering 11 per cent of the 832 bombers despatched.[94] However, worsening weather in Europe as the autumn took hold meant precision targeting became less possible. Area targeting was, therefore, included in the 25 September directive issued by Bottomley to Harris, though it was a residual target in the event of poor weather. Oil became the unequivocal priority target.[95] Harris wrote to Churchill on 1 October 1944 stating:

> You will note that the whole of the Boche revelation to the Jap centres round retrieving air supremacy. So the Boche and the Jap realise what happened to the German Armies in France – even if our own military minds do not yet quite grasp it. Our armies have had one or two (no more) really tough local battles in France. They have not yet had as many killed

---

92 Webster and Frankland, *The Strategic Air Offensive*, Vol 3, 27.
93 Davis, *Bombing the Axis*, 358.
94 Probert, *Bomber Harris*, 307.
95 Hastings, *Bomber Command*, 331; Probert, *Bomber Harris*, 306.

as on the first day of the Battle of the Somme. They have not yet had as many killed as Bomber Command in its past efforts to make the invasion practicable. At Le Havre and Boulogne, for instance, we have taken these vital and heavily defended ports with nearly 20 000 prisoners at the cost of less than 150 of our men killed in fierce fighting. Why these extraordinary discrepancies? The answer is Air power. When these facts are hoisted in, the probabilities of the future begin to clear. From now on, as in the past, our fortunes depend on whether we can maintain our Air supremacy. That is what the Boche admits to the Jap in these ULTRA papers. I agree with him ... We should now get on and knock Germany finally flat. For the first time we have the force to do it. Opportunities do not last forever and this one is slipping ... If we do not take full advantage now of the vast Allied Air superiority, we shall lose the opportunity. With the lost opportunity, we shall lose the effect upon the land battles. We must therefore at any cost nip in the bud any possibility of the German regaining a serious footing in the air ...[96]

Churchill responded, 'I agree with your very good letter, except that I do not think you did it all, or can you do it all. I recognise, however, this is a becoming view for you to take. I am all for cracking everything in now on to Germany that can be spared from the battlefields.' He added to his military chief of staff, Hastings Ismay, 'I do not rate the share of the Air Force as high as he [Harris] does.'[97] The damage, however, was done. With Churchill overtly authorising Harris to recommence the city bombing campaign, Harris could interpret Portal's preferred priority to hit oil targets loosely.

Portal had committed himself to prioritising oil targets at the Second Quebec Conference in September 1944, during which he and Arnold had taken back joint control of bomber assets from Eisenhower. Harris remained unconvinced attacking single target sets could be effective, despite the obvious and ironic fact that his obsession with Berlin was exactly that. Portal was intent on doing what the CCS had prescribed. Trouble was brewing.

---

96 Saward, *Bomber Harris*, 264.
97 Churchill to Ismay, 1 Oct 1944, Chartwell Papers, Churchill College, Cambridge (hereafter referred to as CHAR), CHAR/20/153/4; Saward, *Bomber Harris*, 264–265.

Strategic differences rumbled following a Bomber Command attack on Cologne on 30–31 October. Bomber Command committed a rather paltry 6 per cent of attacks against oil targets that month despite its primacy in priority, and Portal considered that Harris's rhetoric was being matched in reality of effort. Portal wanted to know why the synthetic oil facilities in the Ruhr had not been targeted in preference, stating his belief that the oil campaign gave the Allies the best chance for a quick victory.[98] Portal regarded Harris's response, which highlighted Cologne to be an important communications centre, as unsatisfactory. Harris's further explanation regarding weather in the respective areas did nothing to ameliorate his chief's concerns. Responding to a further Harris letter from 1 November, Portal wrote:

> In the closing paragraphs of your letter of the 1st November you refer to a plan for the destruction of the 60 leading German cities, and to your efforts to keep up with, and even to exceed your average of 2½ such cities devastated each month. I know that you have long felt such a plan to be the most effective way of bringing about the collapse of Germany. Knowing this, I have, I must confess, at times wondered whether the magnetism of the remaining German cities has not in the past tended as much to deflect our bombers from their primary objectives as the tactical and weather difficulties which you described so fully in your letter of 1st November. I would like you to reassure me that this is not so. If I knew you to be as wholehearted in the attack on oil as in the past you have been in the matter of attacking cities I would have very little to worry about.[99]

The effect of Portal's critique was immediate. Bomber Command carried out wholesale destruction of Ruhr oil targets in the following weeks, putting all synthetic oil production facilities out of commission. Bomber Command attacked in all but the most adverse weather conditions. Portal may not have endeared himself to Harris, but Harris nevertheless provided the military results Portal wanted. Yet, strategically the two remained divided, as evidenced by Harris's letter dated 12 December:

---

98 Portal to Harris, 5 November 1944, RAFM/H83/86.
99 Portal to Harris, 12 November 1944, RAFM/H83/89.

You will recall that in the past M.E.W. experts have never failed to overstate their case on 'panaceas', e.g., ball-bearings, molybdenum, locomotives etc., in so far as, after the battle has been joined and the original targets attacked, more and more sources of supply or other factors unpredicted by MEW have become revealed. The oil plan has already displayed similar symptoms. The benzol plants were an afterthought. I am quite certain that there are dozens more benzol plants of which we are unaware and if and when we knock them all out I am equally certain we shall eventually be told by M.E.W. that German MT [motor transport] is continuing to run sufficiently for their purpose on producer gas, steam, industrial alcohol, etc., etc. However, we should be content if we can deprive them of adequate supplies of aviation fuel. That in itself will take enough doing.[100]

The description of oil as a panacea got Portal's attention. He responded, 'I am profoundly disappointed that you still appear to feel that the oil plan is just another "panacea". Naturally, while you hold this view you will be unable to put your heart into the attack on oil.'[101] Harris bit back on 28 December, saying:

You are quite wrong to say that if I hold that view I will be unable to put my heart into the attack on oil. It has always been my custom, and it is one that I will never relinquish, to leave no stone unturned to get my views across, but when the decision is made, I carry it out to the utmost and to the best of my ability. I am sorry that you should doubt this, and surprised indeed, if you can point to any precedent in support of your statement. I can certainly quote precedent in the opposite sense … While doing my utmost to push this plan to the conclusion sought, it does not relieve me of my duty to inform you that like all previous panaceas so enthusiastically put forward by the MEW, the basis of the plan is wrong in the

---

100 Harris to Portal, 12 December 1944, RAFM/H83/105.
101 Portal to Harris, 22 December 1944, RAFM/H83/106.

light of all the factors involved, and its pursuance is, and will prove to be, chimerical.[102]

The exchange between the two men continued through January 1945, with neither giving ground. Portal argued strongly in favour of the oil campaign; Harris agreed to pursue the approved strategy loyally despite his concerns. It is unclear whether Portal was simply needling Harris into greater effort, or trying to convince him of the veracity of the intelligence reports supporting the assigned targeting prioritisation. If the former, Portal's tactic largely worked, since Harris did all that was asked of him in the first months of 1945. The results were apparent to Portal by 20 January, when he wrote:

> I willingly accept your assurance that you will continue to do your utmost to ensure the successful execution of the policy laid down. I am very sorry that you do not believe in it but it is no use my craving for what is evidently unattainable. We must wait until after the end of the war before we can know for certain who was right, and I sincerely hope that until then you will continue in command of the force, which has done so much towards defeating the enemy and has brought such credit and renown to yourself and to the Air Force.[103]

Harris immediately expressed his regret at the disagreement. His force subsequently prosecuted a highly successful campaign that severely hampered the mobility of the Wehrmacht, a crucial enabler of the 8 May 1945 Allied victory.

The Portal–Harris relationship survived the most extreme pressures imaginable. Their mutual respect played an important part in this, with Portal's self-confidence allowing him to maintain Harris in situ. Harris was unquestionably the right man to take over Bomber Command in 1942, as he proved instrumental in revolutionising the command and ensuring its grand successes in 1942 and 1943. Harris also developed an exceptional relationship with the Eighth Air Force commanders and enjoyed the confidence of Churchill, who later cynically threw him under the bus to protect his own post-war legacy.

---

102 Harris to Portal, 28 December 1944, RAFM/H83/107.
103 Portal to Harris, 20 January 1945, RAFM/H84/10.

The letters Harris and Portal exchanged from late 1944 through early 1945 demonstrate the character of both men; they further highlight Portal's comparative strategic flexibility, the source of most of his disagreements with Harris. Portal came to believe the CBO to be an enabling rather than a war-winning campaign; Harris simply could not abandon his view of the path to victory. Portal was frustrated at his inability to educate Harris, while Harris remembered it as the only occasion in the war when Portal lost his temper with him.[104] Yet Harris's job was never under serious threat. Portal kept Harris in place because Harris enjoyed the confidence of Churchill, the Americans, and his Bomber Command subordinates, and because he oversaw tremendous strides at Bomber Command. Portal believed it would have been 'monstrously unjust' to replace Harris after all he had done for Bomber Command.[105] According to Dermot Boyle, a future Chief of Air Staff, who observed Portal keenly during the war, 'If Portal had thought that Harris was not doing well for the country, Harris would have been out in five minutes.'[106] It is the mark of both men that their relationship endured to the end of the war and beyond. On 9 May 1945, Portal wrote to Harris:

> My Dear Bert,
> All official congratulations are going out in the name of the Air Council, but I would like to send you a personal note to tell you how deeply and sincerely grateful to you I feel for all you and your Command have done. It has been truly magnificent.
>
> I also want to thank you for never letting the inevitable differences of opinion in a long war affect our personal relationship and I would like also to say how tremendously I admired the way you refused to let ill-health affect your grip and mastery of your great three-year battle. For the support you have always given me, and for your tremendous personal contribution to the achievements of the RAF in this war I can never adequately thank you.[107]

Harris humbly replied:

---

104 Hastings, *Bomber Command*, 334.
105 Ibid.
106 Richards, Denis, 'Portal, Harris and the Bomber Offensive', *RAF Historical Society Journal*, No. 6 (September 1989), 15.
107 Probert, *Harris*, 342; Richards, *Portal of Hungerford*, 327.

Thank you for your letter – which I do not deserve altho' my crews and others do. If we had differences of opinion, they were not personal – and in the outcome you were always right on the things that mattered. The burden, which you have so well supported, far exceeded mine but I am of the lesser stature. I regret indeed occasions on which I have been crochety and impatient – I was the closest to the urgencies of my Command and, frankly, borne down by the frightful inhumanities of war. Thank you for all you did for us and the Country.[108]

If any words sum up Portal's monumental contribution to Britain's wartime effort, they appear in Harris's missive. 'In the outcome you were always right on the things that mattered.'

---

108 Harris to Portal, 10 May 1945, CC/2/A/2/20.

Chapter 8

Aftermath

To the Victor go the spoils.

Senator William L. Marcy

With his customary grace and humility, Portal retired from the RAF at the end of 1945. 'He engaged in no polemics. He (uniquely among his colleagues) wrote no contentious and self-laudatory memoirs. He neither thumped his chest nor beat his breast. He took his laurels and left. Not everyone in the RAF, or in the country, appreciated the debt they owed him; but this seemed to worry him not one whit.'[1]

Victory brought a surfeit of honours Portal's way. He had already been awarded a KCB and GCB in 1940 and 1942 respectively, as well as awards from Poland, Czechoslovakia, and Norway. Victory brought many more.[2] King George awarded Portal the Order of Merit on 1 January 1946, the day after Portal's retirement from the RAF. The only other recipient on the list that year was Churchill. He was made Baron Portal of Hungerford on 17 August 1946 and, absent any sons, requested that a special remainder be granted for his daughter Rosemary.[3] Prime Minister Atlee gladly submitted this to King George VI, who approved it. This was an unusual mark of respect for Portal, as similar requests were customarily denied. Portal also had his Barony upgraded to a Viscounty, alongside Alan Brooke and

---

1 'Lord Portal: Marshal of the Royal Air Force, *The Wykehamist*, No. 1199, 2 June 1971.

2 Knight Commander of the Order of the Bath (KCB) and Knight Grand Cross of the Order of the Bath (GCB) respectively. The latter was a promotion in rank in the fourth highest order of chivalry in the British Empire (behind the Most Noble Order of the Garter, the Most Ancient and Most Noble Order of the Thistle and the Most Illustrious Order of St Patrick [dormant]).

3 Richards, Denis, *Portal of Hungerford: The Life of Marshal of the Royal Air Force, Viscount Portal of Hungerford, KG, GCB, OM, DSO, MC.* New York, N.Y.: Holmes & Meier, 1977, 340.

Andrew Cunningham. He was awarded honorary degrees from numerous universities, including both Oxford and Cambridge, and was promoted to the Order of the Garter at the end of 1946.[4] The US, France, Belgium, and Greece awarded further accolades, giving Portal recognition on an unprecedented but fully deserved scale.

On 12 June 1946, the British wartime COS met once more as each received the Freedom of the City of London. Their unity on display, they arrived in a carriage specially made for the occasion; it allowed them to sit alongside one another rather than one behind the other two, which might have inferred a seniority none felt. Portal spoke with great eloquence on the occasion, as usual putting forward the contribution of others, rather than himself. In particular, he wished:

> To put on record my humble tribute to those members of the Royal Air Force whom I had the privilege of leading in the war and on whose behalf I receive with pride and gratitude the Freedom of this City and its Sword of Honour ... It is they who have earned the load of Honours heaped upon my person – a load that would be unbearable were it not spread, as in truth it is spread, among the scores of thousands who died in the fight, among the scores of senior commanders and Staff officers whose wisdom and experience directed their operations.[5]

Portal's particular reference to the RAF was deliberate, as he insisted that Alan Brooke make similar mention of the British Army in his own speech.[6] It was a final example, in uniform, of Portal's joint perspective. 'To share this occasion with my former colleagues multiplies threefold the happiness which it gives me, not only for personal reasons but also because our joint appearance seems to give recognition, as a fact, to the thing for which above all else we strove – the welding of the three Services, with all their diversity of function and of tradition, into one great fighting instrument.'[7]

---

4 Richards, *Portal of Hungerford*, 340–341.
5 Speech: Sir Charles Portal on receiving the Freedom of the City of London, 12 June 1946, in Alanbrooke Papers, King's College London (hereafter referred to as KCL/AB), KCL/AB/9/1/4.
6 Letter: Portal to Brooke, 27 March 1946, KCL/AB/9/1/4.
7 Speech: Sir Charles Portal on receiving the Freedom of the City of London, 12 June 1946, KCL/AB/9/1/4.

Portal's approach echoed the thoughts of Churchill, who shortly after VE Day had opined:

> And here is the moment when I pay my personal tribute to the British Chiefs of Staff with whom I worked in the closest intimacy through these heavy, stormy years. There have been very few changes in this small, powerful and capable body of men who, sinking all Service differences and judging the problems of war as a whole, have worked together in perfect harmony with each other. In Field Marshal Brooke, in Admiral Pound, succeeded after his death by Admiral Andrew Cunningham, and in Marshal of the Air Portal, a team was formed who deserved the highest honour in the direction of the whole British war strategy and in its relation with that of our allies.[8]

After a brief spell of inactivity, Portal accepted Churchill's invitation to become the Controller of Atomic Energy, within the Ministry of Supply. In this role, Portal advanced the argument for Britain to gain an atomic weapon and thus, a seat at the top table.[9] He held the post for five years before later becoming the Director of British Aluminium Co. He also held a series of directorships elsewhere, including Barclays Bank, Commercial Union Assurance and at the Ford Motor Co. In all these roles his calm management delivered effective results, though nothing as dramatic as those of his wartime service. To many, his integrity, kindness, and transparent honesty shone through every communiqué.[10] His post-service behaviour reflected his time in uniform; there was only one, authentic, Charles Portal.

As well as business activities, Portal enjoyed more leisurely pursuits. Of particular joy must have been the year he spent as President of the Marylebone Cricket Club (MCC), a distinct honour for a keen cricketer. He volunteered actively for the RAF Benevolent Fund and the Nuffield Trust, and supported the reconsecration of the RAF church at St Clement Danes. He went about his work quietly, with a poise that stayed with him to the end. In early 1971 doctors informed him he had an inoperable cancer. Sir

---

8 Churchill, Winston, *Great War Speeches*, World Broadcast, 13 May 1945, 360.

9 Denis Richards' notes on Portal, in Portal Papers, Christ Church College Oxford (Hereafter referred to as CC), CC/3/X.

10 Edwards, Sir George, 'An Appreciation of Sir Charles Portal', *Airframe*, June 1971, CC/3/X.

Charles Portal died peacefully at home on 22 April 1971, the last surviving member of the both the British COS and CCS Committees.

Charles Portal was instrumental in winning the war, yet he has been largely forgotten. He is lauded neither as strategist, nor diplomat nor leader. To some he is merely a peripheral figure, to others deeply flawed. Individual quotes are taken to erroneously represent his whole contribution, such as Portal's desire for 4,000 to 6,000 heavy bombers to win the war. Perhaps though, it is the historical view of the CBO that has most adversely coloured opinions of Portal. If the CBO is viewed as a failure, or worse a non-starter, then Portal's judgement must have been seriously awry, and he could not have been an effective strategist.

Those who consider the CBO to have failed are making a fantastical logical leap. They associate the inability to achieve strategic bombing's initial goal, to have the Germans capitulate before military victory in the land domain was achieved, with the overall ineffectiveness of the CBO. This logic is missing several steps to make it compelling. Firstly, it does not ask what contribution the CBO made to destroying German industry, to having that industry spread out rather than concentrated, to assisting the Soviets in the East, or to preventing the Wehrmacht from providing reinforcements following the OVERLORD landings. As the official history concludes, the CBO contributed hugely in all of these ways and was a vital cog in Allied victory in the European theatre of operations (ETO).[11] Portal was indeed inextricably linked to the bomber offensive, but it was not the failure often presented.

Adam Tooze presents a compelling case for the CBO's effectiveness in *The Wages of Destruction*. The text offers substantiating evidence of strategic bombing's impact on the German wartime economy. The predominant critique of the CBO highlights Germany's continuing industrial output as a mark against strategic bombing's effects. This critique omits mention of what German production would have been absent the CBO. As Tooze notes, 'For six months in 1943 the disruption caused by British and American bombing halted Speer's armaments miracle in its tracks.'[12] Tooze goes on to describe the 1944 'revitalisation' of the German war economy: faced with apocalyptic oppression, the population produced outdated aircraft, which

11 Webster, Charles Kingsley and Frankland, Noble, *The Strategic Air Offensive against Germany, 1939–1945. History of the Second World War Vol. 3*; United Kingdom Military Series. London: H.M. Stationery Office, 1961., 288–289.

12 Tooze, *The Wages of Destruction: The Making and Breaking of the Nazi Economy.* Penguin: New York, 2006, 671.

Allied fighters subsequently destroyed in droves. Following the Eighth Air Force's spectacular 'Big Week' in February 1944, German *Jaegerstab* (fighter staff) leaders toured German aircraft factories and 'dispensed summary justice' on those managers deemed to have failed.[13] Speer's 1944 miracle did not signify the CBO's failure, but a failing autocracy's last-ditch effort to stave off inevitable defeat.

Like Tooze, Phillips O'Brien attributes the degradation and eventual destruction of the German war economy to the CBO. O'Brien's *How the War was Won* depicts the service chiefs' contending views of strategic bombing. Alan Brooke, O'Brien notes, simply never realised strategic bombing's potential.[14] Portal questioned the merits of 'morale bombing', consistently inserting references to oil and transportation targets (which Harris derided as panaceas) into documents purporting to support city bombing.[15] O'Brien also highlights the CBO's contribution to Russian success in the East. By the end of 1943, 70 per cent of German fighters were either defending Germany or the Western Front, leaving only eleven weak fighter *Gruppen* on the whole Eastern Front.[16] This left Eastern Front German troops largely undefended from attack by the reinvigorated Red Air Force. Over Germany and the Mediterranean, Allied bombers destroyed 4,732 German aircraft in the second half of 1943.[17] This incredible level of attrition ensured that Germany could not replace its experienced pilots. Likewise, the 1944 oil campaign, prosecuted as part of the CBO, curtailed training for new Luftwaffe pilots. Though German fighter production peaked in 1944, the Luftwaffe was a paper tiger by then: a fighter force of embryonic pilots flying outdated models patched together from scrap. The CBO attrition campaign had enormous effects on the war in Europe. The failure of its loftiest aim, to win the war through strategic bombing alone, ought not to cloud the truth of its disparaging effect on German industry.

Two further myths cloud the CBO's historical record. The first is that the Eighth Air Force practised high-altitude daylight precision bombing in Europe. The reality is that the Eighth Air force often resorted to area attacks on

---

13 Tooze, *Wages of Destruction*, 628.
14 O'Brien, Phillips Payson, How the War Was Won: Air-sea Power and Allied Victory in World War II, Cambridge Military Histories. 2015, 163.
15 Ibid., 164.
16 Ibid., 291.
17 Ibid., 292.

cities.[18] Bomber Command, despite the ironic protestations of its commander, was mostly more accurate than the Eighth when weather conditions allowed precision bombing. In no small part, this was due to the ORS in Bomber Command, whose insightful analysis informed improvements in both tactics and equipment. However, over northern Europe, where cloud cover was typically heavy, neither Bomber Command nor the Eighth Air Force could, for practical reasons, carry out precision bombing.

The second slight against Bomber Command hinges on the morality of the campaign. As Max Hastings wrote, 'February 1945 marked the moment when farsighted airmen and politicians began to perceive that history might judge the achievements of strategic air power with far less enthusiasm than their own Target Intelligence departments.'[19] It was in fact late March, not February, when Churchill penned a minute stating, 'The destruction of Dresden remains a serious query against the conduct of Allied bombing ... I feel the need for more precise concentration upon military targets, such as oil and communications behind the immediate battle-zone, rather than on mere acts of terror and wanton destruction, however impressive.'[20] Portal, with customary magnanimity and poise, claimed the PM must have been tired when he drafted it, and that it would be unfair to the PM to allow it to stand.[21] Portal subsequently approached Churchill alone and persuaded him to withdraw the minute, another example of his remarkable influence on Churchill. The PM had Ismay redraft the minute to finish, 'We must see to it that our attacks do not do more harm to ourselves in the long run than they do to the enemy's immediate war effort.'[22] Despite the withdrawal and redraft, the original minute remains central to the story of the war and perceptions of a government to Air Ministry divide that did not exist. The original minute has even been quoted in a recent *Air Force Magazine* article.[23]

---

18 Biddle, Tami Davis, Rhetoric and Reality in Air Warfare: The Evolution of British and American Ideas about Strategic Bombing, 1914–1945, 1st. pbk. ed. Princeton Studies in International History and Politics. Princeton, N.J.; Woodstock: Princeton University Press, 2004, 292.

19 Hastings, Max, Bomber Command, New York: Dial Press/J. Wade, 1979, 343.

20 Webster and Frankland, *The Strategic Air Offensive, Vol. 3*, 112.

21 Richards, *Portal*, 192.

22 Webster and Frankland, *Strategic Air Offensive Vol. 3*, 117.

23 Correll, John T., 'The Allied Rift on Strategic Bombing,' *Air Force Magazine*, 1 December 2020, at 'The Allied Rift on Strategic Bombing – *Air Force Magazine*', accessed on 30 June 2021.

The US JCS proved much more aware of bombing's moral ambiguity than some British commanders; both Arnold and Eaker insisted the USAAF had conducted precision bombing whenever questioned. Other than Hawaiians and Alaskans, American civilians were never attacked during the war, and likely held a different view of strategic bombing than the British public. In contrast, Harris's honesty was jarring: 'I would not regard the whole of the remaining cities of Germany as worth the bones of one British grenadier.'[24] His words became even more stark as time passed, particularly as perspectives towards the German people softened after the Berlin Airlift. Yet a true assessment of morality can only be conducted considering what was known at the time, and what the conditions of war were.

The Allies fought an existential war against an abhorrent ideology. According to prevailing Just War theory, conditions of existential war, or 'supreme emergency,' leave the fighter with a single duty: survival.[25] The Second World War left Britain with no other options for attacking Germany; as such, there was no question of immoral action. As an industrialised country, Germany's cities – comprising transport hubs, industrial centres, power networks, government, and morale – were legitimate targets. Given Bomber Command's limitations at the time, area bombing was a strategic necessity. Portal's decisions to prosecute strategic area bombing were entirely morally appropriate.

Even the much-decried Dresden raids of February and March 1945 were grounded in significant military justification. Firstly, they aided the Russian advance and, according to George Marshall, the Russians requested them. Secondly, Dresden was both industrially significant and a virgin target. Thirdly, the war was not over. Land battles would still be fought at Nuremburg, Hamburg and Berlin until April–May 1945. The absence of effective air defences made Dresden appear defenceless. Yet, Bomber Command planning included a major accompanying raid on the Bohlen oil refinery, to divide Luftwaffe fighter attention, and significant spoofing. The expectation was that German air defence would be significant.[26] That this did not materialise was a pleasant surprise for the beleaguered crews of an exhausted command. The devastating

---

24 Hastings, *Bomber Command*, 344.
25 Walzer, Michael, *Just and Unjust Wars: A Moral Argument with Historical Illustrations* Fifth edition. New York, NY: Basic Books, a member of the Perseus Books Group, 2015, 251–255.
26 Verrier, Anthony, The Bomber Offensive. London: Batsford, 1968, 313.

results of the raids highlighted Bomber Command's achievement of both enhanced accuracy and the death of the Luftwaffe. The raids were not, however, immoral. Such views belie the reality and uncertainties of war. Portal's continued, and nuanced, support for the CBO writ large was entirely strategically apposite, and not the aberration of a man unable to escape the arguments of interwar air theorists. His judgement, though not faultless, is beyond reproach.

Portal also demonstrated excellent judgement in the prioritisation and apportionment of his assets. Perhaps the mark of his excellence is the critique levelled at him by all and sundry in this regard. He was roundly criticised by the Navy for a lack of support to the Battle of the Atlantic; by the Army for a lack of support to Army Co-operation Squadrons; implicitly by Tedder for a lack of support to North Africa; and by Harris for a lack of support to the bomber offensive. In all of these areas, only Tedder had real cause for complaint. Fighter Command assets, and in particular Spitfires, would have been of inestimable value in North Africa in 1941. They were, at the time, being used in ill-conceived operations over northern France to try to draw German fighter squadrons away from the Eastern Front. This was a misstep in which Portal supported the analysis of Leigh-Mallory and Douglas.

Crucially, from a strategic perspective, the Allies lost neither the Battle of the Atlantic nor the war in North Africa. The bomber offensive took its toll in 1943 and 1944 despite Harris's obsession with Berlin, and the Army got the co-operation it needed to prepare for OVERLORD. While no command or service received exactly what they wanted, each received what was needed. In strategy, it is more important to avoid defeat, rather than to pursue victory. Portal played a canny and patient game, while he awaited the American industrial juggernaut. He withstood withering critique from the narrow-minded and the uninformed, demonstrating significant fortitude in the process.

Portal also opposed certain campaigns he knew would overstretch British forces. He argued against both the debacle in Greece in 1941 and the Dodecanese in 1943. Ever pragmatic, Portal saw the deficiencies of such actions. He considered matters from a balanced standpoint. Because he did not consider Britain obligated to assist the Greeks, his strategic judgement remained unaffected. The Greek action was doomed from the start because of the long lines of communication. Portal rejected the action for this reason, but also because it unnecessarily degraded the strength of British forces in North Africa. Because he thought Turkey unlikely to join the war, he saw no strategic purpose for action in the Dodecanese. He also knew it would unnecessarily strain Alliance relations. The incursion into the Dodecanese was damned from the moment the Americans decided not to support it, as was inevitable.

Portal's outlook extended beyond the air war; he was a joint strategist who took full part in all strategic military decisions. Again, he got most of the big decisions right. Portal and Brooke's plan to attack the 'soft underbelly' of Europe via North Africa, Sicily and Italy was a strategic masterstroke. Both men understood that France could only be liberated by severely weakening German forces (to which the CBO contributed greatly). Portal knew that getting Italy out of the war would leave German divisions stuck in Italy, unable to support the Western Front in 1944. Moreover, Portal refused Arnold's bait of a pure air offensive against Italy, preferring a joint campaign. He knew the value of joint operations and eschewed any RAF-centric temptations. The hard fighting in Italy proved the necessity of such action, and OVERLORD's success was vindication for Portal's and Brooke's overall European strategy.

Another important aspect of Portal's strategic success was the selection of his subordinate commanders. This book discusses two in great detail: Arthur Tedder and Arthur Harris. These were both fantastic appointments. However, Portal's appointment of Wilfrid Freeman as his deputy in the Air Ministry was a real masterstroke. Nobody knew the RAF better than Freeman, and Portal needed someone to carry out the day-to-day business of the service while he concentrated on the COS Committee and higher strategy. Moreover, Freeman's expert knowledge of the MAP ensured effective oversight of the RAF's procurement programme. The appointment was another demonstration of Portal's humility, as well as his self-awareness in grasping that he could not do everything.

Tedder was, perhaps, the outstanding operational air commander of the war. Both he and his field commander 'Mary' Coningham worked wonders in North Africa and the Mediterranean. Tedder's appointment was confirmed against Churchill's wishes, but he was an outstanding success, so much so that Tedder elicited a rare apology from Churchill later. Portal was, under the most extreme pressure, willing to replace Tedder in November 1941. This would have been a mistake, which Auchinleck was instrumental in preventing.

In a theatre that needed a great organiser and collaborator, but also someone with an appreciation for joint operations, Tedder excelled. Despite being frequently starved of air assets due to crises in other theatres, Tedder's ingenuity and ability to make the most out of a very difficult situation really shone through. His frank correspondence was also vital in providing Portal with insight into the real problems in North Africa, which the other services initially blamed on the RAF. Under Tedder and Coningham this narrative changed. Even Montgomery was forced to acknowledge the phenomenal efforts of the Desert Air Force. On 2 November 1942, at the height of the Battle of El Alamein, he commented, 'They are winning this battle for me. The RAF are doing a wonderful job.'[27]

Throughout the war, Portal used his bluntest instrument, Arthur Harris, brilliantly. Harris was central to the successes Portal's Bomber Command enjoyed in the Battles of France and Britain. His No. 5 Group aircraft led the raid on Berlin that changed the course of the Battle of Britain, and together the two men developed technological advances important later in the war. Harris was an effective DCAS, acting as an agent of change in the bloated Air Ministry before Portal sent him across the Atlantic to further solidify UK–US relations. Harris' technical expertise and belief in bombing forged key relationships in America. When he returned to Bomber Command, he embodied the passionate command needed to reenergise an ailing force, and skilfully integrated the Eighth Air Force into the forthcoming CBO. Later in the war they disagreed about the best way forwards, yet Portal was able to ensure that Harris carried out Bomber Command's designated tasks, even when Harris believed the missions were not the best use of his forces.

The men above represent the most important of Portal's subordinates, but Portal also occasionally had to work to ensure the wrong appointment was not made. Churchill was insistent in 1943 that Sholto Douglas be appointed the new Vice Chief of Air Staff. He wrote, 'There is only one place for Douglas, that of Vice Chief of Air Staff … I trust you will meet my strong views on this matter.'[28] This note was written to the Secretary of State for Air, Archie Sinclair. Portal persuaded Sinclair to stand fast and have Douglas Evill appointed, who was a much more amiable character, if less forthright. This reality reflected the fact that Portal had to also manage the careers of those who did not possess the capabilities of Tedder, Freeman or Harris. Finding senior appointments was a challenging task, and not an exact science. Portal's one misstep may have been assigning Leigh-Mallory as the tactical air commander for OVERLORD. He undoubtedly had the expertise to conduct the role, but he lacked the interpersonal skills to be successful in such an important Allied position.

---

27 Orange, Vincent, Coningham: *A Biography of Air Marshal Sir Arthur Coningham, KCB, KBE, DSO, MC, DFC, AFC*. Washington, D.C.: Center for Air Force History, 1992, 115.
28 The National Archives, Kew (hereafter referred to as TNA), TNA/PREM/3/15.

Portal's importance to British strategy was matched by his overall contribution to the Alliance. Allied strategy was not decided purely upon a rational basis during the Second World War. Since the rational ends of the United States and the United Kingdom were not precisely alike, this would have been impossible. Charles Portal was well aware of this and worked to ensure a strategy was implemented that would prove acceptable to all parties. This was an extraordinarily difficult task because Portal had to first get Brooke to agree, then Churchill, and finally the US JCS. At CASABLANCA it was Portal who saw the immediate value of a paper drafted by Slessor, which subsequently overcame disagreements between the UK and US regarding the allocation of forces to the ETO and the Pacific respectively. Portal also produced the compromise course of action at CASABLANCA when agreement regarding operations in Italy could not be reached. He suggested Sicily be next, and pushed the decision about Italy to the future. In the end it became obvious that operations in France in 1943 would be impossible, so the Americans ultimately agreed to operations in Italy. Compromise was essential as the participants basic convictions were unchanged. Brooke described his appreciation of the respective views following the Washington Conference in May 1943:

> King still remains determined to press Pacific at the expense of all other fronts. Marshall wishes to ensure cross Channel operation at expense of Mediterranean. Brooke still feels that Mediterranean offers far more hope of adding to final success. Portal in his heart feels that if we left him a free hand bombing alone might well win the war. And dear old Dudley Pound when he wakes up wishes we would place submarine warfare above all other requirements. Out of the above compromise emerges and the war is prolonged, whilst we age and get more and more weary![29]

Fatalistic and downtrodden as Brooke was, he illustrated the clear necessity of compromise, and the importance of Portal's presence on the CCS Committee. Ismay thought Portal 'was instrumental in smoothing over many difficulties,' necessary as some members of the CCS Committee were

---

29 Alanbrooke, A., Todman, Daniel, and Danchev, Alex, *War Diaries, 1939–1945: Field Marshal Lord Alanbrooke*. Berkeley: University of California Press, 2001, 411.

much more truculent than Portal.[30] Portal could also be quick-thinking in resolving disagreements, as he was when Mountbatten proposed an assault on the Andaman Islands (OP BUCCANEER). Rather than merely stating that the islands had no strategic value from an air perspective, Portal went on to suggest an alternative course of action to President Roosevelt: a 'hit and run' raid elsewhere to appease the Chinese. It was another example of Portal just seeking a way forward for the Alliance.

While patient, Portal was not immovable. His strategic paper of autumn 1942 proposed courses of action (COAs) that he initially considered mutually exclusive. However, he did not blindly adhere to these views once written, and Alan Brooke slowly convinced him this was not the case during October 1942. Portal subsequently realised heavy bombing could be a preparatory phase for the invasion of France, not an alternative, and presented this COA to Churchill. The official history critiques Portal's consideration of the COAs as mutually exclusive, but not for possessing the magnanimity to support the changes once made.

Portal also quickly altered RAF support to the Battle of the Atlantic once evidence showed a better way forward in early 1943. In doing so, Portal showed he was unconcerned with saving face, but solely with making the correct decisions. Moreover, he demonstrated that his strategic acumen stretched to the naval realm, as well as the land and air domains he so clearly mastered. This breadth of knowledge, underpinned by his extraordinary intellect, ensured he played a full part in all military decisions as one of Churchill's key advisors.

Portal knew the vital importance of his relationship with Churchill and spent hours and hours responding to the endless stream of minutes emanating from the PM's office. He did so both to establish credibility early on in his tenure, but also as a mark of respect for a man whose responsibilities dwarfed all others. Portal maintained a prodigious level of personal correspondence during the war, even writing to his VCAS's wife to apologise for keeping him (Wilfrid Freeman) away from home so much. He wrote informally to Hap Arnold on several occasions during the war, and visited him in hospital following Arnold's second heart attack.

Portal and Brooke argued for most of 1942 about strategy, but Portal never lost his calm. He rarely, if ever, did. When things start to go wrong during war, a kneejerk reaction is the most natural of human responses.

---

30 Ismay, Hastings Lionel, *Memoirs*, New York: Viking Press, 1960, 318.

Portal never suffered from this affliction. He remained remarkably steady throughout the war, never vacillating from a strategic course of action, but never so wedded to one he was unable to see potential alternatives. Even in their early discourse, when Churchill questioned strategic bombing as a war-winning approach, Portal did not give a closed-minded defence of the strategy. He simply pointed out that other strategies would require a different air force to the one that was currently being built. His strategic patience also allowed him to see that results might not come as quickly as desirable, but that did not mean they would not come. Portal's early discourse with Churchill is littered with examples of his patient approach, of him choosing to stay the course rather than making a quick change to appease his fickle master. The discussion about the Middle East theatre epitomises this approach. As Portal knew how difficult it would be to reinforce the theatre if things went awry, he had no wish to change the allocation of forces to make rapid gains elsewhere. He knew it was a zero-sum game.

Portal's patience and calm also shone through in his regard for the Eighth Air Force's bombing efforts in 1942. Portal was prepared to wait for the effects that might be delivered through success, because he knew the pay-off could be huge. General Sir Leslie Hollis, Senior Assistant Secretary to the War Cabinet, wrote that Portal was:

> Another calm character with a brain like a rapier. I never saw him ruffled even under vicious and uninformed attacks on the Air Force. He would sit surveying the critic coldly from beneath his heavy-lidded eyes, never raising his voice or losing his temper, but replying to rhetoric with facts. A great man, Portal, who enjoyed the complete confidence of the US Air Chiefs.[31]

Alongside his calmness, Portal's humility set him apart from others. Because he was unconcerned with being right all the time, he was able to moderate his views as soon as a more informed one came along. Similarly, in correspondence, he was willing to admit to being wrong where others would not. His letters to Tedder at the beginning of 1945, in the shadow of

---

31 Leasor, James, *War at the Top: The Experiences of General Sir Leslie Hollis*, London: Michael Joseph Ltd, 1959, Introduction.

the OCTAGON Conference, demonstrate this trait perfectly. He held his hands up that he had written something in error and apologised to Tedder, his subordinate, unreservedly. This incident also demonstrates Portal's empathetic nature; he could always see the other side's perspective. This may have been the character trait that enabled him to remain so calm under the most extreme pressure. However, it was his transparent honesty that the US JCS found so appealing. Portal never made an argument for personal gain, only for the betterment of the Alliance. He held to the higher ideal at all times. It is this factor, above all others, that made him an incredibly important and effective leader.

Portal's breadth of engagement at the highest levels made him easily the most important Royal Air Force officer of the war. It is important to recognise that myriad great leaders were needed to defeat the Axis powers. Charles Portal was one of these great leaders, and his influence was prodigious. He embraced the nature of his appointment, successfully guiding the RAF through the war. As service chief, Portal had unfettered access to all the key players; his influence was inherently greater than any subordinate officers, if not always as apparent. Portal's role was not primarily to inspire, but to organise, to strategise rather than to lead. Yet, his leadership was also tangible in how he dealt with people on a daily basis. He was central to the execution of British strategy due to his close relationship with Churchill, and his position on both the COS and CCS Committees, where British and Alliance grand strategy were conceived and agreed. Portal's contribution spans several vital and interconnected areas: strategy, diplomacy and leadership.

One of the largest factors enabling Portal to influence Britain's war effort to such a degree was the relationships he built that form the backbone of this book. In an age of joint operations and coalition warfare, this assertion rings true. To be truly effective at the top levels of the military, leaders must be able to deal effectively with sister services, the industrial sector, the civil service, subordinates, political leadership, and perhaps even the general public. A complex web of relationships that must be managed to get things done in the modern world. Charles Portal provides an excellent case study of a man who built productive relationships with his colleagues, superiors, and subordinates.

A brief examination of the relationships in this book illuminates Portal's interpersonal skills and personality traits. To work effectively with Churchill, Portal needed huge reserves of stamina simply to keep up. He also had to be a subject matter expert on all RAF matters, so a high intellect was essential. The endless questioning from the Prime Minister could easily cause capitulation, so Portal had to be both forthright and resolute, though not to the point of obdurate stubbornness. Perhaps, above all, he needed patience, because Churchill rarely accepted a first answer and frequently reintroduced ideas and strategies that the COS thought had been rejected.

Alan Brooke was highly intelligent, but often abrupt, with very definite ideas about how the war should be fought. Portal's fortitude, intelligence and good humour won him a lifelong friend; the two men came to respect one another greatly. They did not agree strategically, but Portal's ability to maintain calm during heated debates ensured compromise was achieved. More importantly, their discussions never boiled over, as they did between Brooke and Ernest King at the Tehran Conference in late 1943. Portal demonstrated his infinite patience in dealing with the other services more generally. He was again resolute, yet logical and calm when explaining why the demands of the Royal Navy for the Battle of the Atlantic, and the British Army for co-operation training were not fully met. He understood their parochialism but could not afford to share it.

Portal's relationship with Tedder was relatively easy to manage despite the enormous operational challenges the latter faced. Their honest correspondence greatly assisted both men through difficult times. Portal was shrewd in perceiving Tedder's talents, and pushed those talents to the very edge with his meagre apportionment of aircraft. He trusted Tedder to get the job done, as well as to improve the organisation. Tedder proved to be a man who could do more with less, and he was equally firm in dealing with the other services. Portal's astute political sense was on full display in this relationship as he won Tedder over, and ensured the RAF version of events was available to the COS, or at least to Portal. Portal knew the tendency of the other services to blame the RAF for operational failures, and Tedder was his bulwark against biased operational reporting, and his natural successor as CAS.

Building a productive relationship with Hap Arnold was a distinct challenge. Portal's charm and charisma are most apparent here. He had to be at his best to win the Anglophobic Arnold over. Moreover, Portal once again demonstrated both his higher strategic vision and his empathy in understanding the problems of others. Portal knew Arnold resented sending his flying armada across the Atlantic, so was always gracious in communications. Portal knew how to get what the RAF needed from Arnold, and he was willing to give Arnold access to jet engine technology as the beginnings of a *quid pro quo* with his American colleague. Portal was deliberate in promoting rare early American bombing successes to Churchill, but firm in abjuring an air-only assault on Italy in 1943. Portal knew the value of joint action.

Portal's relationship with Harris was the most controversial, yet the two men remained friends despite heated debate. Portal again chose the right man for the job in the determined and diligent Harris, who revolutionised Bomber Command's output and capabilities. Harris was exactly who Portal needed to minimise the critique coming from Churchill, who was unimpressed with Bomber Command's efforts early in the war. Moreover, Harris worked exceptionally well with Ira Eaker and the American Eighth Air Force. Later, when Portal and Harris disagreed vociferously about the operational use of Bomber Command, Portal's temperance was on full display. He did not fire Harris, which would have been the easy thing to do, but not a course of action he considered fair. Portal's sense of justice kept Harris in post, but he was unarguably incredibly patient in dealing with a subordinate who was sometimes obstinate, closed-minded, and rude.

Charles Portal possessed a rare combination of personality traits that made him one of Britain's finest wartime leaders. Portal's minute to Churchill in 1942, prior to Arnold's second visit to London, perfectly encapsulates Portal's strategic, diplomatic and leadership abilities at work. He encouraged Churchill to build bridges with Arnold rather than seeking to maximise the output of Lend-Lease for the Royal Air Force. It took great self-confidence to send the minute in the first place, but Portal's strategic awareness, patience and willingness to compromise were all vital. Portal understood America would enter the war on its own terms, and realised that a productive relationship with America was in Britain's best long-term interests, even though this delayed the build-up of British military capability, and Bomber Command in particular. Portal was rightly concerned with being able to strike Germany with an enlarged bomber force, but he prioritised grand strategic calculations. He supported the American point of view, even though this meant a significant loss for the Royal Air Force in having its bomber allocation shredded. Portal pursued a grand strategic bargain that proved instrumental in the Alliance relationship, but must have been, at some level, a bitter pill to swallow.

It was this minute more than anything that resulted in the composition of this book. In carrying out early research on Portal, a sense of the great man was there, but there was no hard evidence, as I had not yet read the Portal Papers at Christ Church. One day, while reading Huston's description of Arnold's second trip to London, I sensed that Churchill's behaviour during the meetings with Arnold had been guided by outside intervention. I travelled to Oxford in the hope, but not necessarily the expectation, of finding a note from Portal to Churchill telling him that histrionics would not work, and that the British needed to keep Arnold onside for the long-term strategic benefits this would deliver. Finding that minute was the moment Portal emerged as a statesman with rare personal qualities. It was the moment I knew Portal's story had to be told again. Sir Charles Portal was a great man and a great leader, deserving of recognition and study as one of most important figures of the Second World War. He merits much more than being simply another unknown victor.

Coda

It is sincerely appropriate that the statues of the man who more than any other established the RAF on a permanent basis, and of the man who more than any other guided its efforts in the years of its greatest test and triumph, should now stand side by side.

Prime Minister Harold Macmillan
21 May 1975

Bibliography

Unpublished Sources and Archives

Air Force Historical Research Agency, Maxwell AFB, Alabama:
Hap Arnold Papers.
Henry L. Stimson Diaries.
Christ Church College, Oxford: Charles Portal Papers
Churchill College, Cambridge: Chartwell Papers
Imperial War Museum, London: Dudley Clarke Papers.
Liddell Hart Centre for Military Archives, King's College London: Alan
   Brooke and Hastings Ismay Papers.
The National Archives, Kew: CAB 79, CAB 80 and AIR archives.
RAF Museum, Hendon: Arthur Harris, Norman Bottomley and Arthur
   Tedder Papers.

Published Sources

Books
Alanbrooke, A., Todman, Daniel, and Danchev, Alex, *War Diaries,*
   1939–1945: Field Marshal Lord Alanbrooke. Berkeley: University of
   California Press, 2001.
Allison, Graham T. and Zelikow, Philip, *Essence of Decision: Explaining*
   the Cuban Missile Crisis. 2nd ed., New York: Longman, 1999.
Arnold, Henry Harley and Huston, John W., *American Airpower Comes of*
   Age: General Henry H. 'Hap' Arnold's World War II Diaries, Maxwell
   Air Force Base, AL: Air University Press, 2001.
Arnold, Henry Harley, *Global Mission,* London: Hutchinson, 1951.
Balfour Harold, *Wings over Westminster*, Hutchinson: London, 1973.

215

Ben-Moshe, T., *Churchill, Strategy and History*. Boulder, Co.: Lynne Rienner, 1992.

Bercuson, David Jay and Herwig, Holger H., *One Christmas in Washington: Churchill and Roosevelt Forge the Grand Alliance*. Toronto: McArthur, 2005.

Biddle, Tami Davis, *Rhetoric and Reality in Air Warfare: The Evolution of British and American Ideas about Strategic Bombing, 1914–1945*, 1st. pbk. ed. Princeton Studies in International History and Politics. Princeton, N.J.; Woodstock: Princeton University Press, 2004.

Boyle, Andrew, *Trenchard*, London: Collins, 1962.

Broad, Charlie Lewis. *Winston Churchill: A Biography*. New York: Hawthorn Books, 1958.

Brodhurst, Robin, *Churchill's Anchor: The Biography of Admiral of the Fleet Sir Dudley Pound*, Barnsley: Pen & Sword Maritime, 2015.

Bryant, Arthur and Alanbrooke, Viscount Alan Brooke, *The Turn of the Tide: a History of the War Years Based on the Diaries of Field-Marshal Lord Alanbrooke, Chief of the Imperial General Staff*. 1st ed. Garden City, N.Y.: Doubleday, 1957.

Bryant, Arthur and Alanbrooke, Viscount Alan Francis Brooke, *Triumph in the West: A History of the War Years Based on the Diaries of Field-Marshal Lord Alanbrooke, Chief of the Imperial General Staff*. 1st ed. Garden City, N.Y.: Doubleday, 1959.

Buell, Thomas B., *Master of Sea Power: A Biography of Fleet Admiral Ernest J. King*. 1st ed. Boston: Little, Brown, 1980.

Bungay, Stephen, *The Most Dangerous Enemy: A History of the Battle of Britain*. London: Aurum, Press, 2001.

Busch, Fritz-Otto, *Prinz Eugen*. London: First Futura Publications, 1975.

Butler, James Ramsay Montagu, Gwyer, J.M.A., Ehrman, John and Howard, Michael. *Grand Strategy: History of the Second World War Vol. IV*, United Kingdom Military Series. London: H.M. Stationery Office, 1956.

Butler, James Ramsay Montagu, Gwyer, J.M.A., Ehrman, John and Howard, Michael. *Grand Strategy: History of the Second World War Vol. V*, United Kingdom Military Series. London: H.M. Stationery Office, 1956.

Butler, James Ramsay Montagu, Gwyer, J.M.A., Ehrman, John and Howard, Michael. *Grand Strategy: History of the Second World War, Vol. VI*, United Kingdom Military Series. London: H.M. Stationery Office, 1956.

Charmley, John, *Churchill: The End of Glory: A Political Biography*. London: Hodder & Stoughton, 1993.

Churchill, Winston, Roosevelt, Franklin D., Kimball, Warren F., *Churchill & Roosevelt: The Complete Correspondence*, Princeton, N.J.: Princeton University Press, 1984.

Churchill, Winston, *Great War Speeches*, World Broadcast, 13 May 1945.

Churchill, Winston, *Lord Randolph Churchill*, New ed., London: Odhams Press, 1952.

Churchill, Winston S., *The Second World War, Vol. II, Their Finest Hour*, The Educational Book Company Ltd: London, 1951.

Churchill, Winston S., *The Second World War, Vol. III, The Grand Alliance*, The Educational Book Company Ltd: London, 1951.

Churchill, Winston S., *The Second World War, Vol. IV: The Hinge of Fate*, The Educational Book Company Ltd: London, 1951.

Coffey, Thomas M., *HAP: The Story of the U.S. Air Force and the Man Who Built It, General Henry 'Hap' Arnold*, New York: Viking Press, 1982.

Connelly, Mark, *Reaching for the Stars: A New History of Bomber Command in World War II*. London; New York: I.B. Tauris. Distributed by St Martin's Press, 2001.

Corum, James S. and Johnson, Wray R., *Airpower in Small Wars: Fighting Insurgents and Terrorists*. Modern War Studies. Lawrence, Kan.: University Press of Kansas, 2003.

Cohen, Eliot A., *Supreme Command: Soldiers, Statesmen, and Leadership in Wartime*, 1st Archor Books ed., New York: Anchor Books, 2003.

Copp, DeWitt S., *Forged in Fire: Strategy and Decisions in the Air War over Europe, 1940–45*. Garden City, N.Y.: Doubleday, 1982.

Crane, Conrad C., *Bombs, Cities, and Civilians: American Airpower Strategy in World War II*, Lawrence [Kan.]: University Press of Kansas, 1993.

Danchev, Alex, *Very Special Relationship: Field-Marshal Sir John Dill and the Anglo-American Alliance, 1941–44*, 1st ed. London; Washington: Brassey's Defence Publishers, 1986.

Daso, D., *Architects of American Air Supremacy: Gen. Hap Arnold and Dr Theodore von Kármán*. Maxwell AFB, Ala.: Air University Press, 1997.

Daso, Dik A., *Doolittle, Aerospace Visionary*, Military Profiles. Washington, D.C.: Brassey's, 2003.

Daso, Dik A., *Hap Arnold and the Evolution of American Airpower*. Washington, D.C.: Smithsonian Institution Press, 2000.

Davis, Paul K., *Masters of the Battlefield: Great Commanders from the Classical Age to the Napoleonic Era*. New York: Oxford University Press, 2013.

Davis, Richard G., *Bombing the European Axis Powers: A Historical Digest of the Combined Bomber Offensive 1939–1945.* Maxwell Air Force Base, Alabama: Air University Press, 2012.

Davis, Richard G., United States Air Force. Office of Air Force History, A.F.C.H.O. and Afcho, *Carl A. Spaatz and the Air War in Europe.* General Histories. Washington, D.C.: Office of Air Force History, U.S. Air Force, 1993.

Dobson, Alan P., *US Wartime Aid to Britain*, 1940–1946. New York: St Martin's Press, 1986.

Douglas, Sholto, *Years of combat; the first volume of the autobiography of Sholto Douglas.* London: Collins, 1963.

DuPre, Flint O., *Hap Arnold: Architect of American Air Power.* Air Force Academy Series. New York: Macmillan, 1972.

Eden, Anthony, *The Reckoning; the Memoirs of Anthony Eden, Earl of Avon.* Boston: Houghton Mifflin Co., 1965.

Ehlers, Robert, *The Mediterranean Air War: Airpower and Allied Victory in World War II.* Lawrence, Kan: University Press of Kansas, 2015.

Eisenhower, Dwight D., *Crusade in Europe,* (Garden City, N.Y.: Doubleday), 1948.

Eisenhower, Dwight D., (Dwight David) and Robert H. Ferrell. *The Eisenhower Diaries,* 1st ed. New York: Norton, 1981.

Fraser, David, *Alanbrooke.* London: Bloomsbury Reader, 2013.

French, David, *Raising Churchill's Army*, Oxford: OUP, 2011.

Furse, Anthony, *Wilfrid Freeman*, Spellmount, 2000.

Gentile, Gian, *How Effective Is Strategic Bombing? Lessons Learned from World War II to Kosovo.* New York: NYU Press, 2001.

Goebbels, Joseph, and Lochner, Louis Paul, *The Goebbels Diaries, 1942–1943.* (1st ed.). Garden City, N.Y.: Doubleday, 1948.

Harriman, W. Averell and Abel, Elie, *Special Envoy to Churchill and Stalin, 1941–1946,* New York: Random House, 1975.

Harris, Arthur, *Bomber Offensive*, Barnsley: Pen & Sword, 2005.

Haslop, Dennis, *Britain, Germany and the Battle of the Atlantic: A Comparative Study,* London: Bloomsbury Academic, 2013.

Hastings, Max, *Bomber Command,* New York: Dial Press/J. Wade, 1979.

Hastings, M., *Winston's War: Churchill, 1940–1945* (1st Vintage Books ed.). New York: Vintage Books, 2011.

Hayes, Grace P., *The History of the Joint Chiefs of Staff in World War II: The War against Japan.* Annapolis: Naval Institute Press, 1981.

Horne, Alistair, *To Lose a Battle: France 1940*. Rev. ed. London: Penguin, 2007.

Hughes, Terry and Costello, John, *The Battle of the Atlantic* New York: Dial Press/J. Wade, 1977.

Huntington, S., *The Soldier and the State; the Theory and Politics of Civil-Military Relations*. Cambridge: Belknap Press of Harvard University Press, 1957.

Ismay, Hastings Lionel, *Memoirs,* New York: Viking Press, 1960.

Janowitz, M., *The Professional Soldier, a Social and Political Portrait*. Glencoe, Ill.: Free Press, 1960.

Jenkins, Roy, *The Chancellors*. London: Macmillan, 2015.

Jones, H. and Raleigh, Sir Walter Alexander, *The War in the Air: Being the Story of the Part Played in the Great War by the Royal Air Force: Appendices* (History of the Great War). Oxford: Clarendon Press, 1937.

Kane, Robert B., *So Far from Home: Royal Air Force and Free French Air Force Flight Training at Maxwell and Gunter Fields during World War II,* 2016.

Kennedy, John, *The Business of War; the War Narrative of Major-General Sir John Kennedy,* London: Hutchinson, 1957.

Kimball, Warren F., *Churchill and Roosevelt, Volume 3: The Complete Correspondence – Three Volumes*. Princeton, NJ: Princeton University Press, 2015.

Kimball, Warren F. and Kimball, Warren F., *The Most Unsordid Act*, Baltimore: The Johns Hopkins Press, 2019.

Kuter, Laurence Sherman, *Airman at Yalta*. 1st ed. New York: Duell, Sloan and Pearce, 1955.

LaSaine, John T., *Air Officer Commanding: Hugh Dowding, Architect of the Battle of Britain,* Lebanon, NH: ForeEdge, 2018.

Leasor, James, *War at the Top: The Experiences of General Sir Leslie Hollis*, London: Michael Joseph Ltd, 1959.

Lewis, Cecil, *Sagittarius Rising*. Great Novels and Memoirs of World War I, Harrisburg, P.A.: Stackpole Books, 1967 and republished Barnsley: Pen & Sword, 2009.

MacIsaac, David, *Strategic Bombing in World War II: The Story of the United States Strategic Bombing Survey,* New York: Garland Pub. Co., 1976.

May, Ernest R., *Strange Victory: Hitler's Conquest of France*. 1st ed. New York: Hill and Wang, 2000.

Meilinger, Phillip S., *Airmen and Air Theory: A Review of the Sources*. Maxwell Air Force Base, AL: Air University Press, 2001.

Mets, David R., *Master of Airpower: General Carl A. Spaatz*. Novato, CA: Presidio Press, 1988.

Miller, Russell, *Boom: The Life of Viscount Trenchard: Father of the Royal Air Force,* London: Weidenfeld & Nicolson, 2016.

Moorehead, Alan, *Desert War: The North African Campaign 1940–1943*, Penguin: New York, 2001.

O'Brien, Phillips Payson, *How the War Was Won: Air-sea Power and Allied Victory in World War II*, Cambridge Military Histories. 2015.

O'Hara, Vincent P., *Torch: North Africa and the Allied Path to Victory*. Annapolis: Naval Institute Press, 2015.

Orange, Vincent, *Churchill and His Airmen,* London: Grub Street, 2013.

Orange, Vincent, *Coningham: A Biography of Air Marshal Sir Arthur Coningham, KCB, KBE, DSO, MC, DFC, AFC*. Washington, D.C.: Center for Air Force History, 1992.

Orange, V., *Tedder: Quietly in Command* (Cass series – studies in air power, 9), London; Portland, OR: F. Cass, 2004.

Overy, R.J., *The Bombers and the Bombed: Allied Air War over Europe, 1940–1945*. New York: Viking, 2014.

Overy, R.J., *The Bombing War: Europe 1939–1945*, London: Penguin, 2013.

Owen, R., *Tedder.* London: Collins, 1952.

Parton, James and Air Force Historical Foundation, '*Air Force Spoken Here': General Ira Eaker and the Command of the Air.* 1st ed. Bethesda, M.D.: Adler & Adler, 1986.

Paterson, Michael, *Winston Churchill: Personal Accounts of the Great Leader at War,* Cincinnati: F&W Publications, 2005.

Playfair, Ian Stanley Ord, Molony, C.J.C. and Jackson, W.G.F., *The Mediterranean and Middle East: Volume II,* London: Naval & Military Press, 2004.

Playfair, Ian Stanley Ord, Molony, C.J.C. and Jackson, W.G.F., *The Mediterranean and Middle East: Volume III*, London: Naval & Military Press, 2004.

Playfair, Ian Stanley Ord, Molony, C.J.C. and Jackson, W.G.F., *The Mediterranean and Middle East: Volume V,* London: Naval & Military Press, 2004.

Pogue, Forrest C., *George C. Marshall: Ordeal and Hope 1939–1942*, New York: Viking Press, 1963.

Pogue, Forrest C., Bradley, Omar Nelson and Brėdli, Omar. *George C. Marshall: Organizer of Victory, 1943–1945*. New York: Penguin Books, 1993.

Porch, Douglas, *The Path to Victory*, New York: Farrar, Strauss and Giroux, 2004.

Probert, Henry, *Bomber Harris: His Life and Times: The Biography of Marshal of the Royal Air Force Sir Arthur Harris, the Wartime Chief of Bomber Command*. London: Greenhill, 2006.

Rostow, W.W. (Walt Whitman), *Pre-Invasion Bombing Strategy: General Eisenhower's Decision of March 25, 1944*. 1st ed. Austin: University of Texas Press, 1981.

Royal Air Force Historical Society, *Seek and Sink: A Symposium on the Battle of the Atlantic*, 21 October 1991, Bracknell: UK, 1992.

Rawson, Andrew, *Organizing Victory: The War Conferences 1941–45*, The History Press: Stroud, 2013.

Read, Simon, *The Killing Skies: RAF Bomber Command at War*. Stroud (England): Spellmount, 2006.

Richards, Denis, *Portal of Hungerford: The Life of Marshal of the Royal Air Force, Viscount Portal of Hungerford, KG, GCB, OM, DSO, MC*. New York, N.Y.: Holmes & Meier, 1977.

Richards, Denis and Saunders, George, *Royal Air Force 1939–1945 Vol. I: The Fight at Odds*, London: York House, 1953.

Richards Denis and Saunders, George, *Royal Air Force 1939–1945 Vol. II: The Flight Avails*, London: York House, 1954.

Richardson, Charles, *'From Churchill's Secret Circle to the BBC: The Biography of Lieutenant General Sir Ian Jacob,'* London: Brassey's, 1991.

Roberts, Andrew, *Masters and Commanders: How Roosevelt, Churchill, Marshall and Alanbrooke Won the War in the West*, London: Penguin, 2008.

Robertson, Scot, *The Development of RAF Strategic Bombing Doctrine, 1919–1939*. Westport, Conn: Praeger, 1995.

Rolfe, Mel, *Looking into Hell: Experiences of the Bomber Command War*. London: Arms and Armour, 1995.

Rommel, Erwin and Liddell Hart, Basil Henry, *The Rommel Papers*. (1st American ed.). New York: Harcourt, Brace, 1953.

Rubin, Gretchen Craft, *Forty Ways to Look at Winston Churchill: A Brief Account of a Long Life*. 1st ed., New York: Ballantine Books, 2003.

Saward, Dudley, *Bomber Harris: The Story of Marshal of the Royal Air Force, Sir Arthur Harris ...* 1st ed. in the U.S.A. ed. Garden City, N.Y.: Doubleday, 1985.

Schoenfeld, Maxwell Philip, *Sir Winston Churchill: His Life and times*. 2nd ed. Malabar, Fla.: R.E. Krieger Pub., 1986.

Sherwood, Robert E., *Roosevelt and Hopkins: An Intimate History* (New York: Harpers & Bros), 1948.

Slessor, John Cotesworth, *The Central Blue; Recollections and Reflections,* London: Cassell, 1956.

Smith, Perry M., *The Air Force Plans for Peace, 1943–1945*. Baltimore: Johns Hopkins, 1970.

Speer, Albert, *Inside the Third Reich: Memoirs*. New York: Macmillan, 1970.

Stewart, Herbert Leslie, *Winged Words: Sir Winston Churchill as Writer and Speaker*. New York: Bouregy & Curl, 1954.

Strauss, Barry S., *Masters of Command: Alexander, Hannibal, Caesar and the Genius of Leadership*. 1st Simon & Schuster hardcover ed. New York: Simon & Schuster, 2012.

Sun Tsu, *The Illustrated Art of War*, trans. by Samuel B. Griffith, Oxford: OUP, 2005.

Taylor, A.J.P. et al, *Churchill Revisited: A Critical Assessment*, New York: The Dial Press, 1969.

Tedder, A., *Air Power in War* (The Lees Knowles lectures, 1947). London: Hodder and Stoughton, 1954.

Tedder, Arthur William, *With Prejudice: The War Memoirs of Marshal of the Royal Air Force, Lord Tedder.* London: Cassell, 1966.

Terraine, J., *A Time for Courage: The Royal Air Force in the European War, 1939–1945*. New York, N.Y.: Macmillan, 1985.

Tooze, Adam, *The Wages of Destruction: The Making and Breaking of the Nazi Economy.* Penguin: New York, 2006.

Tweddle, Paul, *The Other Battle of Britain: 1940 Bomber Command's Forgotten Summer*, Stroud: The History Press, 2018.

United States Department of State, *Foreign Relations of the United States: The Conferences at Washington, 1941–1942, and Casablanca, 1943,* Washington, D.C.: U.S. Government Printing Office, 1941–1943.

Verrier, Anthony, *The Bomber Offensive*. London: Batsford, 1968.

Wakelam, Randall T., *The Science of Bombing: Operational Research in RAF Bomber Command* Toronto: University of Toronto Press, 2009.

Walzer, Michael, *Just and Unjust Wars: a Moral Argument with Historical Illustrations* Fifth edition. New York Basic Books, a member of the Perseus Books Group, 2015.

Warner, Philip, *Auchinleck: The Lonely Soldier*, Barnsley: Pen & Sword, 2006.

Webster, Charles Kingsley and Frankland, Noble, *The Strategic Air Offensive against Germany, 1939–1945. History of the Second World War*, United Kingdom Military Series. London: H.M. Stationery Office, 1961.

White, David Fairbank, *Bitter Ocean: The Battle of the Atlantic, 1939–1945*, New York: Simon & Schuster, 2006.

Wilson, Theodore A., *The First Summit; Roosevelt and Churchill at Placentia Bay 1941*. Boston: Houghton Mifflin, 1969.

Yenne, Bill, *Hap Arnold: The General Who Invented the U.S Air Force*. Washington, D.C.: Regnery History, 2013.

Articles

Baxter, Christopher J. (1997), 'A Question of Blame? Defending Britain's Position in the South China Sea, the Pacific and South-East Asia, 1919–1941,' *The RUSI Journal*, 142:4, 66–75.

Bell, Christopher M., 'Air Power and the Battle of the Atlantic: Very Long Range Aircraft and the Delay in Closing the Atlantic "Air Gap,"' *Journal of Military History*, 79, No. 3, July 2015, 691–719.

Benbow, Tim, 'Brothers in Arms: The Admiralty, the Air Ministry, and the Battle of the Atlantic, 1940–1943,' *Global War Studies*, 11(1), 2014, 41–88.

Betts, Richard K.,'Is strategy an illusion?' *International security* 25, No. 2 (2000), 5–50.

Burls, Nina, 'RAF Bombs and Bombing 1939–1945,' *The Royal Air Force Historical Society Journal*, 45, 2009.

Correll, John T., 'The Allied Rift on Strategic Bombing,' *Air Force Magazine*, 1 December 2020, at The Allied Rift on Strategic Bombing – Air Force Magazine accessed on 30 June 2021.

Costigliola, Frank, 'Pamela Churchill, Wartime London, and the Making of the Special Relationship,' *Diplomatic History*, September 2012, Vol. 36, No. 4, 753–762.

Cox, Sebastian (1994), '"The Difference between White and Black': Churchill, Imperial Politics, and Intelligence before the 1941 Crusader Offensive,' *Intelligence and National Security*, 9:3, 405–447.

Goette, Richard, 'Britain and the Delay in Closing the Mid-Atlantic "Air Gap" During the Battle of the Atlantic,' *The Northern Mariner*, XV No. 4 (October 2005), 9–41.

Goulter, Dr Christina J.M., 'RAF Coastal Command's Anti-Shipping Operations in North-West Europe, 1940–1945,' *The Royal Air Force Historical Society Journal*, 33 (2005).

Milner, Mark, 'The Battle of the Atlantic,' *The Journal of Strategic Studies*, 13:1 (1990), 45–66.

O'Connell, John F., 'Closing the North Atlantic Air Gap: Where did all the BRITISH Liberators Go?,' *Air Power History*, Vol. 59, No. 2 (Summer 2012), 32–43.

Peake, Air Commodore Harald, 'Marshal of the Royal Air Force Lord Portal of Hungerford,' *The Royal Air Forces Quarterly*, Vol. 11, No. 3 (Autumn 1971).

Duncan Redford, 'Inter- and Intra-Service Rivalries in the Battle of the Atlantic,' *Journal of Strategic Studies* 32, No. 6 (2009): 899–928.

Redford, Duncan, 'The March 1943 Crisis in the Battle of the Atlantic: Myth and Reality,' *History*, Vol. 92, No. 1 (305) (January 2007), 64–83.

Richards, Denis, 'Portal, Harris and the Bomber Offensive,' *RAF Historical Society Journal*, No. 6 (September 1989), 8–32.

Schep, Leo J., Slaughter, Robin J., Vale, J. Allister & Wheatley, Pat (2014), 'Was the death of Alexander the Great due to poisoning? Was it Veratrum album?,' *Clinical Toxicology*, 52:1, 72–77, DOI: 10.3109/15563650.2013.870341

Schmalenbach, Paul, 'KM Prinz Eugen,' *Warship Profile 6*. Windsor: Profile Publications, (1971), 121–144.

Smith, Malcolm, 'The Allied Air Offensive,' *The Journal of Strategic Studies*, 13:1 (1990), 67–83.

Strang, G. Bruce, '"The Worst of All Worlds:" Oil Sanctions and Italy's Invasion of Abyssinia, 1935–1936,' *Diplomacy and Statecraft* 19, No. 2 (2008): 210–235.

Thomas, Group Captain Andrew, 'Arthur Tedder – Air Power Maestro,' *The Royal Air Force Historical Society Journal*, 50 (2011).

Trainor, Tim, 'How Ford's Willow Run Assembly Plant Helped Win World War II,' *Assembly Magazine*, 3 February 2019, found at, How Ford's Willow Run Assembly Plant Helped Win World War II 2019-01-03 |ASSEMBLY (assemblymag.com)

Young, R.J., 'The Strategic Dream: French Air Doctrine in the Interwar Period, 1919–39.' *Journal of Contemporary History*. 1974; 9(4): 57–76.

Index

INDEX